The Coming Struggle for Peace

The Coming Struggle for Peace

ANDRE VISSON

NEW YORK : THE VIKING PRESS : 1944

To my son Philip

Acknowledgments

I want to express my sincere gratitude to Harold K. Guinzburg, my publisher and friend, whose welcome to the very idea of this book encouraged its preparation; to the editorial staff of the Viking Press for most friendly and enlightening assistance; to Miss Ellen Smith, my personal assistant, whose devotion did so much to speed up the realization of my assignment; to my brother Vladimir whose sound judgment and constructive criticism have helped to circumvent many difficulties; and especially to my wife who has been my first reader, first critic, and often also first editor. I am equally indebted to many good friends for their generous help both in research and advice.

Part of the material in the chapter "The Cornerstone" appeared previously in my article, "Suspicions Old and New," published in *The Atlantic Monthly*, whom I want to thank for their courtesy in authorizing its use. I wish to extend my thanks also to the *New York Herald Tribune* and the *Washington Post* for having given me the opportunity to discuss in my Sunday column many of the problems which are analyzed more at length in this book.

A. V.

Contents

ix

Introduction

THE somewhat provocative title of this book should not lead the reader to expect to find in it more than it contains. This is not a book on peace, nor is it a blueprint for a new postwar order. It does not even attempt to survey the innumerable peace schemes proposed with equal zeal and conviction by professional and amateur planners alike. This book is simply a study of some of the internal problems of the United Nations, problems which have to be solved —and satisfactorily—if the peace which the United Nations intend to win is to become an enduring peace. And considering the short life of the United Nations as a unit, there is an abundance of these problems.

The "United Nations" dates back only to January 1, 1942, the day its birth certificate was registered in Washington, D. C., its birthplace. It was on the first day of the first year of the coalition war—less than a month after Pearl Harbor—that representatives of the three great powers, Great Britain, Soviet Russia, and China, came to the White House to sign with President Roosevelt the joint declaration which for the first time used the term "United Nations." With President Roosevelt acting as godfather, Assistant Secretary of State Adolf Berle, in the role of birth registration clerk, the next day invited to the State Department representatives of the other members of the association to be known as the United Nations.

The press did not immediately become aware of the historical significance of this new document. It took several days for the commentators and editors, and even longer for the public, to realize that a new attempt was being made to create a really New World Order after the victory that would end the war. Most people believed, and some of them still believe, that President Roosevelt was the father spiritual of the United Nations. This notion contributed to the confusion surrounding the United Nations' first tottering steps.

Neither President Roosevelt nor representatives of the other

1

signatory nations brought the United Nations to life. It was brought to life by Adolf Hitler who perversely built up the family of the United Nations by attacking one country after another. We must not forget that only two countries—Great Britain and France—were compelled to take the initiative technically in declaring war upon Hitler. All the others were brought into the war gradually and generally against their wills by the successive assaults of Hitler or his allies. The United Nations is, consequently, not a coalition created spontaneously by the common agreement of its members; it is rather the result of the aggressor's actions revealed in the union of the member nations for the common defense of their individual interests.

History proves that while every coalition has the advantage over its enemy in time of war because its common resources permit a greater, united effort, every coalition is bound to find itself seriously handicapped at the peace conference. In losing the war to the coalition, the enemy has a chance to win the peace which he must negotiate with the coalition because of the individual and frequently conflicting objectives and interests of its members. The biggest question facing the United Nations now is the question of winning the peace. Having been brought to life by Adolf Hitler, will the coalition be able to survive him?

As the war moves closer to its end in a United Nations' victory, it becomes more obvious that the conflicting interests of the coalition's members will find sharper and sharper expression. United in the face of common danger, the United Nations has the natural but regrettable tendency to disunite as the danger appears to decrease. This inevitably results in the expansion of each nation's aspirations, which are in turn justified through partisan evaluation by that nation of its contribution to the common cause. And it is only too human for every member to overestimate his own contribution and to underestimate the contribution of his allies.

The United Nations had neither the time nor the courage in the speed of its emergency organization to elaborate a common program for lasting co-operation. Taking first things first, it proceeded with the most urgent problem: the organization of the common war effort. The first attempts to continue into the postwar world the solidarity established by the necessity of war were not made until the Moscow Conference and the later meeting of the leaders of the Big Three at Teheran.

At the climax of the fighting, the brunt of the war lay on the shoulders of the four big powers—the United States, Great Britain, the Soviet Union, and China—solely because of the fortunes of war and the material advantage springing from numeric strength. But this fact will unquestionably increase the natural tendency of these four nations to consider themselves responsible for the reorganization of the postwar world. And this is a situation that may lead to serious trouble, for failure of these leaders to agree among themselves on the postwar pattern of the world will make it impossible for the junior members to solve their problems. This is already evident in a theory held by some official circles in Washington that as long as the Big Four cannot agree, the junior members must not dare to interfere because their conflicting voices would only complicate the arrival at a solution.

The junior members refused to accept this theory, claiming that those who would find a solution of the general world problem must first consult them, for their particular difficulties are interlocked with the world puzzle. They go so far as to assert that the prerequisite for an adequate solution of the general problem is a satisfactory resolution of the local troubles. This feeling is especially strong in French circles which still believe it is France's right to be considered as a great power. Thus the United Nations face trouble at their own conference tables even before the conquered enemy is admitted to negotiations, even before the enemy is conquered.

The three principal areas in which the United Nations will find their most complicated postwar problems are Europe, the Near East, and the Far East. The situation in the Far East appears now to be the most nebulous. Because of the overlapping national, racial, and economic issues which will be stirred up by the application of the Atlantic Charter, it seems likely that the solution of the underlying problems in the Far East will not be easy to achieve. The situation in the Near East will be no less unhappy. For here the Arab-Moslem world, sadly deceived after the First World War, will claim once more—this time in the name of the Atlantic Charter —satisfaction for what it believes to be its justifiable objectives.

But it is Europe, where the lines of basic conflict are sharpest and the various protagonists most outspoken, which harbors the chief problems for the United Nations and the greatest potential destructive factors. For with few exceptions, every European member of the United Nations has its own external and internal problems which will serve to make infinitely difficult the attainment of a lasting peace.

Europe has been the main source of our civilization for the last two thousand years. She has given birth to all the moral, political, and social doctrines of that civilization. Amazingly enough, despite devastating wars and ever sharpening national conflicts, Europe still continues to contribute a large share to our civilization and culture. If we have not always been able to discern Europe's tremendous sources of creative energy, it is because all of us, Americans as well as Europeans, have accepted at face value the terms "Old" and "New" Worlds. The New World, which gave to humanity in the nineteenth century a new expression of the age-old dreams of the pursuit of happiness, has created new and successful technical means and weapons for the realization of those dreams. Proud of its successful formula, the New World gradually began to liberate itself from the feeling of admiration for the Old World, while the latter looked with growing envy at the social and technical accomplishments of the New World.

Today, however, we discover this amazing paradox. The New World, now satisfied with its achievements, has grown conservative and is preoccupied with maintaining them intact; while the Old World, more turbulent than ever and more than ever in search of new formulas, is spurred onward in this search as never before by the eternally opposed elements of its own conservative and revolutionary forces.

It is interesting to note that the four major members of the United Nations are non-European powers in the strict sense, a fact that may furnish the greatest obstacles to the solution of Europe's problems by this coalition. Two of these four powers, the United States and China, are extra-European powers; Great Britain and

Russia are semi-European and because of their geographical positions have many, if not most, of their political and economic interests outside Europe.

The two great European powers were unquestionably Germany and France. Germany will come to the peace conference a defeated enemy, a more or less passive attendant at the negotiations. She will have to accept and execute the program to be worked out by the United Nations. France left Europe with a huge political vacuum when she lost, after her collapse, her centuries-old position as a great Continental power. Her prolonged absence from Europe's political field threatens to aggravate the already extremely complicated problems which the United Nations face there. Those official circles in Washington that are convinced that France cannot recover her freedom and her independence except through the efforts of the senior members of the United Nations are correct in their belief. But they are seriously in error when they overlook the uncontrovertible fact that France will be the last European country to accept with resignation her new status as a subordinated nation, and one subordinated to non-European powers.

In this connection, we must remember that the Soviet Union, a multi-national state, is a kind of federation that entertains a desire to create the strongest possible defense line in the West while many of her political aspirations turn to the East. Great Britain is geographically and politically closer to Europe than any other of the Big Four, for until the seventeenth century she had an exclusively European history and she still has a wholly European civilization.

The United States is in a much less advantageous position than either Britain or Russia. American public opinion has a definite tendency to consider Europe's nationalisms as obsolete and destructive. This tendency goes back to the founding of this country, which was created by Europeans who wanted to break free from the ties of European nationalisms. It was the greatest effort ever made to escape from Europe's political, religious, and social conventions, and the United States has reason to be proud of her political and social freedom. But she must not overlook the historic truth that the nationalisms which are Europe's greatest danger because of their continuous upheaval of destructive forces are at the same time Europe's most powerful creative sources.

European nationalisms in their continuing evolution found their modern expression as late as the nineteenth century. Although the Napoleonic Wars were considered the peak of Europe's nationalistic era, the present war and the evolution of Soviet Russia have proved the extreme vitality and durability of European nationalisms. Hitler has been able to overrun nearly all of Europe, to conquer almost every European country; but he has not been able to break or even dominate a single European nationalism. On the contrary, he has strengthened them by oppression and has built them up to a level of potentially explosive wrath unknown in European history. The implications of this condition are extremely serious in the light of the postwar problems which confront the United Nations.

While Britain is closer to Europe geographically, America is closer to Europe ethnographically. More than thirteen million foreign-born Americans, to whom should be added twenty-two million second-generation Americans, assure a living bridge between the homes of their fathers and their new fatherland. The fate of Eastern Europe, of Germany, and of Italy is much closer to the hearts of Americans whose origins are in those countries than it is to the hearts of the British. At first glance it would seem that this element would give the United States an advantage over Britain in helping to organize postwar Europe. However, this is not the case, for America's foreign-born groups constitute a serious handicap to the establishment of proper relations between this country and Europe. Most of these Americans left their native lands in the nineteenth century or in the first years of this century. Consequently, they belong to a social and intellectual atmosphere which has become obsolete in their old countries. American Poles, for example, came here for the most part before Poland's rebirth in 1919. The Czechs and Slovaks migrated to the United States before Czechoslovakia was created. The Croats, Slovenes, and the smaller number of Serbs now living here never did live in Yugoslavia; most of them were subjects of the Austro-Hungarian Empire. The same anachronism in political and social ideas applies to Italian-Americans and even to German-Americans. Many

Italian-Americans still live with the ideals of Garibaldi and Mazzini, while large numbers of German-Americans still subscribe to the ideology of the liberal Germany of 1848. The foreign-born American, whose influence in American life forms one of the lesser known but most interesting chapters in modern American history, represents a factor which must not be overlooked in a study of United Nations' problems. He is one of the many factors which give us reason to believe that the United States may come upon dangers in Europe about which the American people should be advised in advance.

Among these dangers is the possibility that American troops may be more welcome in enemy countries than in Allied countries. In enemy territory the American soldiers are expected to bring liberation from totalitarian dictatorships and assurances of political equality and justice. They will be welcomed both by the anti-totalitarian elements and by those conservative elements which may have sympathized and collaborated with the dictatorships but which will be grateful to the American Army for saving them from political and social chaos. They will be received as defenders of all those who fear England's imperialism and the Soviet Union's expansion, as well as those who do not want to be drawn into Russian or English spheres of influence.

The situation will be different in the liberated countries of our Allies. If at first their peoples are thankful for the freedom from oppressors the American soldiers have brought them, and for the food and relief that follow, they cannot help but resent in the long run their obligation to foreigners, even to friendly and allied foreigners, for their liberation. They will resent their own weakness that made this necessary, and there is grave danger that because of this resentment they may misunderstand and misjudge American policy. Unfortunately good intentions are not always accompanied by the necessary knowledge of Europe's basic trends.

Conquerors have rights; friends have only obligations. Europe's gratitude for all she expects from her powerful American ally will certainly be equaled by her resentment because she has to expect so much. The experience with the French has proved that this danger already is acute, and that it can lead to undesirable and regrettable consequences.

American policy makers and American public opinion as well must be made aware in advance of the impossibility of imposing by external force any general plan upon Europe's traditionally rebellious, independent, and freedom-loving peoples. Not only that great power of yesterday, France, but even tiny Luxembourg with her minute population of three hundred thousand will never accept an administration imposed upon her by the political machinery of the United Nations. Luxembourg's motto, "We want to remain what we are," holds true for all European nations, great and small. In addition, some of the United Nations are divided within themselves by racial, social, or religious differences. These internal conflicts will of necessity complicate their external problems.

One may well wonder, therefore, whether it is either timely or wise to point out and analyze present and potential problems, since their discussion will necessarily disclose serious dissensions that exist now or will inevitably arise within the United Nations. This author hardly needs to assure his readers that he has no intention of writing a single line that would give the slightest comfort to the enemy. He is, however, firmly convinced that no problem can be solved merely by ignoring it. And he is also firmly convinced that the American public is entitled to at least as much information on the problems it must help solve in the postwar world as the enemy already possesses. It is fundamentally the basic strength of the democracies that permits them to reveal their divergencies and dissensions even in wartime.

"Wars cannot be run by a debating society," Major Atlee, leader of the Opposition, rightly remarked in the House of Commons. But peace must be prepared during the course of war and we know from our tragic experience that the basis of a sane and lasting peace cannot be laid down without the approval of all the peoples concerned in its establishment. The American people will be called upon to approve by their votes a number of vital decisions made by the Administration long before the fighting ceases. How can they express an opinion if they are not provided with all available information about these vital problems?

Even those who are hostile to any peace programs which involve entering into the internal, domestic problems of other nations should have before them all the ethnographical, political, and moral facts which concern our Allies and their peculiar problems. Even this group, which believes that America's postwar role should be restricted only to surveillance of the international behavior of other governments, might be interested in objective information on the national and social structure of our fellow-members in the United Nations.

Many Americans may not be at all interested in knowing whether the Czechs and the Slovaks, the Serbs and the Croats, wish to live together in the postwar world, or whether they prefer to live apart. Many Americans may not care to know whether the Poles will seek to set up a genuine democratic regime in the postwar world, or whether the French will strive to re-establish the Constitution of the Third Republic or build a Fourth Republic. But they must—if they would think at all of a postwar world of peace and harmony—be interested in these seemingly remote questions, for Europe's problems are tragically intermingled. If the Serbs and the Croats fail to iron out their difficulties, the whole organization of Danubian Europe will have to be changed about. If the Croats and Slovenes should be separated from the Serbs, the Slovaks may follow their example, and the Vatican-sponsored plans for a Central European Catholic Federation may have important repercussions in the political alignment of Central and also of Western Europe, and thus indirectly affect the future of America.

The problem of Germany's place in the postwar world is not discussed in the following pages. That is a problem in which all of the United Nations are interested directly or indirectly. Its solution will be the final test of the stability of the peace. Moscow even goes so far as to consider all other problems, especially those of the relation of the Soviet Union to her western neighbors, subordinate to the agreement among the Big Three of the United Nations—the United States, Great Britain, and Russia—on postwar Germany. But although this problem is connected with many internal or inter-member problems of the United Nations, the latter are generally considered in Washington and London to be the primary test of the sincerity and solidarity of the United Nations in their desire to build a lasting peace.

The Moscow and Teheran conferences left unsolved the question of Germany's postwar status. It is highly regrettable that the conferences also left unsolved many of the United Nations' pressing internal problems. The leaders of the Big Three had to be satisfied with a kind of general, political groundwork indispensable for their agreement on vital military strategy.

The Italian problem, less complicated and less important than the German one, also does not find its place in this book; neither does the question of Spain. Spain attracted attention by her tragic curtain-raiser to the present war, but it is difficult to conceive how she might play a significant part in the struggle for the peace, although she is important as a cultural channel between Europe and Latin America. It looks now as if General Franco will try to utilize Spain's eccentric geographic position for the conservation of Fascist or semi-Fascist ideology. However, it seems most likely that the future of Spain will be determined by the general political face of postwar Europe. The problems of Spain, Italy, and Germany are external problems.

The survey of Far Eastern problems in this book may appear rather summarized as compared with the more detailed discussions of Europe and the Near East, but it is not because the problems of the Far East are less important. This is a global war, and the peace which will follow must be a global peace or it will be no peace at all. The Far Eastern problems, if we can believe those who have devoted all their lives to a study of them, are less complicated, less enmeshed in conflicting nationalisms, and less imbedded with centuries-old racial hatreds than the issues which confront Europe and the Near East.

Furthermore, the problems analyzed in this book are examined from their political and psychological angles. The author is all too well aware of the extreme importance of the economic angle in international relations; he knows that a lasting peace must have sound economic foundations. But he believes that the discussion of the economics of international problems should be left to those who are more qualified than he. However, he could not ignore economics in the chapter on British-American relations, in which the economic problems may well constitute the supreme test. In all the other chapters, this book confines itself to a survey of the principal political problems of the United Nations.

This author does not pretend to have at hand the solutions for all the problems of Europe. He does not know all the answers. However, he is thoroughly acquainted with those European areas in which most of today's perplexing problems have arisen, and what he has tried to do here is to present a substantial but condensed survey of the internal problems of the United Nations, those problems which the average American will come up against when he is required by his free vote to decide the fate of his country and of the world.

The author views this book as a guide through the labyrinth of the United Nations. He views it, also, as his modest contribution to the great effort of this great country in behalf of peace. He believes in this country, and feels that should this belief ever be lost, there would no longer be any hope of finding a workable formula that would assure this war-torn and socially disturbed world of ours a sane and lasting peace.

I: The Cornerstone

British-American Relations

BRITISH-AMERICAN solidarity is supposedly the cornerstone of the United Nations. No one can or does question their determined unanimity so far as the winning of the war is concerned. However, bilateral solidarity on this limited objective does not necessarily exclude occasional differences in the conception of the strategy with which this common goal can best be achieved. And, even more important, it does not exclude different conceptions of the postwar world. The United States and Great Britain have been able to agree on unconditional surrender as the only terms for the armistice that will end this war. It is generally believed that they will also agree on the peace terms to be imposed upon the defeated enemy. The important question then, important not only to the United Nations but to the entire world, is whether the two Atlantic powers so closely united in the war will continue to agree on the maintenance and guaranteeing of the peace.

Both encouraging and disquieting omens can be found in the background of modern relations between Britain and the United States. Twice in our generation we have seen this country come to Britain's assistance. But we have also seen American public opinion, disappointed by European power politics in which Britain played a determining part, turn back after the last war to isolationism.

The necessities of political world developments gradually brought the two countries together again, imposing solidarity upon them from without. The growth of common threats to their existence and to their ways of life expedited the process. But this hard won solidarity often has been strained, fortunately not yet to the point of cleavage, by basic psychological differences and conflicting economic interests. The manifestations of successful British-American co-operation certainly make a long and impressive list, but an account of their mutual suspicions is equally long and impressive.

It was after the War of 1812 that the two English-speaking democracies reached a kind of tacit understanding. Common enemies in the last war and in the present one brought them closer together into the formal relationship of allies. These co-operative experiences and their respective awareness of common dangers in the past and in the future should contribute to the strengthening of British-American solidarity which is certain to be put to a very serious test.

The relative power of the two nations already has undergone great changes and is bound to undergo still greater ones in the near future. Britain was leading the British-American team at the end of the last war. Now Britain and the United States are partners, but if the British have managed to maintain an appearance of leadership because of their "front line" position and their greater freedom of action in the diplomatic field, they have had to recognize the superiority of the United States assured by her ever growing economic and military potential. In the postwar world the United States is bound to become the leader of the American-British team, and the British will have to adapt their political mentality, and perhaps also their economy, to this radically altered relationship. The Americans will have to assume new responsibilities which many of them are not at all eager to take on.

In one of the most lucid current analyses of American-British relations, Walter Lippmann finds them now "so numerous and so complicated that it is meaningless today to ask whether they are good or bad. The point is that they are permanent and that they cannot be severed, and above all, that our interests are now so deeply engaged that they are no longer, in the conventional and traditional sense, foreign relations." This interdependence of Anglo-American relations is generally recognized in both the United States and in Britain, and certainly by the Germans, judging by the desperate effort of their propagandists to prove the contrary.

A study of German shortwave broadcasts to the United States and Great Britain reveals a concentrated attack on what the German psychological warfare experts apparently believe to be the most vulnerable points on the British-American psychological front. These are, according to Berlin, the imperialistic rivalry of the two allies, their insistence on mutual economic exploitation, their disagreement over war strategy and political policies, and disunity within the combined military command. Dr. Goebbels neatly summarizes these points by telling the Americans that "Britain will fight to the last American" and explaining to the British that in their exposed position they have become "America's aircraft carrier."

The Nazi propagandists further itemize the potential points of friction in their domestic broadcasts. German audiences are told in detail of American criticism of Britain's Indian policy, of the American-British rivalry for control of North Africa and the Near East, the disagreements inside the Supreme Command over Allied operations in the Mediterranean, Australia, and Burma. They are encouraged to take hope from the disturbances allegedly caused by American troops training in Britain, and from discussions as to which ally is getting the greater advantage out of Lend-Lease, which country is doing more, paying more, building more ships and weapons, contributing more oil and resources to the joint war effort, and what is going to be done about war debts.

It is interesting to note that in combing the British and American press and parliamentary speeches for statements to support these allegations, the Nazi propagandists quote more often from American sources than British. One explanation for this is that because of the newsprint shortage, British newspapers cannot devote as much of their half dozen pages to these discussions as can newspapers printed on this side of the Atlantic. A more important psychological reason arises from the fact that geographical necessities which determine the social life of the British people in their overcrowded island have imposed upon them for generations a certain caution in the expression of their opinions. They have learned to be careful of their immediate reactions so as not to hurt the feelings of their neighbors. And they instinctively carry this attitude over into their international relations. If they had as much elbow room, geographically, at home as the Americans, they too probably would be less restricted in what they say and how they phrase it.

Despite the skill and experience of Dr. Goebbels' aides, they have not succeeded in weakening British-American united determination to win the war. It would be a dangerous error, however, to ignore this propaganda completely, because it constantly and consistently is seeking to aggravate mutual prejudices and to exploit actual and potential sources of friction between the two countries.

No comprehensive analysis of mutual complaints and fears has yet been made in either country and many people doubt the wisdom of listing them and publicly discussing them. However, a frank discussion of America's complaints in relation to Britain and of Britain's complaints in relation to the United States can only contribute to the strengthening of British-American solidarity. Such a study is both appropriate and important in this consideration of the potential obstacles to peace.

Public opinion surveys have indicated that about 25 per cent of the American people are more or less unfriendly toward Britain. The source of much of this feeling may lie in the hatred of the British which has been fostered for generations among the Irish-Americans. Whatever its original source, most of the anti-British sentiment in the United States finds its foundation in the circulation of these complaints:

Britain is imperialistic and has developed an unprogressive colonial system which she hopes to preserve after the war. The fact that the natives of Malaya and Burma did not fight on the British side is new evidence, in addition to the Indian problem, to prove the failure of Britain's colonial policy.

Britain has not yet pulled her full weight in the war. She has kept most of her troops at home and wants America to win the war for her.

The $6,353,143,000 allotted to Great Britain and her empire out of total lend-lease aid of $8,252,733,000, is a great drain on American resources and is involving the United States increasingly in "Britain's war." This problem of Britain's lion's share of Lend-Lease is frequently confused with her failure to pay her First World War debts.

There is a certain traditional American prejudice against the

British, their aristocratic society and their "old-school ties." They are accused of being superior, condescending, Machiavellian.

Britain cannot be trusted to co-operate in the postwar world for her aims are "selfish and imperialistic." Her bankers and industrialists will resume their fight against American competitors in the world markets in order to maintain their centuries-old privileged position while British diplomats continue to outsmart their American colleagues.

The British answer these complaints by asserting that their empire cannot be described as unprogressive, for Australia, Canada, Eire, New Zealand, and South Africa represent the largest federation ever achieved by free peoples in the modern world. The Dominions are, indeed, in no sense subject to Great Britan. Australia, Canada, and New Zealand entered this war voluntarily; Eire, as voluntarily, stayed out. In further support of their argument, the British stress their surrender of the Iraq mandate in 1930, their recognition of Egypt in 1922 as an independent sovereign state, their agreement upon certain restrictions of their military and naval forces in Egypt in 1932 and 1936.

Though recognizing that the Malayan and Burmese natives did not fight on their side while the Filipinos fought with and for the Americans, the British note that the Filipinos had almost five centuries of Christian civilization behind their decision, whereas the Malayans are profoundly Oriental and as profoundly pacifist in the Oriental sense. They readily admit that their failure to develop in the Malayans a sense of responsibility was their own fault. But, they insist, if they had organized a native army in Malaya, they would have been attacked at home by the Church, the Liberals, and all their own homegrown pacifists.

The British usually are not too anxious to discuss their policy in India. They will, however, point to the technical progress which they have achieved there during the last fifty years. They emphasize India's old internal conflicts which, they say, would plunge the four hundred million Hindus into devastating civil war the moment Britain leaves India to her fate. However, many British are not too happy about their Indian policy and they protest that it is unfair to judge their imperialism solely by their treatment of that country. Others avoid discussion of this situation by declaring that it is as difficult for Americans to appreciate the Indian problem as for the British to understand the Negro problem in America.

As for their war effort, the British say they entered the war just as unprepared as the United States and that they too had suffered from an isolationist sentiment. After Dunkirk they had left less than one armored division with which to defend their island. Nevertheless, they sent troops to Libya and Abyssinia; and if the assistance they gave Greece was not sufficient, it at least helped to buy invaluable time for the Russians. For a year and a half their navy, without aid, patrolled and kept free 125 million square miles of water. Even today it carries the major burden of Atlantic convoys from the United States to the Soviet Union and the Far East. The British provided the bulk of the transports and the naval escorts for the North African campaign.

The Royal Air Force has materially reduced German war production and weakened civilian morale, thus indirectly assisting Russia. British troops held in England were expeditionary forces training for the invasion of Western Europe. The British marshalled their wartime manpower to such an extent that less than three million, including children, sick, cripples, and aged, did not engage in some form of national service. The average working week in Britain was fifty hours, and many worked from sixty to seventy hours.

To the complaints about Lend-Lease, the British reply that these transfers were not commercial loans; they were contributions of material into a common pool to wage a common war. From the report given by Edward R. Stettinius at the conclusion of his services as Lend-Lease Administrator, hardly anyone can consider Lend-Lease a "one-way traffic." British purchases for cash in the United States amounted to more than seven billion dollars, far exceeding by November 1942 the value of goods exported to that date under Lend-Lease.

The British particularly resent American complaints about the "ossified British social system." In rebuttal they refer their critics to an American opinion held by Allan Nevins, who wrote that Britain is now a land of "fierce and urgent economic democracy.... Ideas thought radical in America appear conservative in England." They believe that they can make a good case on the record of their social progress as compared with America's, merely by comparing the dates of adoption of various reforms and advances in the two countries:

Britain recognized trade unions by the Trade Union Act of 1871; the United States gave them similar recognition in 1933.

Britain provided old age pensions in 1908; the United States in 1935.

Britain's national health insurance was established in 1911; the United States still has no comparable program.

Britain started national unemployment insurance in 1912; the United States went into it in 1935.

Maternity care and welfare work for children under five became a British public service in 1918; it became an American public service in 1935.

In the important problem of housing, Britain claims an advantage in that more than one-third of her homes were built between 1918 and 1939.

Eighty-five per cent of England's purchasing power is now in the hands of those earning less than $4,000 a year.

In the process of leveling off income, only eighty persons in all of Britain now enjoy a net income of $25,000 a year, compared to seven thousand in 1939; the income tax was boosted to a 50 per cent standard plus surtaxes, which at the highest rate brings the total income tax to 97 per cent.

The Beveridge Report would carry all these advance steps in social security and reform many steps ahead, making them so all-inclusive that it has become known as the "cradle to the grave" plan.

All these differences and disagreements appear insignificant against the most serious American complaint concerning British-American relations: doubt as to Britain's sincerity in postwar world co-operation. All the traditional prejudices and inevitable frictions between two peoples compelled to adjust their individual efforts to a common aim could not affect the solidarity of these two nations on the point of winning the war. But should doubts of Britain's sincerity become more widespread in this country, that sturdy solidarity might well be hopelessly compromised as far as the winning of the peace is concerned.

The tremendous potentiality of this danger was graphically demonstrated by the "secret criticisms" disclosed by five United States Senators upon their return from a tour of the battlefronts in the autumn of 1943. At that time British-American relations were in one of their "perfect honeymoon" stages. In a speech that was applauded by highest Administration circles, Prime Minister Churchill had just suggested that the combined Chiefs of Staff of the American and British military commands be maintained for a "good many years" after the war. He hailed the "gift of a common tongue" as the "priceless inheritance" of the British and American peoples and as a possible "foundation of a common citizenship." At this same time the proposal for a military alliance with Britain, then put forward unofficially, was favored, according to a Gallup poll, by 61 per cent of American public opinion.

Into such a friendly atmosphere criticisms of the British which had been circulated for months in Washington's "well-informed" quarters were exploded in public debate for the first time, with the combined authoritative prestige of legislators and eyewitnesses to support them. The British were accused of having hoarded their manpower in India and their oil in Persia; of assuring themselves an economic edge over the Americans in the postwar world, and of even using for that purpose American Lend-Lease. Their businessmen, assisted by well-trained foreign service agents and old established and highly efficient news services, were charged with trying to consolidate everywhere their existing economic positions and to build up new ones whenever possible.

Although the Administration and a part of the press sturdily defended the British, explaining that the Senators' information was incomplete and could not therefore give an accurate picture of the situation, these well-worn, standard criticisms nevertheless provoked serious reactions in two quite different sectors of American public opinion. Isolationist circles, traditionally suspicious of the British, naturally jumped at them as evidence that their suspicions of British sincerity were correct. On the other hand, those who think of the postwar era in terms of Wendell Willkie's *One World*, and whose postwar ideal is collective security, found in these criticisms support for their skeptical view of a British-American alliance in the postwar world. They feared such an alliance would result in an attempt to build up an "Anglo-American century" which would be unacceptable not only to the Russians but to many other European peoples, and which would inevitably become a marriage between British insularism and American isolationism. They, too, suspected British sincerity in the shaping of a "really decent and moral" postwar world, and the Senators' criticisms spurred them to renewed insistence upon "collective security" as the only foundation for the "One World" of the postwar era.

American doubts about British sincerity on this important question are the more serious because the British answer that they entertain exactly the same doubts about American sincerity—or capacity, as some of them put it—to continue in postwar times the co-operation established during the trying years of the war. The Senate incident revived and reinforced all their suspicions and apprehensions as well. Remembering America's withdrawal after the last war, London developed considerable anxiety about the 1944 Presidential election.

Every prominent British visitor to this country inquired anxiously about the Republican stand on international affairs, for in England they interpreted the Republican gains in the 1942 and 1943 Congressional elections as indicative of a coming "isolationist reaction." The British readily revealed their apprehension that "big business" would dominate America's postwar foreign policy. Naturally, it was the Labour Party that was especially worried about this possibility although the Conservatives also were disturbed lest American big business emerge in the postwar world much stronger than Britain's big business. This even led to speculation in London that the appointments of Mr. Stettinius, Leo G. Crowley, and W. Averell Harriman to high posts in American diplomatic and economic agencies were inspired by the alleged desire of American business to insure itself in advance of key positions in the shaping of its country's postwar foreign policy.

Meanwhile, in the United States people were wondering whether British big business would try to revive after the war the "liberal, benevolent" imperialism of Cecil Rhodes, or even to resume with new vigor the shrewd economic competition which resulted in 1920 in the complete elimination of American oil interests from the Near East by the Royal Dutch-Shell trust. The oil problem, with the proposed American move to the Near East where a government-built pipeline will further the development of the United States' oil concessions in Saudi-Arabia and at Kuwait on the Persian Gulf, will itself be a critical test of American-British economic solidarity.

The American people would have felt better about the British as allies if they had, for example, announced the abandonment of their bases at Hong Kong and Singapore. The British indicated they would gladly have given America this satisfaction early in the war if the United States could and would have guaranteed her co-operation in the establishment of international, worldwide security. The British have said that if they continued to play their traditional role as "go-between" for the United States and other foreign powers—as they did with the Fighting French, the Near Eastern peoples, and Russia—it was mainly because they felt that, in the absence of definite guarantees from the United States as to her postwar co-operation, they had no choice but to improve their diplomatic positions throughout the world. They do not always say this, but the British universally believe that their long experience in international politics entitles them to play this part not only for their own benefit but also for that of the United States.

The British have an equally ready answer to those Americans who hesitate about commitments on co-operation because of their ally's future economic and trade policies. They point out that when they accepted the idea of the United States as "Democracy's Arsenal," and later lend-lease, they exposed themselves to the danger that the United States would thereby come out of the war with a much more powerful industry than Britain's and a correspondingly greater competitive advantage in the struggle for world markets. But they comforted themselves with the idea that they had and still have the advantage over the United States in world trade. They believe that their two hundred years of experience, their worldwide mercantile organization, and the flexibility of British industry, accustomed to the individual treatment of customers in all parts of the world, will in the long run help to counterbalance the dynamic power of American industry, specialized as it is in standard production.

Concerning Lend-Lease, they felt originally and still feel that it might enable the United States to impose a number of crippling obligations upon them after the war—the United States might demand repayment in commodities (tin and rubber) or in territories (more naval and air bases) or in the control of the seas or the airways. And indeed, during the Senate discussion in October 1943 of lend-lease expenditures, Senator Allen J. Ellender of Louisiana demanded permanent possession of strategic Allied bases used in this war by the American Navy and Air Force, in return for lend-lease aid. The British press bristled in immediate reaction to this suggestion, which was given a highly unfavorable reception over there. Another proposal by the same Senator for Allied concessions in oil, tin, iron ore, and rubber in order to enable the United States to replenish her natural resources depleted by the war effort, also caused considerable concern among the British who are particularly sensitive to American ambitions in the field of international aviation and shipping.

British shipbuilders were deeply stirred by the frank statement by Rear Admiral Howard L. Vickery, Chairman of the United States Maritime Commission, who merely declared that the United States intended to become a maritime nation with or without the co-operation of Britain. The General Council of British Shipping hurried to answer that they were willing to co-operate with the United States "in the spirit of the Atlantic Charter," but that they wanted to make clear that "however important the possession of an adequate merchant marine may be to the United States, to Britain it is a vital necessity."

Early in the war the United States and Britain agreed that the British were to build war vessels while the Americans concentrated on cargo ships. Admiral Vickery revealed that despite the original agreement, America had had to put more emphasis on strictly emergency vessels such as the Liberty ships, while the British in the meantime were beginning to build large and fast ships which could engage in commercial competition after the war. This change naturally worried American shipping circles, which feared that the United States would be left with a fleet of useless Liberty ships, while Britain after the war would have a modernized and enlarged merchant marine. The General Council was able to explain the change in America's original plans by the submarine menace, which necessitated emphasis on quantity instead of quality. This explanation was undoubtedly correct, but it left open the problem of postwar co-operation between American and British shipping.

In the field of civil aviation, the British were no less anxious to maintain their position. American production facilities and the flying experience gained by American military pilots disturbed them just as British control of the world's principal bases outside of Europe made American aviation interests uneasy. An American civil aviation official described the situation perfectly in this evaluation of the reasons for mutual mistrust: "We have the edge in equipment and operating methods; the British have the edge in geography."

In this connection, the British Independent Committee on the Future of Civil Aviation pointed out that "the British Empire comprises about a quarter of the world's surface; no territories comprised in it are separated by more than 2,000 miles, and, consequently, it includes convenient stages for the operation of airlines over most of the globe." This is perfectly true, and so is the fact that the shortest route from any point in the United States to most of the places on the globe usually crosses territory of the British Empire.

On the other hand, the United States is now producing fifteen thousand transport planes yearly, including flying boats, an impressive output with which the British cannot compete either in quantity or quality. While she recognizes American superiority in production, Britain is alarmed by American ambitions for the high place in international commercial aviation to which this productive ability entitles her—alarmed to the point where an RAF officer has publicly demanded that Britain and her Dominions tell the United States "that the Empire is not willing to be pushed off the map."

However, British opinion generally favors an agreement between the two countries, for the British realize that such a pact, based on the "free air" principle—the only one acceptable to the United States—would provide the best means of helping Britain maintain her position in international aviation. And the British and American governments seem to be equally anxious to work out such an agreement. It would assure Britain that America's powerful aviation industry would not "push the British Empire off the map," and it would guarantee American planes use of British Empire bases.

In the first two years of the war, the United States invested more than a billion dollars in foreign air bases. Their construction was dictated solely by military expediency and many of them will have no postwar commercial value, although a few do have great commercial possibilities. No American can understand why such bases, built or modernized with American money, should be closed to American planes six months after the end of the war. Nor can any American understand why Britain, who is anxious to have the United States continue as a world power, should not recognize America's right and duty to maintain a large merchant marine.

No American can understand why the British should object to American attempts to recruit business in Latin America or in any other part of the world. Nor why the British should retain their monopoly of Lloyd's reinsurance transactions, or of the world's diamond industry. And certainly no American can understand how his objections to British monopolies and his search for trade outlets could be branded by the British as an "explosion of economic nationalism in the United States." All these are matters of strong and sincere feelings of self-interest on both sides of the Atlantic Ocean. They are, too, potential thunderheads of misunderstanding.

This study of British complaints or fears in relation to the United States reveals that the British are particularly concerned about the postwar period. Their complaints about the present are chiefly minor psychological grievances. They feel that the United States should have come into the war sooner; they resent Americans playing up their equipment as though every weapon used for victory was made in the United States; they dislike the attitude of American white troops toward colored troops, and contrast it with American criticism of the British policy in India. They were happy to have an opportunity in North Africa to emphasize the American policy of "selling democracy and France to Vichy officials," thus giving expression to their resentment about American attacks on their former appeasement policy. In Italy, however, they had no objections to the acceptance of the Badoglio regime, which was along the same line of "military expediency" as that pursued in North Africa.

The British are understandably irked by the inability of certain Americans to comprehend that if Great Britain is to survive as a great power after the war, the Empire will have to survive in some form or other. For the Empire is to the English the geographical solution of their economy. It was the prosperity created by her imperial markets that allowed Britain to increase her population fivefold during the last century. Loss of these markets without economic compensation would ruin England. Thus the political question is fundamentally an economic question. And it was certainly not merely for rhetorical effect that Winston Churchill confounded certain American critics of British imperialism with the retort that he "did not become the King's First Minister in order to preside over the dissolution of the British Empire."

Consequently, the British are apprehensive lest "idealist and internationalist" America force them to make many political and economic sacrifices which a possible "isolationist" America of the future may refuse to acknowledge in assuring necessary American support to Britain. The principal American complaint is that the British are too slow to make these concessions, which Americans consider necessary, in India, the Near East, and the Far East.

Great Britain views without any sympathy proposals that American capital replace British investments in Latin America, for they fear that American goods would follow American dollars, and they are most anxious to maintain their position in Argentina and to recapture all other Latin-American markets as soon as possible. Plans for the return to these Western Hemisphere markets are overshadowed by the fear that American industry might prepare, behind high tariff walls, a massive drive for the conquest of these outlets, heretofore assured British trade through Britain's investments and her import demands.

As a result of her large imports, countries which furnish her necessary materials have a supply of British currency that encourages them to become British customers. The United States, on the other hand, maintains a large export surplus and there is a shortage of American currency in world markets. There is a grave possibility that after the war sterling will be still more widely offered while the dollar will become even more scarce. Obviously it will not be easy to co-ordinate British and American trade and financial interests, even though such co-ordination is vitally important to prevent a commercial rivalry that could seriously endanger the political and diplomatic relations of the two countries.

The British are anxious also to defend their economic and political positions in the Near East. They deeply regretted that Wendell Willkie listened to the grievances of Arab leaders, which resulted in certain passages in his book. Mr. Willkie has faith in the British Commonwealth of Nations, but his observing eye noted all the sore spots of the British colonial system in the Near East, and he found that system "completely antipathetic to all the principles for which we claim we fight."

The British still resent that "reservoir of good will" which this country continues to have, as Mr. Willkie had opportunity to discover, in the Near East. They resent the fact that while British subjects cannot easily obtain visas to Ibn Saud's Saudi-Arabia, citizens of the United States are able to get there without difficulty for the development of important American oil interests; and that Americans have practically taken over control of Iran's public finances.

While Americans have already forgotten British criticisms of the United States' policy in North Africa, they remember that the British lost no time in resuming their control of the coal, grain, and sugar trade in North Africa. The United States Chamber of Commerce has proposed that American businessmen be allowed to go into war zones to recruit business before peace comes—if the British can do it, why can't Americans?

The real problems of British-American relations, as we have seen, concern postwar co-operation. The British want to be assured that the Americans will co-operate with them for international security and for the creation of a free but co-ordinated trade which would enable Britain to maintain her standard of living. The Americans expect British statesmen to guarantee that the old imperialism has gone and that a new Anglo-American ideal will be created out of the present international chaos, an ideal which will express all that is best in the traditions common to England and America.

An intelligent and courageous Englishman, Mr. Geoffrey Crowther, wrote: "The American people have to learn the responsibilities of their strength; the British people have to learn the limitations of their weakness." An equally witty and intelligent American diplomat, John C. Wiley, has conceived this excellent formula to explain the chaos which preceded this war: "In the years between the two wars, the British knew what they wanted and knew how to get it. But they always wanted the wrong things. We, however, could not get what we wanted, simply because we did not know what to wish for."

This time let us hope that the British will want the "right things" and that the Americans will know what they want, because once they do know it, they will know how to get it without having to be drawn into another war.

II: The Crucial Problem

The Soviet Union and Her Allies

If British-American solidarity is the cornerstone of the United Nations, the Russian problem—or more precisely, the problem of the co-ordination of Anglo-American and Russian war strategies and postwar aims—is the crucial problem confronting the Allies. For if the Soviet Union recognizes that the United Nations can assure her security in the postwar world, the United Nations will survive the defeat of Hitler. But if the Soviet Union comes to the conclusion that the United Nations are unable or unwilling to build a postwar world in which she will be secure from any aggression, then she will try to achieve her security—even if it be only temporary—by all available means, and the United Nations will be doomed.

The first half of this problem, the question of co-ordinating war strategy, was disposed of by the Teheran Conference, but not before the dispute over the second front had raged through two years of common fighting against Hitler and had developed into a serious handicap to the formulation of a more vital general agreement on postwar aims. Although the United States, Great Britain, and Russia had long been in agreement on the absolute necessity of defeating their common enemy and destroying Nazi Germany, this was only a *limited* war objective. The unity of the three major members of the United Nations on this point was of a destructive rather than constructive character. They were able at Teheran to unite on the strategy by which Nazi Germany could be quickly destroyed, yet they still did not know whether they could agree on the Germany which should succeed the defeated Nazi regime; whether they could agree on the postwar world which they must build in order to apply the principles of the Atlantic Charter and to assure their own security and that of the nations now dependent upon them.

29

This original lack of understanding on strategy can be partially explained by the fact that the Big Three did not enter the war against the Axis simultaneously. Great Britain realized the failure of appeasement and found herself obliged to declare war on Hitler on September 2, 1939, when he attacked Poland. Soviet Russia became involved in the war on June 22, 1941, when Hitler's armies rolled across the Soviet Union's newly extended borders. The United States was dragged into the war on that fateful Sunday afternoon of December 7, 1941, a date never to be erased from American memories.

Thus 1942 was the first year of the coalition war; it was then that American and British military experts began mapping their grand strategy in preparation for future military operations, while on the Eastern Front Russia was bearing the whole weight of Hitler's formidable war machine. The Russians ceaselessly urged Washington and London to establish as quickly as possible a second front in Northwestern Europe in the belief that this would relieve the pressure on them by compelling Hitler to withdraw fifty or sixty divisions from the Russian front. During the decisive battle of Stalingrad in that year they appealed desperately for a second front. They argued bitterly in 1943 that the opening of the second front in co-ordination with their summer offensive could bring about the early collapse of Hitler.

Irritated by the criticisms implicit in Moscow's demands, many Americans, especially among the former isolationists, pointed belligerently to the ever-increasing figures of lend-lease aid to Russia and to her insistence on neutrality toward Japan. For those Americans who considered the war against Japan as the only "American" war, the Soviet Union could not become a true ally so long as she was not fighting the enemy in the Pacific. But Churchill, in his address following the Quebec Conference in August 1943, refused to "blame the Russians for what they say" because he recognized that in the light of their heroic fighting and the enormous casualties they had inflicted upon Germany's military strength "nothing they [the Russians] could say in honest criticism of our strategy or the part we have so far been able to take in the war, would be taken amiss by us or weaken our admiration for their own martial courage and achievements." Many British and many more Americans, however, have not shown Churchill's understanding of Russia's reproaches.

The problem of the second front almost developed into an American domestic issue. Mutual partisan reproaches were exchanged, and they were sharpened by domestic political passions. Many unfortunate and frequently irresponsible statements were made on the radio, in the press, and on Capitol Hill. The makers of United States foreign policy and high-ranking military leaders were accused publicly of hoping in secret that both "Nazi Germany and Soviet Russia will bleed white." There were accusations that an enormous American army was being raised not so much to win the war as to police the world after the United Nations' victory, in order to prevent revolutionary chaos and guard against the spreading of Communism. All these did much to foster mutual mistrust between Russia and the United States. The polls on "Are we going to—and should we—fight Soviet Russia after this war?" had a similar effect. These polls, incidentally, were organized with the best possible intentions along the lines of traditional freedom and frankness of American discussion. Their organizers were convinced that they were rendering a real service to the United Nations by proving to Soviet leaders that the overwhelming majority of Americans rejected even the possibility of a conflict with Russia.

However, it was difficult for Soviet leaders, who for twenty-five years shaped the foreign and domestic policies of their country without a free press and who practically suppressed what the Western democracies know as public opinion, to understand the very structure of public opinion and a free democratic press. They simply could not realize that editorials and columns critical of the Soviet Union were really free expressions of American public opinion and not inspired hints and warnings issued through semi-official channels. They suspected that the sponsors of these polls were primarily interested in finding out not how many Americans were opposed to an eventual conflict with the Soviet Union but how many Americans believed that this conflict was inevitable or even indispensable.

On the other hand, the record of Russia's relations with the outer world, including her present allies, was certainly not without its shadows, and some of them appeared to be rather disturbing. The

Comintern is now disbanded, but it is not easy to forget how it was used for many years in a number of foreign countries, and how it weakened French resistance in 1939. The magnificent resistance of the Red Army to the Nazis succeeded the pact with Nazi Germany, but that resistance has not erased the prior and disturbing fact of the pact's existence. Moscow's reluctance to permit the Allies to use Russian bases in the Caucasus for the bombing of Rumania can perhaps be explained by the innate Soviet distrust of establishing foreign military missions in the area in which Britain and France tried in 1919-1920 to obtain for themselves control of Russia's richest oil fields. However, this distrust was not of a nature to inspire the confidence of the Allies in Soviet Russia.

Unfortunately, instead of applying the searchlight of honest and objective thinking to dispel our own capitalistic-democratic shadows, as well as those we have discovered on Russia's record, we have erred in both directions by exaggerating one day the lights of the two countries and by blackening the next day their shadows. We were and we still are approaching the problem of relations between Soviet Russia and our democratic, capitalistic world on an emotional rather than a political basis, apparently forgetting that these relations developed in the poisoned climate of mutual prejudices and suspicions. But even so, this we do know: No responsible present-day political leader in Washington or London believes that it is possible to exclude Soviet Russia from the postwar world organization.

Because of the traditional American preoccupation with the moral character of political issues, and because of the indirect but important influence of foreign-born groups whose origins were in Eastern and Central Europe, there is a natural desire in this country that Russia's postwar aims comply with the principles of the Atlantic Charter. This desire and hope have developed a somewhat defensive attitude in American circles. But even the most friendly defensive attitude appears to be suspected by Moscow of concealing potentially aggressive intentions. For the Soviet's leaders still cannot forget the foreign interventions of 1918.

In prewar 1938, a Russian citizen, "Comrade Ivanov," wrote to Stalin to ask him "whether the Soviet Union could devote herself entirely to the building of socialism in one country, while living in capitalistic encirclement." And Stalin answered that while living in a "capitalistic encirclement" Soviet Russia cannot consider the "victory of socialism" complete unless she "protects herself completely from the dangers of intervention and destruction."

This old apprehension of possible encirclement apparently still motivates Russia's categoric opposition to all schemes for an "East European Federation," which the Soviet leaders view as merely a camouflaged version of the worn-out *cordon sanitaire*. Both Washington and London consider this fear absolutely unjustified and many observers consequently question its sincerity. Nevertheless, it is one of the most important clews to the understanding of Soviet foreign policy for it distorts the Russian leaders' otherwise natural and legitimate desire to assure the security of their country. They needed this security yesterday for the "building of socialism in one country." They will need it still more urgently tomorrow for the rehabilitation of their land, now so terribly devastated by Hitler's invasion.

In the absence of "nuclear alliances," such as Walter Lippmann proposes, or of a practical form of collective security, such as Sumner Welles advocates, every great power is naturally anxious to assure its proper security by all available means. But the idea of security for a great power does not necessarily exclude the idea of expansion. Makers of foreign policy sometimes view security as a consolidation stage to prepare for an eventual expansion. And security may also be viewed as a determinant of a certain expansion believed indispensable to the achievement of that security. Now, everyone recognizes the right of Soviet Russia to assure her own security after her present ordeal. But many people in Great Britain, and even more in the United States, would be greatly disturbed if Russia should attempt to guarantee that security by imposing her domination either directly or in disguise upon a Europe just liberated from Nazi domination.

The new Soviet Constitution may be a very clever move for the most efficient development of the many nations which constitute the Soviet Union. It may be a logical evolution of the Soviet Union in her permanent search for the consolidation of her achievements. The new administrative decentralization, which does not alter the political, social, and economic unity of Russia, may be merely the expression of their legitimate desire to develop new national individualities within the Soviet commonwealth. But the Soviet trend toward unilateral settlement of existing problems has caused some observers to wonder anxiously whether the new Constitution may not eventually become an extremely flexible and, therefore, particularly dangerous bit of machinery for use in the Soviet Union's expansion. It may, indeed, replace the old-fashioned "policy of expansion" by a new "policy of attraction."

How, then, is Russia to achieve her security? Or, more important to the United Nations, how does Russia intend to achieve it? What are her postwar aims and what tactics will she use to establish them? Will she be able to reconcile and co-ordinate her postwar objectives with those of the other major members of the United Nations? The latter is the crucial problem; its solution will measure the success or failure of the United Nations. Perhaps the answers to these questions may be found by examining the Soviet Union's methods and tactics as they were registered during the years on her foreign record.

As long as the post-Versailles Germany was possessed of her complex of "frustrated nationalism," Moscow considered her as a possible ally against the "powerful, satisfied" Western democracies. But when Hitler's arrival to power converted Germany into a potential danger, Soviet Russia began searching for collective security, only to find the doors to such an international arrangement effectively closed at Munich in September 1938. In the summer of 1939 the British and French tried to reopen them in desperate negotiation for an urgent alliance with Russia. Thereupon Stalin, almost as suspicious of the British and French after Munich as he was of the Germans, made his deal with Hitler. He must have known the temporary character of that deal, but it gave him additional time and certain territories which he was able to incorporate "constitutionally" into Soviet Russia's framework. Like all leaders of revolutionary origin, Stalin has always been very anxious to legalize by a "constitutional" record all annexations or re-annexations.

Concurrent with his search for collective security, Stalin had to resurrect Russian nationalism, after having previously protected and co-ordinated the national individualities of hundreds of non-Russian minorities. He expected Russia to find herself fighting a "patriotic national war." Moreover, European revolutions, regardless of their origins, their causes, and ideologies, always have had nationalistic conclusions. Just after Hitler's arrival to power in 1934, for the first time the term "Our Fatherland" was permitted to reappear in the Union of Socialist Soviet Republics. This program also entailed the rehabilitation of Russian history which was so thoroughly discredited in the first years of the Revolution.

Already in 1929, Count Alexey Tolstoi, in his historical novel, *Peter the First*, had suggested a psychological link between Stalin and Russia's revolutionary Czar who brutally closed the Muscovy chapter of Russian history by establishing a Russian Empire with a window open to Europe on the Baltic shores. Tolstoi wanted to convey the impression that Stalin, who brutally closed the capitalistic chapter and the window to capitalistic Europe, was the historical successor of Peter the Great.

With the growth of external danger a restoration of Russian nationalism was intensified. Soviet historians were instructed by their government to stop the wholesale discrediting of former Russian rulers and to bring out the unchanging patriotic ideal which throughout the centuries guided all those who built first the Russian State and later the Russian Empire. Moreover, they were instructed to mark, whenever possible, the conflict between Russia's "westernized" emperors and their "genuinely" Russian generals. They found an excellent opportunity to bring out this conflict in the study of the "Fatherland's War" of 1812.

The Russian historian Eugene Tarlé published in 1938 a great political book entitled *Napoleon's Invasion of Russia,* recounting how Alexander I, who read his *Evangile* in French, allowed himself to be seduced by the idea of becoming the liberator of European peoples conquered by Napoleon. After defeating Napoleon in Russia, he became involved in the Holy Alliance, which established a reactionary order in Europe. The utterly Russian Marshal Kutuzov, whose strategy of retreat defeated Napoleon, became suspicious of Alexander's British ally and argued that Russia's victorious army should be kept at home and not sent to fight beyond their country's borders.

A Soviet film, *Alexander Nevski,* celebrated, also in 1938, a Russian grand duke who in 1242 defeated the Teutonic knights whose brutality and "master-race" conceptions were to be revived seven centuries later by a little Baltic-born teacher of design, Alfred Rosenberg. And he, in turn, was to become in 1941 by Hitler's will the Vice-Fuehrer of the conquered Russian territories. Alexander Nevski, having defeated the Teutonic knights, magnanimously sent their soldiers home, declaring that his people wanted to live in peace with all their neighbors and had no desire to continue fighting even their enemies once they left Russian soil. In the same film Alexander Nevski made another significantly revealing remark. When his friends complained about the Tartars who were oppressing the Russians, he replied, "Let us first defeat the Germans, who are the principal enemies. Then we will be able to take care of the enemy in the East." This remark was passed by the Soviet censor and it may have prophetic political importance.

One would, of course, never dream of trying to discover the future trends of American foreign policy through an analysis of an American historical novel, or by an interpretation of a Hollywood movie. In the Soviet Union, however, films and historical books follow more than closely along the official state policy line. Hence the significance of the idea expressed as early as 1938 in both the book and the film that "once the aggressor has been defeated and repulsed beyond Russian borders, the Russian Army should turn back and remain at home." This may not, in the final analysis, become the guiding idea of Stalin's foreign policy. The idea, however, was undoubtedly still alive after three years of exasperating struggle against the German oppressors, who certainly are hated more violently in Russia than in any other European country.

We can hear different echoes of this same idea coming out of Moscow—in Stalin's speech of November 6, 1942; in Soviet broadcasts to Germany during December 1942; in Stalin's Order of the Day of January 25, 1943; and finally even in the "Free Germany" manifesto of July 21, 1943. Russia fights the Nazi aggressors, but not the German people. The first objective of the Russian Army is to repulse the invaders "over the boundaries of our motherland." Nevertheless, there are many in Europe and also in the United

States anxiously wondering whether Stalin, who in 1942 could be compared to the 1812 Alexander I, would not try in 1944 to become the Alexander of 1814, attempting by means of some "holy" or "unholy" alliance to settle the fate of Europe. But judging so far as we can from the record of Stalin's foreign policy, it appears that the Georgian revolutionary who became the absolute ruler of Europe's greatest continental power prefers Alexander Nevski, who stayed at home, to Alexander I, who pushed on to Paris and, inspired by the Austrian Metternich and the Frenchman Talleyrand, presided over the Congress of Vienna. What are, however, Stalin's reasons for preferring Alexander Nevski to Alexander I and what does he understand to be his home? The answer to the first question will help us to understand the basic trend of Russia's foreign policy. The second and much more important question concerns the potential, and at certain points already actual, dissension between the Soviet Union and the other United Nations.

Why should Stalin want both his allies and the German enemy to know in advance that he is not too anxious to have his victorious army cross Russia's restored and somewhat expanded borders and push on to Germany? His feelings toward Germany must be somewhat mixed. Revenge is a sacred duty for every Caucasian-born man and he certainly must hate the Germans as much as he incites his soldiers to hate them. On the other hand, he has always suspected that the Western democracies might eventually co-operate with a defeated Germany and he would like to insure himself against just such a possibility. He is afraid that after the war the Atlantic powers may feel much closer to a "redemocratized" Germany than to Soviet Russia. He knows that the German Lutheran Church already has established contacts in Sweden and Switzerland with representatives of the American Lutheran Church, looking forward to the moral rehabilitation of a defeated Germany. He knows that this certainly was not done without the knowledge of the Gestapo. He knows also that the Catholic Church works along the same lines, and this knowledge may be one of the reasons for Moscow's attack on Vatican foreign policy.

The problem before Stalin is, then: How can he prevent religious, social, economic, and eventually political co-operation between the Atlantic powers and Germany, who will then be speaking the same democratic and capitalistic language? There are two possible courses of action. He can either bolshevize Germany or seduce her by offering her in advance more favorable conditions than those she might hope to obtain from the Atlantic powers.

The bolshevization of Germany would be truly a radical solution, offering Soviet Russia a complete guarantee against any possible "anti-Soviet" coalition. But it would have this very serious disadvantage: A German Soviet Socialist Republic with seventy or eighty million Germans incorporated in the U.S.S.R. would have a natural tendency to take over first the economic and later the political leadership of the Union. The Russians now are numerically, economically, and culturally superior to all other Eastern European or Asiatic nations and tribes incorporated in the Soviet Union, but inclusion of a German Soviet might well endanger their internal leadership.

Moreover, a Communist revolution in Germany might well reopen the revolutionary volcano inside the Soviet Union, which Marshal Stalin succeeded in extinguishing, to the bitter disappointment of some of his early revolutionary companions who accused him of having sacrificed the Party to the Army. Consequently, the German Soviet solution would be acceptable to Stalin only when and if he completely loses faith in the Atlantic members of the United Nations. So long as he remains only suspicious of their possibly "unfriendly" relations, he will satisfy himself with playing a complicated diplomatic game in which he reserves for himself the greatest possible freedom of action, and for Germany the part of a possible junior partner with Soviet Russia.

As for the seduction of Germany, the Russians have for generations specialized in the psychology of the "humiliated and insulted" and Stalin must believe that his people will be in a much better psychological position than the dignified Anglo-Americans to win over the sympathies of a beaten Germany, humiliated once again in her frustrated nationalism. Stalin is, therefore, disposed in advance to flatter—if it will serve his interests—that thwarted German nationalism just as he already is flattering France by treating with General de Gaulle and his Algiers Committee in a manner much more becoming to a great power than that employed by either the United States or Britain. The German Liberation Committee created in Moscow is consequently a clever blow in the psychological warfare Stalin is waging against both the Germans and his allies. It may speed Germany's collapse; it may also accelerate the recognition by the Atlantic powers of the Soviet Union's part in the war and her postwar objectives.

But there are other important reasons sufficient to convince Stalin to stay "at home." To him and to the present Russian generations Central and Western Europe is definitely a strange, foreign, and unsympathetic part of the world. Those Russians who since early in the nineteenth century had begun to feel equally at home in Paris, Berlin, Vienna, and Rome, disappeared with the storm that swept Russia in 1917. Those now in power do not know Western Europe, do not like it, do not trust it. But they are not going to ignore it after this war. On the contrary, they believe—and they already make declarations to this effect—that as Europe's greatest continental power, Soviet Russia will be entitled to "one of the leading parts in the organization of postwar Europe and the world." (*War and the Working Class*, Moscow, August 1943.) In Russia's first public forum on postwar policies, held in July 1943, Nikolai Malinin, a Soviet writer, went so far as to specify that Russia will be interested not only in the future of Italy and of other vassals of Germany, but also in the problems of the colonies lost by the British, Dutch, and French in the war.

Having taken all necessary measures to insure her security in the West through participation in the reorganization of Europe, Russia then will be able to look eastward for her economic and political expansion. The East, from Iran up to Manchuria, is very close to the hearts of Russia's present rulers, and it is, moreover, in the traditional line of expansion of the Russian Empire. The Russians realize that they cannot hope to assimilate the more highly cultured Western and Central Europeans. In Asia, however, they feel themselves able to fulfill a real mission by civilizing the Asiatics as they expand their empire economically and politically. The East is rich, it is seductive; it has space, appeal, constructive possibilities. To the Russians the East is what the West was for the American pioneers of the last century. The all-important prerequisite for Russia's opening up of the East—blocked now in "Manchukuo" by Japan and in Turkey and Iran by the British—will be her security in the West.

Where, however, will the Soviet Union in its search for security establish its "West Wall"? Along what borders? The answer was not forthcoming at either the Moscow or Teheran conferences because the Allies preferred not to ask for it. But the answer is not as mysterious as is generally implied. We have already seen the basis for it in Soviet films and literature. The Marshal Stalin who orders his historians, novelists, and film producers to picture him as Alexander Nevski, Peter I, or Marshal Kutuzov, without a doubt feels compelled to restore the borders that Lenin's revolution took over from Nicholas II, Russia's last Czar. Even as Napoleon could not give up the territories conquered by the French Revolutionary Army, so Stalin considers himself both the conclusion of the Russian Revolution and the successor to all Russian Empire builders who preceded the Revolution. To begin with, Stalin will claim his historic right and obligation to recover Russia's 1914 borders. Furthermore, he might find himself compelled, always in search of security, to continue, with new tactics, all the old expansion policies which were dictated by the national interests of the old Empire.

Following the pattern of historical evolution, the Soviet Union was bound to develop from a revolutionary state with underlying nationalist conceptions into a multi-national state with underlying revolutionary aspirations. The defensive, patriotic character of the present war merely accelerated this joint evolution. "Imperialist" and "imperialism" still are disparaging terms in Soviet political language. But it was inevitable that the Soviet Union in its nationalistic evolution should travel—though often unconsciously—in new communistic vehicles along the old roads of policy staked out by the Russian Empire.

Empires evolve. But whether they transform themselves into "Commonwealths" or "Federations of Soviet Republics," they must, if they would survive, obey their organic laws. The political and social coloring of their missions may change but the framework for the realization of the revised missions must be conserved and, whenever necessary, extended. This phenomenon explains away the paradoxical situation now existing between Great Britain, the Soviet Union, and the United States. Great Britain and the Soviet Union, two evolving empires, may be divided by the traditional conflicts of their interests in the Balkans and the Near East, but they instinctively understand each other. Each realizes the growing necessity of co-operating with each other, else peace cannot be preserved.

The United States and Russia never conflicted in their past relations. On the contrary, as Mr. DeWitt C. Poole, American diplomat who served in Russia after the last war, notes in his study *Russia and the United States,* each country "has always wished the other to be strong" because each regarded the other as "a potential friend in the rear of potential enemies." Mr. Poole points out that the Americans never have liked "the governments which the Russians have permitted to rule over them" while both the Czarist and Soviet governments had little sympathy for American democracy. Despite these mutual ideological antipathies, during the War of Independence the Continental Congress looked for the assistance of Russia, and in the Civil War Czar Alexander II considered the preservation of the union so imperative for Russia's welfare that he dispatched warships to New York and San Francisco as a warning to London and Paris not to recognize the Confederacy. In return the United States in 1918 firmly opposed dismemberment of Russia and insisted on the withdrawal of Japanese troops from Siberia. This country was the last great power to recognize *de jure* the independence of the three Baltic republics, not acting until July 1922.

There still are no "boundary disputes" between the United States and Russia and, as Walter Lippmann stresses, there is "no American territory which Russia covets, no Russian territory to which the United States has ever laid any claim whatever." Nevertheless, relations between the two countries became much less satisfactory than between Russia and Great Britain. Americans are basically opposed to and critical of all imperialism, and especially to an imperialism distorted and camouflaged by a social ideology that is unacceptable to an overwhelming majority of them. As the only great power built originally on a "moral" rather than a "national" concept, the United States is more anxious than other nations to co-ordinate the realistic necessities of foreign policy with strictly moral considerations. Often overlooked in this respect is the political importance of millions of Americans who were born in Eastern Europe and are hostile to both Czarist and Soviet Russia.

Outspoken British imperialists, such as Lord Beaverbrook, and "neo-idealists" like Anthony Eden, are convinced defenders of a British-Russian alliance because they have come for different reasons to the same conclusion. On the eve of Mr. Eden's departure for Washington early in 1943 the London *Times* said editorially, "There can be no security in Western Europe unless there is also security in Eastern Europe, and security in Eastern Europe is buttressed by the military power of Russia." The same editorial, developing the need for closer British-Russian postwar collaboration, concludes that after the war Russia will be in a position "to assure her security, as she understands it, and that it would be therefore wise for Great Britain to recognize in advance Russia's sphere of influence in Eastern Europe."

This same newspaper sees British diplomacy facing two essential tasks: To "develop a spirit of growing confidence in Anglo-Russian relations" in order to destroy the seeds of all Russian suspicions, and to "interpret to the United States the common interest of Britain and Russia in European security and the means of attaining it."

Thus some British circles have come to the conclusion that the nineteenth-century balance of power has been irretrievably destroyed. They realize that "the continental nations, hopelessly divided, are now no match for Germany." But if Britain should decide to abandon her traditional policy of supporting the "second strong" nation on the Continent, she would like to be able to maintain her traditional role of "honest broker," this time between two great powers—the United States and the Soviet Union.

The great paradox of current history is that Great Britain's Tory government should become an intermediary between the Soviet Union and "New Deal" America. It is equally paradoxical that Britain, which for generations considered Russia her rival in Asia, has become more aware of Russia's important role in world security than has the United States, which has virtually never had a serious dispute with Russia and may even need her to help curb Japanese imperialism.

The reasons for this paradox, as we have analyzed them, are principally of a moral character. To them we must add a "technical" consideration. The Constitution of the United States does not permit this country to enter into treaties such as the Russian-British twenty-year alliance of June 1942. Moreover, American public opinion, if we can safely judge by a Gallup poll taken on the eve of the Moscow Conference, is divided on the issue of a permanent military alliance with Soviet Russia. This poll showed 61 per cent in favor of a permanent military alliance with Britain but only 39 per cent supporting a similar alliance with Russia, whereas 37 per cent of those canvassed were against such an American-Russian treaty, and 24 per cent were undecided.

The principal objections raised by those opposing a Russian alliance were, first, the ideological antagonism between the two countries; second, a deep mistrust of Russia expressed in the suspicion that she would not honor such a pact; and third, the fear that, because of Russia's geographic position in Europe and her dealings with neighboring countries, America would run the risk under such an agreement of being almost continuously entangled in foreign wars.

The Soviet Union and her allies are equally tortured by the same legacy of suspicion. Their postwar co-operation is threatened by the disruptive forces of this legacy. They can overcome those forces only by a frank and sincere presentation not only of their respective postwar aims but also of the methods by which they hope to achieve those aims.

It is permissible to assume that the Soviet Union, along with her allies, is primarily interested in her postwar security. But even should the Soviet Union and her allies become equally convinced of their equal interest in security—and thus dispel much of their mutual distrust—they would still need to agree on the methods they intend to apply for the realization of their common aim. Those methods should not interfere with their respective approaches to foreign policy problems.

The foreign policy of a nation is, indeed, the political expression of its instinct for preservation. It is determined by geography, partly by history, to a great extent by economy, and especially by changing conditions in the outer world. A foreign policy therefore is necessarily subject to change and is of temporary character. But a national approach to foreign policy problems is basically and essentially permanent, so far as the national temperament is permanent.

The co-ordination of Soviet foreign policy methods with American and British national approaches to foreign policy is of paramount importance. Thus the Soviet Union's dealing with her neighbors—especially with Poland, which is a member of the United Nations—holds first place on the list of the internal problems to be resolved by the United Nations.

III: The Open Wound

Poland

THE Polish problem has become the open wound on the body of the United Nations and until this wound is healed the United Nations will be grievously sick. Poland's problem is closely interrelated with that of Russia and with the entire structure of nations known as the Allies, for Poland was the first victim of Hitler's military aggression. As such she can truthfully claim that Great Britain and France took up arms against Hitler, at least officially, to fight for the preservation of Polish independence.

Poland has suffered more than any other nation under the Nazi yoke and she is proud of being the only enslaved nation without a Quisling. Even when conquered, she never gave up the fight. She must realize, however, that only through the victory of the United Nations can she recover her freedom and independence. She should, therefore, be more interested than any other member in the solidarity of the United Nations.

Yet, unfortunately, it was in the Polish-Russian sector of the United Nations that Dr. Goebbels' propaganda machinery was able to register its only major victory—the Russo-Polish split over the mysterious deaths of ten thousand Polish officers near Smolensk. When relations between Russia and the Polish Government-in-Exile in London were severed in April 1943, Foreign Commissar Molotov attributed it officially to the fact that the Polish government, giving credence to Nazi propaganda charges that the Russians had murdered ten thousand Polish officers in Russian territory, asked the International Red Cross to investigate the Nazi-reported discovery of their graves in Smolensk.

These officers were reportedly interned in three Russian concentration camps after the Russian-German partition of Poland and all trace of them was lost after April 1940. As soon as the Poles in exile had resumed relations with Russia, following the Nazi invasion of the Soviet Union, they tried to locate their missing officers for humanitarian reasons and to staff their reorganized army. Polish Ambassador Stanislaw Kot repeatedly brought the matter to the attention of high Soviet officials, including Stalin himself. The late General Wladyslaw Sikorski, Poland's Prime Minister, personally handed Stalin a list of 4,000 names of officers who had been detained in one of the three camps, and an additional list bringing the total to 8,700 was presented later.

In November 1941, Soviet authorities declared that "all Polish officers in the U.S.S.R. have been released" and flatly denied Polish reports that some of the officers might have been scattered in the northern regions of Russia. The Poles claimed that in the discussion that followed the Russians admitted that many of their officers must have been dispersed throughout the Soviet Union and that some of them might have fled from Siberia to Manchuria. In the spring of 1942 Russia permitted a Polish commission to visit her concentration and war prisoner camps but it was unable to locate the missing officers. The commission, however, did succeed in arousing the suspicions of Soviet officials who were inclined to take all inquisitive foreigners for spies.

The Poles refused to abandon their search and repeatedly asked influential British and American visitors to Russia to help them locate their missing men. The Nazis very cleverly turned this incident to their uses, stressing reports that the Russians had cold-bloodedly murdered the Polish officers. Finally they revealed the discovery of the site of the mass execution and the graves themselves, producing evidence which the Nazis claimed proved the Russians were responsible. It was on this so-called evidence that the Poles in London appealed to the International Red Cross to intervene and make the investigation.

There were, however, two other, more substantial reasons for the severance of diplomatic relations. One of them—expressed indirectly in Molotov's note—was the fundamental conflict over Russian-Polish boundaries. The other was Moscow's strong distrust of the Polish government in London and the desire to see this government replaced by a "friendly" regime which would follow Moscow's foreign policy line.

Poland and Russia were fighting on the same side only because

of Hitler's successive aggressions against them. The only connect-
ing link in this war was their passionate desire to see their common
enemy defeated. Otherwise divided by their history, they had
always viewed each other's foreign policy with suspicion and
mistrust. The Russians cannot forget that during every troubled
period of their history, Polish soldiers appeared on their soil. In
1610, when Muscovite Russia was plunged into anarchy, the Poles
entered Moscow and held the Kremlin. In 1920, when Russia was
divided by civil war, the Poles reached Kiev, capital of the Soviet
Ukrainian Republic and "Mother of Russian Cities."

The Poles, on the other hand, will always remember that Russia
participated in the three partitions of their country during the
eighteenth century (1772, 1791, and 1795) and that the Soviet
Union, which signed a pact with Hitler only a week before he
invaded their country, was paid a month later for that signature
with a share in the fourth partition of Poland. Russia's treatment
of the Poles deported by the Soviet administration from Poland's
eastern provinces when they were incorporated into the Soviet
Union as a result of that partition, certainly did not help to
strengthen Polish sympathies for the Russians.

British diplomacy, therefore, could consider the Russian-Polish
agreement signed in London on July 30, 1941, as a miraculous
achievement. Since Hitler's Russian invasion the British Foreign
Office had most anxiously sought to regulate relations between
these two neighbors which, divided by centuries of unceasing
struggle for the borderlands of White Russia and the Ukraine, suddenly found themselves in the same camp.

The Russian-Polish agreement was made possible mainly because of the strong personal influence Winston Churchill exercised
on General Sikorski. He convinced Sikorski, for whom Germany
always has been Poland's chief enemy, that Russian-Polish co-
operation was the best if not the only defense of Poland's national
interests. By signing this agreement, General Sikorski rendered a
most important service to the cause of the United Nations five
months before the Allies were officially organized as such. Sikorski
sincerely believed that he was also, if not primarily, serving the
interests of his country.

He believed that he would be able to improve immediately the

fate of those of his compatriots who were then held by Russia
in either war prisons or concentration camps. He believed, too,
that he would be able to prepare the best possible moral climate
for postwar solution of the Russian-Polish boundary problems left
open by the London agreement. He actually did bring some sev-
enty-five thousand Polish soldiers out of Russia to become the
nucleus of the new Polish army since created in the Middle East.
He was to be deceived, however, about the determination of Poland's eastern boundaries.

In the London agreement the Soviet government recognized "the
Soviet-German treaties of 1939 as to territorial changes in Poland
as having lost their validity." This carefully worded statement was
the most that Sikorski could obtain. As additional satisfaction on
the day the treaty was signed, Anthony Eden handed the Polish
Prime Minister a note which assured him that "His Majesty's Government do not recognize any territorial changes which have been
effected in Poland since August 1939." This was to be expected
from Great Britain, which had in the summer of 1939 committed
herself to guarantee Poland's independence and integrity in the
last desperate Franco-British diplomatic move to avert Nazi aggression in Eastern Europe.

But the very next day Mr. Eden explained in the House of
Commons that the "British government did not guarantee Poland's
pre-war boundaries." If Mr. Eden meant it to be understood by
his statement that while England was pledged to the restoration
of a free and independent Poland she considered the fixing of her
postwar boundaries an "open problem," the Soviet press was much
more specific in its comments. *Pravda* wrote: "While the agreement
with Germany was plainly no longer valid, the Soviet government
did not necessarily accept in advance the boundaries with Poland
as they had formerly been drawn."

In other words, this authoritative Soviet newspaper declared
that a victorious Soviet Russia would not accept the Russian-
Polish borders as delimited after the Soviet defeat in the Russo-
Polish War of 1920 and as they existed until 1939. Thus both parties were anxious to have on the record that their agreement in
no way prejudiced their respective, conflicting claims on the eventual settlement of their boundaries.

In the cabinet crises that shook Sikorski's government following this agreement, three ministers resigned in protest, claiming that to leave the boundary question open was detrimental to Poland's interests. Polish political circles in Britain and the United States opened a violent campaign against Sikorski which contributed greatly to the Soviet-Polish crisis of 1943 by undermining his prestige and stirring up further the Russians' innate suspicions of the Poles. But before retracing the events which led to that historic crisis and analyzing the attitudes of the two countries, let us examine the object of their controversy.

The Russian-Polish boundary question is an old, old quarrel, older than the modern Polish state which emerged only after the Allied victory of 1918; older than Soviet Russia which dates back only to the First World War; older even than the Empire of the Czars. It is the struggle between the two neighboring Slavic peoples of Russia and Poland for the domination of White Russia and the Ukraine. In their efforts to create for themselves a "state frame" even before they acquired a "national consciousness" in the modern sense of that term, these ancient peoples have fought for a thousand years in an interminable series of conflicts over this same territory.

From the eleventh to the fourteenth centuries the contested land was more or less under Russian influence and domination, as far as there was at that time any real difference between the Ukrainians and the Russians. In the thirteenth century the Mongols invaded and conquered many Russian grand duchies, of which the Kiev Duchy was the most important and the most closely connected by intermarriage with Western Europe. This decay of Russian duchies facilitated the rise of the Polish state which, after fighting the Germans in the west from the fourteenth to the seventeenth centuries, tried to extend its suzerainty to the divided and weakened borderlands to the east.

In the fifteenth century the emerging Muscovite Czardom began to unite "all Russia," but in 1598 the Muscovite dynasty had already become extinct. Unable to agree on a Russian pretender, the Muscovite boyars in 1610 offered the Russian throne to Prince Vladyslav, son of Poland's King Sigismund. But Sigismund wanted the Russian throne for himself and his attempt to bring the whole of Russia under Polish rule provoked a Russian national revolt. The Poles were driven from the Kremlin and the first Romanov, whose father was at that moment a war prisoner in Poland, was elected to Russia's throne in 1613.

Under the Romanovs Russia began to rise to power, while Poland, weakened by internal dissension and civil wars, began to decline. The Ukrainian Cossacks, headed by Hetman Bohdan Chmielnicki, revolted in 1648 against the Poles, who had exasperated them by the intolerance of Polish Roman Catholic priests toward the Greek Orthodox Church and by the high-handed behavior of the Polish landlords. The Polish gentry and Jesuits were massacred in the Ukraine, and in 1654 Chmielnicki and his Ukrainian Cossacks swore allegiance to the "Muscovite Czar, the Orthodox Czar." In 1667, by the Truce of Andrussovo—which proved to be one of the most enduring peace agreements in history—Poland ended her war with Muscovite Russia. Vitebsk and the province of Polish Livonia were returned to Poland but she ceded "in perpetuity to Russia Smolensk and the whole eastern bank of the Dnieper."

In the eighteenth century, Empress Catherine II of Russia decided to take advantage of Poland's increasing weakness to recover all provinces with Greek Orthodox White Russian and Ukrainian populations. The first partition of Poland in 1772 brought Russia the provinces of Vitebsk and Polock, a territory of 34,616 square miles. The second partition in 1791 increased Russia's territory by another 96,571 square miles from Livonia in the north to Moldavia in the south. The third partition in 1795 marked the end of Poland as an independent state.

Upon emerging in 1918 from their political bondage, the Poles were blinded by the sudden light of freedom and invigorated by the bracing air of independence. They felt themselves free to go as far as they liked in both the West and the East. Poland could not and did not have stable historical boundaries such as the Western European countries could cling to. Her frontiers, especially in the East, had been different in every century. The problem then was to determine where to fix the new boundaries of re-established and independent Poland.

The Poles generally favored the eighteenth-century borders that antedated the first partition. However, many of them, recalling Poland's glory in the fourteenth and sixteenth centuries, were convinced that Poland should extend her possessions from the Baltic Sea down to the shores of the Black Sea. Meanwhile, many European statesmen, diplomats, and military leaders were convinced at that time that Russia had disappeared forever as a great power. Others, frightened by the specter of a Communist revolution in Europe, were only too eager to build up a *cordon sanitaire* against the new Red disease. With the collapse of Russia, France lost the precious Eastern ally so badly needed for her own security, and she became interested in building a *cordon sanitaire* and in discovering a new Eastern ally. Both as that new ally and as the pivot of the *cordon sanitaire*, Poland seemed to be a godsend to France.

A temporary Russian-Polish boundary was proposed in December 1919 by the Allied Supreme Council. It later became known as the Curzon Line, although Lord Curzon, then British Foreign Minister, was not personally responsible for it. He suggested that line, which was established by ethnographic considerations, only as the basis for an armistice in 1920. It was not considered by the Poles or by their friends on the French General Staff as Poland's definite boundary in the East. It was simply a delimitation of unquestionably Polish territories. The fate of territories east of this line—White Russia and the Ukraine with more or less important Polish minorities—was to be determined in the future. Its immediate purpose was to end the skirmishing between Russian and Polish soldiers who were waiting for the determination of a definite boundary.

Unfortunately for the future of Polish-Russian relations, their boundary differences could not be resolved peacefully. On one side was a revolutionary government which boasted that after establishing a Soviet regime in the former Empire of the Czars it would carry the Red banner to all the other countries of the world. On the other was a Polish government inspired by historical recollections, intoxicated by the "unlimited possibilities" which appeared suddenly along with its brand new independence, and encouraged if not incited by the French General Staff.

Without a fixed boundary line, the Soviet Union and Poland

lived in an anomalous relationship that was neither war nor peace. In January 1920, Lenin, Trotsky, and Tchitcherin signed a stern declaration addressed to "the Polish government and the Polish nation." It warned that "Poland is now confronted with a decision that for many years to come may have grave repercussions on the lives of both nations. Everything shows that the extreme imperialists of the Entente, the supporters and agents of Churchill and Clemenceau, are at present directing all their efforts to draw Poland into a futile, ill-considered, and criminal war with the Soviet Union." The declaration further emphasized that the Soviet Union recognized "unreservedly the independence and sovereignty of the Polish Republic." It specified that the Red Army would not cross the then existing front line, and expressed the conviction that all questions between Poland and Russia could be solved peacefully.

However, the Poles allowed themselves, under French influence, to become involved in a joint invasion of Russia. Assisted by Ukrainian nationalists, most of them from former Austrian Galicia, they attacked the Soviet Ukraine in April 1920. They reached the Dnieper and entered Kiev, while White Russian forces headed by General Wrangel were fighting their way toward Kiev from the east.

Just as the presence of Polish soldiers in the Kremlin in 1610 resulted in a Russian national revolt, the appearance of Polish soldiers in Kiev in 1920 provoked a surge of Russian patriotism. General Brusilov, hero of the 1916 offensive, and many other high Czarist officers joined the Red Army to fight the Poles who had seized the shrine of their former masters. The Red Army retook Kiev, routed the Poles and pursued them to the suburbs of Warsaw.

Not only Poland but the whole French system in Eastern Europe was endangered. General Weygand hurried to Warsaw, and the Polish Army headed by Marshal Pilsudski and advised by Weygand counterattacked. The Red Army was obliged to retreat and the "Miracle of the Vistula" saved Poland. "It saved," as official Polish publications in the United States continued to emphasize as late as 1943, "Western Europe from Communism." Moreover, it assured a boundary that gave Poland additional important territories in the East, but which also placed under her rule a Ukrainian minority estimated at from 4,500,000 to 7,000,000 and a White Russian minority of 1,500,000. Thirty million Ukrainians and more than a million White Russians remained as citizens of the "Ukrainian and White Russian Soviet Republics" of the Soviet Union.

The Treaty of Riga, signed in March 1921, under which these settlements were made, recognized the independence of the Ukraine and White Russia, which became incorporated into the Soviet Union. White Russia and the Ukraine abandoned all rights and claims to territory west of the agreed frontier and Poland abandoned in favor of the Soviet Ukraine and Soviet White Russia all rights and claims to territory east of the line.

But the succeeding eighteen years of peace during which Poland's eastern frontier was carefully respected by the Soviet Union, did little to improve the relations between these neighboring countries. Poland mistrusted the Soviet Union's intentions when the latter signed the Rapallo Treaty with Weimar Germany in 1922. The Soviet Union in turn mistrusted Poland, first as the ally of France and then more actively when, in January 1934, Poland became the first European nation to sign a non-aggression pact with Hitler.

When the last prewar Polish envoy to Russia presented his credentials early in 1936, Nikolai Krestinski, as acting foreign commissar, welcomed him with a most undiplomatic speech. He told the Polish envoy that Soviet Russia was working for collective security and was pursuing "an anti-German, anti-Italian, and anti-Japanese policy," and went on to accuse Poland, whose foreign policy then was directed by Colonel Beck, of combatting collective security, of supporting Italy, of sympathizing with Japan, and of being "within the orbit of German policy."

Although Poland accepted in March 1939 French and British pledges of military aid, two months later she rejected Moscow's proposals for a mutual assistance pact or participation in collective negotiations with England and France. Colonel Beck explained that his country's attitude would be conditioned by the result of the Anglo-Franco-Soviet negotiations. It was, more probably, conditioned by Poland's fear that once the Red Army appeared in Polish territory in support of a mutual assistance treaty, it might be unwilling to leave.

Then came the Russian-German non-aggression pact, Hitler's attack on Poland and her quick collapse. About two weeks after war broke out, on September 16, Poland's envoy to Moscow was summoned in the night to Russia's foreign commissariat and handed a short note advising him that the Soviet government considered that the Polish state had ceased to exist. The Soviet government, it went on, could not "view with indifference the fact that the kindred Ukrainian and White Russian people, who live on Polish territory and who are at the mercy of fate, are left defenseless." To that end the Red Army had been ordered to "cross the frontier and take under their protection the life and property of the population of the Western Ukraine and Western White Russia."

The Polish envoy refused to accept the Soviet note but he could not prevent the Red Army from crossing Poland's border two hours later. And on that same day Molotov made a speech declaring that it was the Soviet government's "sacred duty to extend a helping hand to our Brother Ukrainians and our Brother White Russians who live in Poland."

The first German-Russian partition of Poland placed under Soviet rule not only all "Brother Ukrainians and Brother White Russians" but also a considerable number of Poles. A few days later, however, on September 29, the demarcation line was changed in Germany's favor, reducing Russia's share and making it ethnographically more homogeneous, with a smaller number of Poles. Soviet Russia acquired 77,703 square miles with a population of approximately 12,775,000. According to Soviet statistics, more than seven million of these were Ukrainians, about two million White Russians, a million and a half Poles, and about a million Jews. Soviet Ukraine received 35,000 square miles of the new territory with a population of approximately eight million, and 42,000 square miles with a population of four and a half million went to Soviet White Russia. In the "elections" preliminary to their incorporation into the Soviet, the official candidates polled 92 and 90 per cent of the vote respectively.

Polish circles refused to recognize the legality of either the plebiscites or the incorporation acts. The Polish Government-in-Exile pretends that all Poles, regardless of their political or religious creed, are unanimously agreed that Poland's eastern territories were "Polish territories" and should be restored to free Poland. However, the Poles themselves never have claimed a Polish majority in the territories in question.

According to the Polish census of December 1931, only 4,571,-999, or 40.4 per cent, of the inhabitants of her seven eastern provinces were Polish. And this was after ten years of Polish rule and strenuous efforts to increase Polish elements in that area. The Ukrainians numbered 36.6 per cent, according to Polish statistics, although Ukrainian sources gave a much higher figure; the White Russians 6.6 per cent; and the Jews, who are considered a national minority in Poland, constituted 7.9 per cent of the total population. If the eastern provinces could be divided from northwest to southeast into three ethnic regions, according to Polish statistics, the Poles would have 66 per cent of the total population in the first region, 36.6 per cent in the second region, and only 16 per cent of the third area.

Very little has been written about the attitude of the Ukrainians who constitute the most important minority group directly interested in the Russian-Polish controversy. The thirty million Ukrainians who live inside the Soviet Union were considerably Russified in the eighteenth and nineteenth centuries. The Soviet regime later granted them rather generous cultural autonomy and the Ukrainians were gradually "re-Ukrainized" on a cultural level. In this war, the Soviet Union Ukrainians have proved themselves loyal to their country and to the Soviet regime. It is significant that none of the potential Ukrainian Quislings whom Alfred Rosenberg had been building up in Berlin and Vienna since the last war, could be employed there.

The second Ukrainian group, which numbers approximately four and one-half to five million, came under Polish rule after the 1920 Treaty of Riga. They did not amalgamate with the third group—the three million Galician Ukrainians who lived for centuries under the Hapsburgs' rule. They were divided by religion:

those who lived in Russia remained Greek Orthodox, while the Galician Ukrainians were converted into a reformed Catholic Church known as the "Uniate Church," which in Vatican projects was to bridge the gap between the Catholic and Greek Orthodox Churches; and they were separated by their different historical backgrounds. But these two groups were finally reunited by their opposition to the Poles.

The Galician Ukrainians, far more conscious of their Ukrainian nationality than the Russian Ukrainians, have insisted upon complete autonomy. Because of their hatred of both the Poles and the Russians, some of them collaborated with the Germans in the First World War and with the Nazis in the present war. Their extremist organizations were responsible up to 1935 for many acts of terrorism which resulted in Polish punitive expeditions and did little to improve friendly relations. In that year Poland renounced her system of governing through punishing forays and entered the so-called "normalization" era of Polish-Ukrainian relations. Both Ukrainian and White Russian deputies sat in Poland's prewar parliament, but the Polish National Council in London, while demanding the return of these two territories, has been unable to find any Ukrainian or White Russian members to serve in the exiled regime.

The National Council was created by presidential decree in February 1941, with a roster of thirty-one members whose duties are to complete, if not control, activities of the Polish Government-in-Exile. It includes representatives of several conservative and reactionary political parties which always strongly opposed General Sikorski's foreign policy. For he was a moderate conservative, fundamentally anti-German and pro-Ally, and therefore in opposition to the "Colonels' Government" which succeeded the Pilsudski regime and had the support of many of the Marshal's followers. In order to justify themselves and their policy, which had led Poland into war with both Germany and Russia, they were only too glad to help prove that Sikorski's pro-Russian policy could lead only to a new catastrophe.

However, the most violent opponents of Sikorski's foreign policy remained outside the National Council. Stanislaw Cat-Mackievicz, leader of the extreme right group in the Colonels' regime, published monthly pamphlets passionately attacking Sikorski and his cabinet. Zygmunt Novakowski, outstanding Polish journalist, was at least as violent in his *Polish News,* which was finally suppressed by the British in February 1944. Dr. Tadeusz Bielecki, president of the even more pro-fascist O.N.R. (Obos Narodowy Radykalny), dissident wing of the rightist National Democratic Party, never ceased to criticize Sikorski in his newspaper *Mysl Polska* (Polish Thought). *Walka* was another sheet devoted to spreading the O.N.R. fascist ideology. Its attacks against Sikorski became so vicious that the Polish government prohibited its circulation among Polish troops in Scotland and the Near East.

The opposition to Sikorski did not fail to develop its activity among Americans of Polish descent. It was anxious to use the political influence of the American Poles who represent an important element in the political life of this country. The 1940 census reported 2,416,332 persons in the United States whose mother tongue was Polish. The number of Americans of Polish descent is estimated at between three and a half and four million. There were, at the time Sikorski's opponents began their work, ten Congressmen of Polish-American extraction (seven Democrats and three Republicans) and several other legislators had strong blocs of Polish voters in their constituencies. Their potential influence was strong enough to warrant considerable discussion in the press.

The émigré politicians in London moved, therefore, to exert pressure upon the Roosevelt Administration through their countrymen within the United States. If Washington would not take up the defense of Polish interests, they threatened, the American Poles, who constituted a bloc of foreign-born labor which in the Middle West generally favored President Roosevelt, would not vote Democratic in the 1944 presidential election. This foreign-born labor bloc to which they referred is for the most part Catholic and consists not only of Poles but of Lithuanians, Croats, Slovaks, and Slovenes.

Although the London group had not yet been able to get a firm grip on the solid Polish blocs in the Midwest, they were able to permeate the less compact groups in the Eastern states. Colonel

Ignacy Matuszevski, who served as Minister of Finance in Colonel Beck's government, became the chief political writer for New York City's most important Polish language newspaper, *Nowy Swiat*, owned by an American Pole, Maximilian F. Wegrzynek. In 1942 Wegrzynek organized the National Committee of Americans of Polish Descent for the defense of Polish interests. This committee, known as "Knap," its Polish abbreviation, became very active in sending petitions to President Roosevelt and members of Congress, and in sponsoring political advertisements in American newspapers.

Sikorski's critics intensified these attacks both in England and the United States as the Red Army counteroffensives began pushing the Germans back, for they feared that the then academic discussion of Russian-Polish boundaries might be ended in Russia's favor by her advancing troops. These attacks served as well to undermine Sikorski's prestige within his own armies. He was fully aware of the extreme delicacy of Poland's diplomatic position, and during his visit to the United States in March 1942 he appealed to the American Poles to "abstain from raising any territorial issues, especially with regard to Russia, for such problems could have a fatal effect upon the scales of victory."

While all this intra-governmental opposition was developing, Sikorski was suffering as well from the irreconcilable attitude of Soviet diplomacy. When the Prime Minister visited Russia in December 1941, Marshal Stalin told him that he wanted a strong and independent Poland and the two signed a "declaration of friendship." The two men seemed to have impressed each other rather favorably. Sikorski indicated as much to his friends and Stalin told one of the Americans in Moscow that "Sikorski seemed to him to be the only Pole whom he could trust and deal with." But this did not alter Russia's unyielding attitude toward the Poles.

Polish relief administrators seeking to locate and release Polish citizens from Soviet concentration camps ran into all sorts of difficulties, and some were even arrested on charges of espionage. The Soviet limited its recognition of Polish citizenship to the Poles, denying it to the Ukrainians, White Russians, and Jews. And besides, there remained constantly the suspicions and irritations aroused by the mystery of the missing Polish officers.

POLAND
59

The Soviet government endeavored later to justify its stiffening
attitude toward the Poles by accusing the latter of violating the
fourth paragraph of their London agreement which stipulated that
the Polish army to be formed within the Soviet Union would
operate under the Supreme Command of the U.S.S.R., supposedly
to fight on the Russian-German front. The Russians charged that
General Wladislaw Anders' Polish army mobilized in Russia was
unwilling to fight under Soviet leadership and in June 1942 they
halted formation of additional units. Polish demands led to the
authorization to evacuate to the Middle East those units already
activated. Some 75,941 fighting men and 37,756 of their dependents
were granted exit visas, but Soviet authorities declared this incident made them lose confidence in the sincerity of Poland's
supposed desire to collaborate with the Soviet Union.

The situation worsened rapidly when Sikorski came to the
United States late in 1942 to ask the Administration to help Poland defend her vital national interests. High American officials
explained to him that although the United States could not commit
herself on Poland's postwar boundaries, this country was more
than interested in the restoration of a sovereign, free, and independent Poland, and that American diplomacy would not miss any
opportunities to defend Poland's legitimate interests. In return
they asked Sikorski to help American diplomacy work to that end
by avoiding public discussion of the boundary problem on the
grounds that it was not only diplomatically indelicate but theoretical so long as the contested territory was still occupied by the
Nazis.

His opposition in London, however, took advantage of the
Prime Minister's absence to stab him politically in the back, a
gesture in which a member of his Cabinet also participated. The
National Council proceeded to adopt a resolution declaring its intention to hold to the exact basis of the Riga Treaty on the eastern
boundary question. And Professor Stanislaus Stronski, Sikorski's
Minister of Information, publicly discussed a projected Eastern
European Federation to include the three Baltic states, although
he was fully aware that Moscow could consider such a proposal a
"diplomatic provocation." Russia reacted immediately. The Polish
government was soon informed that Moscow considered all Poles

still living within the Soviet Union as Soviet citizens. *Pravda* gave the first of several warnings and Alexander Korneichuk, the Soviet Ukrainian leader, bluntly accused the Poles of entertaining an imperialistic aspiration toward his people.

General Sikorski was in an untenable position. His influence and prestige among his own troops was declining rapidly. The Middle East troops resented the absence of their Commander-in-Chief far away "in the comfort of the London exile." His twelve thousand pilots, many of whom played a glorious part in the Battle of Britain and later in the devastating bombing of Germany, reproached him for not publicizing their war activities sufficiently, and clamored for independent Polish communiqués.

Spurred to action by pressure from his combined opposition, he officially accused Soviet Russia of dropping parachutists in Eastern Poland to wage political warfare behind the lines. He charged that the Kocziusko station, the secret Soviet radio broadcasting in Polish, was deliberately stirring the Poles in occupied territory to revolt prematurely. He recalled Stalin's wish for a strong Poland and pleaded for a boundary settlement satisfactory to his government.

Into this strained atmosphere Soviet authorities tossed a bombshell with the disclosure of the execution fifteen months before of two Polish-Jewish labor leaders, Victor Alter and Henryk Ehrlich. Hardly anyone could accept the official explanation: that the two men had "spread propaganda among Soviet troops for a separate peace with Germany." The real reason probably lay in the deep-rooted hatred Communists have for Socialists, whom they always have considered "traitors to the workers' cause." Alter and Ehrlich were founders of the "Bund," the Jewish-Socialist Party which polled 62 per cent of the entire Jewish vote in the last Polish elections. They were widely known for their opposition to Polish Communism, as well as for similar activity years before in Russian labor circles. Ehrlich had been a member of a Petrograd Workers' Council in the early days of the Russian Revolution and had edited an important Russian newspaper. Alter's brother, a Communist Party member, had served as Soviet Consul General in Paris and New York.

News of this double execution provoked worldwide indignation in labor circles and was immediately turned into new attacks on Sikorski's position. The Polish reactionaries in London could hardly have had any sympathy for these labor leaders; the Polish anti-Semites, who whispered that as bad as Hitler was, he had rendered Poland historical service by exterminating her Jews, could hardly be moved by the fate of Ehrlich and Alter. But any weapons were suited to attack Sikorski's pro-Russian policy.

The National Council formally denied that Poland had "any anti-Soviet tendencies" but affirmed its belief that the "integrity of the Polish Republic in her frontiers of September 1, 1939, and her sovereignty were inviolable and indivisible." Sikorski was compelled to support this with a declaration that "so far as the question of the frontiers is concerned, the status quo previous to September 1, 1939, is in force." The die was cast and Moscow immediately took up the challenge.

Tass, the Soviet Telegraphic Agency, issued a statement claiming "in the name of the Atlantic Charter" the right of self-determination for Ukrainians and White Russians. A Polish language newspaper suddenly appeared in Moscow under the name of *Volna Polska* (Free Poland) published by the "Union of Polish Patriots." Its first editorial declared it would seek to close the "artificial gap" that divided the peoples of Poland, Russia, the Ukraine, and White Russia and insisted that "we Poles have no right to the lands of the Ukraine and White Russia, where we are in the minority."

Volna Polska charged that Sikorski and the Polish fascists in control in London did not represent democratic Poland. The Moscow Union of Polish Patriots, on the other hand, consisted principally of Polish Communists who never had been able to obtain the support of more than 25 to 50 per cent of Polish labor and a small number of the landless peasants. It too could not validly claim to represent democratic Poland. What it actually accomplished was the launching of the new trend of the Soviet Union's Polish policy. Irritated by the increasing agitation of reactionary Polish émigrés and fearful that they might have found in London and Washington some influential supporters for a new version of the *cordon sanitaire*, Moscow decided to make sure there would not be an "unfriendly" government on the other side of her frontier. No longer was it a question only of Poland's eastern boundaries. With the appearance of the Free Poland movement, Poland's independence hung in the balance.

This new Soviet policy was a logical development of the idea contained in the last paragraph of that historic Soviet note given the Poles on the night when the Red Army was ordered to march into Poland. Moscow stressed then the thought that it was acting only to protect the defenseless Ukrainian and White Russian population groups. But the last paragraph added that "at the same time the Soviet government proposed to take all measures to extricate the Polish people from the unfortunate war into which they have been dragged by their unwise leaders, and to enable them to live a peaceful life."

As it was originally constituted, the Union of Polish Patriots could hardly expect to find many followers in Poland. Many of its members had been on the staffs of Jewish language newspapers back in Poland. Wanda Wasilewska, who served as editor of *Volna Polska*, is a godchild of Marshal Pilsudski and the daughter of the well-known Polish labor political leader, Leon Wasilewski, but her marriage to Alexander Korneichuk, the Soviet Ukrainian leader, put her in a rather uncomfortable position from which to defend Poland's national interests.

The Poles in exile were, perhaps, correct in minimizing the political importance of this Polish group, but they were terribly wrong in overlooking the power of the Soviet Union which lay behind it. In disregarding this new warning of grave dangers ahead, they rejected the advice of their American and British friends whose sincerity they had no cause to doubt.

The stage was very well set, therefore, for the Nazi propaganda experts to "discover" at this very moment the graves of the ten thousand missing Polish officers in the forest of Katyn near Smolensk. It is as yet impossible to determine how and when these unfortunate men were killed in a way that made their cause such dangerous international tinder. It is not clear, for instance, why, if they were killed, as the Germans claim, by Russian executioners who had time to shoot ten thousand men and camouflage their common graves by planting trees, they neglected to burn uniforms and identification papers which the Nazis claimed to have discovered three years later.

In any case, it certainly was not up to the Germans, who according to Polish official reports already had a million and a half Polish lives on their consciences, to broadcast pathetic denunciations in all languages to all countries over the assassination of ten thousand Poles. If their purpose was to disturb the unanimity of the United Nations, it succeeded only too well. For whatever the facts in this case were, the disclosure by German sources led the Polish Government-in-Exile to commit its most appalling diplomatic blunder—its appeal to the International Red Cross to investigate German charges of the Soviet massacre without asking at the same time for an investigation into the Nazi massacres.

The Soviet Union naturally jumped at the opportunity. *Pravda* accused the Polish government of "giving direct and obvious aid to the Nazi hangmen of the Polish people" and Moscow broke off relations with the Polish government in London. The Nazi propaganda machinery celebrated its greatest victory in psychological warfare with shortwave broadcasts, noting the political fragility of the "Disunited Nations," Berlin's theme, pounded into the radios of Eastern Europe, was that a victory of the United Nations would mean enslavement of all these peoples under the heel of Soviet Russia.

All efforts of British and American diplomacy to patch this lamentable break failed. Moscow remained firm in her determination although Stalin publicly reaffirmed his desire to see a "strong and independent Poland" whose postwar relations with Russia would be based either on "solid good neighborly relations" or, "should the Polish people desire it," upon a "mutual assistance pact against the Germans." Although the road to an understanding between these two governments remained open in principle, the chances of ever achieving such agreement were greatly reduced by the tragic death of Sikorski in a plane crash near Gibraltar in July 1943.

Sikorski's successors faced an extremely difficult task. The double compromise by which Stanislaw Mikolajczyk, leader of the Peasant Party, became Prime Minister and General Kazimier Sosnkowski Commander-in-Chief, did not satisfy Moscow's foreign

policy makers. Mikolajczyk proceeded to reinforce the leftist elements in his cabinet without excluding, however, the moderate
nationalist members, but General Sosnkowski, who was supposed
to satisfy the nationalistic army and the influential Polish rightists
in London and the United States, was completely unacceptable to
Moscow. Moscow recalled his resignation in disapproval of the
Russo-Polish pact in 1941 and the fact that he was the candidate
of the fascistic *Walka* when that newspaper demanded the resignation in March 1943 of the pro-Russian Sikorski government.

It became an extremely difficult task for London and Washington to re-establish good neighbor relations between the Soviet
Union and Poland. Sikorski—and many of his compatriots shared
his belief—had held that Poland could not afford to have two
such powerful neighbors as Germany and Russia both as enemies.
But even the undaunted heroism of the twelve thousand Polish
pilots, the fighting spirit of one hundred thousand Polish soldiers,
and the ordeal of thirty million Poles in the homeland cannot
change geography. The Poles must attempt to draw their conclusions from Poland's geographical and diplomatic position.

Some Poles may still live with megalomaniac dreams of a
"Greater Poland" stretching from the Baltic to the Black Sea, a
Poland embracing all of White Russia, all of Lithuania, all of the
Ukraine. It is obvious, however, that the tremendous contribution
of the Soviet Union to the United Nations' victory has made all
those dreams impossible. Besides, the majority of Poles did not
indulge in such dreams. They believed they were "reasonably
realistic" in claiming only the restoration of their prewar Russian
boundary and a number of rectifications in favor of their prewar
boundaries with Germany.

While Moscow was rather generously disposed to rectifica-
tion of the Polish-German frontier, the Soviet leaders were as
definitely determined to maintain within the Soviet Union those
Ukrainian and White Russian territories which they obtained in
the fourth partition of Poland. Early in 1944 Moscow gave the
world to understand that if the Poles would accept the general
principles of the Curzon Line, the Soviet Union might consider
certain rectifications of the Molotov-Ribbentrop Line, and would
at the same time support a substantial extension of Poland's west-

ern boundaries. An accompanying condition was stipulated in relation to several members of the Polish regime in London who were persona non grata in Moscow because of their outspoken anti-Sovietism. It was not made clear whether Moscow would be satisfied with their elimination from the Polish regime in exile or whether Moscow was determined to consider the whole regime unacceptable for diplomatic negotiation because of their presence in the cabinet.

Should the latter hypothesis prove to be correct, then there would be no hope whatsoever for a solution of the Polish-Soviet problem so long as Washington and London continue to consider the Polish émigré regime as Poland's legitimate government. If, on the other hand, Moscow accepted the removal of Generals Sosnkowski and Kukiel and a number of anti-Soviet Polish politicians, then some hope still remained for a British-American mediation. In the early part of 1944 this hope seemed to be rather dim. For when the Polish cabinet offered to negotiate "all outstanding questions" with the aid of the United States and Britain, Moscow rejected the proposal, claiming that so long as the Poles did not accept the general principles of the Curzon Line, there were no grounds for further discussion.

Assisted by Washington, London exerted all possible diplomatic pressure on the Polish government, but they succeeded only in having the cabinet withdraw its original instructions that resistance groups in Poland not co-operate with the Red Army so long as diplomatic relations remained severed. Certain members of the cabinet were even prepared to make some concessions in order to work out a fair ethnographical boundary. But there apparently were in London no responsible Polish leaders willing to accept the Curzon Line without a mandate from the Polish people. And there was as little willingness in Polish political circles to revise government personnel to comply with Moscow's demand, which they considered improper and unacceptable interference of a foreign power in their domestic problems.

It was indeed extremely difficult for even those Poles who recognized the urgent necessity of reaching an agreement with Moscow to accept the Curzon Line. Poland's feudalistic history of Polish landlords ruling over Ukrainian, White Russian, and Lithuanian peasants, had resulted in the creation of Polish cities, great intellectual and national Polish centers, completely encircled by villages inhabited by non-Polish peasants. While they readily admitted that Wilna was surrounded by Lithuanians and Lwow by Ukrainians, very few Poles were willing to abandon these two shrines of Polish national glory which lie east and south of the Curzon Line.

The Polish regime in London was also morally if not politically dependent upon the Polish army in Scotland and the troops that were moved from the Near East in February 1944 to Italian battlefields. Most of those soldiers came from provinces which lie east of the Curzon Line. If they were informed that they would never see their old homes again, they might well feel they had nothing to fight for.

Moscow's offer to compensate the Poles for territorial losses in the East by expansion westward at Germany's expense was not particularly attractive. The German territories were certainly richer than those which the Poles would lose in the East, but they were reluctant to replace their Ukrainian and White Russian minorities by a large and much more dangerous German minority. They felt that Russia's policy would transform the Polish problem into a German problem, and they were unable to find either in London or in Washington any definitive statement on Germany's postwar status.

The Poles also felt that by obliging them to annex extensive German territories in the West, the Soviet Union would for generations to come tie them to a huge Slavic bloc headed by Moscow for the sole purpose of making a new German aggression in the East impossible. They were frightened at the notion of becoming the most exposed and the most hated (by the Germans) western outpost of this bloc. They would have liked to have their new western boundary guaranteed by Washington and London, but this was impossible so long as Washington and London could not agree with Moscow on postwar Germany. And they realized that even then it would be very difficult if not impossible to obtain from Washington as definite a commitment on their postwar boundaries as they hoped to obtain from London.

England had pledged herself in March 1939 to help in the

restoration of Poland, for which she went to war, but she never guaranteed any definite frontier line. Eden had pointedly recalled that fact after the signing of the Soviet-Polish agreement, and Churchill re-emphasized it in his report on the state of the war in February 1944. In that speech Churchill, paying the usual tribute to Poland, recalled that the Curzon Line was "impartial" and that Russia's "demands for reassurances about her western frontiers" did not go "beyond the limits of what is reasonable or just."

The United States has made no commitments whatever to Poland save those inherent in the very general and vague principles of the Atlantic Charter. Nevertheless, the Polish politicians expected greater assistance from the United States than from Britain. They had hoped that President Roosevelt would consider in the election year the Americans of Polish descent as a potential pressure group favoring Poland's restoration within her prewar boundaries. However, it appeared that the Poles had overestimated the political importance of their national groups in the United States. And that while Soviet leaders trusted and sympathized with President Roosevelt, they were less interested than the British in his re-election and were certainly not disposed to sacrifice for the sake of his re-election what they considered to be their "vital interests."

Unwilling and unable to make any final decisions on their post-war boundaries, the Poles tried desperately to postpone the hour of decision until the end of the war, when all boundary problems would have to be solved simultaneously. They refused to discuss even their minor quarrel with Czechoslovakia over the tiny province of Teschen, which they seized in March 1939 from Hitler's carving table. They feared that even a minor concession—little more than 100 square miles—might establish a dangerous precedent and involve them in much more important concessions. Meanwhile, it was becoming more and more clear that the crux of their conflict with Russia was not the eastern boundary but the place which Moscow was reserving for them in postwar Europe. The "friendliness" of Poland's government was apparently of greater importance to Moscow than her boundaries.

Now centuries-old suspicions were bearing their poisoned fruit. Marshal Pilsudski and the French General Staff advisers, who in

March 1920 approved his war against the newly created and still chaotic Soviet Union for the conquest of the Ukraine, assumed a tragic responsibility for their own and the world's history. The appearance of Polish soldiers in Kiev resulted, as we have seen, in the rebirth of the new Russian, revolutionary-styled nationalism.

Moscow had to accept the border established by the Riga Treaty and she signed other treaties and non-aggression pacts with Warsaw, but no one could compel her to stop mistrusting Poland. Until 1930 Moscow believed her neighbor was the eastern outpost of the French General Staff, and after the Nazi-Polish pact of 1934 she considered her as Hitler's potential ally. We have seen the basis of Poland's hate for Russia as her historic jailer. The new Soviet Constitution, which enlarged the autonomy of the Ukrainian and White Russian Soviet Republics and gave the Soviet Union a new weapon for the legalization of her incorporation of these territories, appeared to the Poles to constitute a new threat to their sovereignty. And it did look that way when examined in the light of the report that a Moscow-sponsored Polish National Council was to succeed the Moscow-created Union of Polish Patriots.

Polish optimists believed this Polish National Council would be only a stronger lever for Soviet pressure to obtain greater territorial concessions and a more "friendly" Polish government in London. The pessimists were convinced it would simply be a channel for the incorporation of a "strong and independent" postwar Poland—as Stalin had promised—into the Soviet Union. But both the optimists and the pessimists agreed that the year 1944 would prove which was correct in their estimation of the Soviet Union's ultimate objectives. And both agreed that the real independence of Poland could be assured only within the framework of a general agreement among the Big Three over Europe's fate.

If the Soviet Union and the Atlantic powers come to an understanding over the future status of Germany, if the Soviet Union is satisfied that there will no longer be a strong Germany, that Britain will not try to balance Europe's powers with a strong Reich, and that there will be no need to restore a strong Germany for Russia's own interests—then Moscow's policy makers no longer will have any reason to suspect Poland either as a German outpost or as a nucleus of an anti-Soviet Eastern European Federation. Then and then only will it be possible for Washington and London to insist upon and to obtain from Moscow the assurance of Poland's independence. And then and only then will the open wound on the body of the United Nations be healed.

IV: Moral Problems on Baltic Shores

Finland and the Baltic States

THE problem of Russian-Polish relations has a counterpart on the shores of the Baltic Sea—a counterpart, not a replica, for these problems differ essentially from the original pattern of the Russian-Polish conflict. Here the three tiny Baltic states, Latvia, Estonia, and Lithuania, which emerged as did Poland after the last war, have already disappeared in World War II through incorporation in August 1940 into the Soviet Union. The independence of Finland, which also came out of the last war as an independent state, is not directly threatened, although Finland knows, just as Poland knows, that Russia will insist on her 1940 and not on her prewar boundaries.

But there is an important difference between the status of Poland and that of the four Baltic states so far as the United Nations are concerned. Poland, the first victim of Hitler's armed aggression, has by her continued resistance assured herself a special place in the ranks of the United Nations. The Baltic states, knowing full well that Hitler's victory would mean for them what it meant for many other small European nations—the complete loss of their recently acquired independence—were unable to take sides in the world conflict. They looked toward Britain and especially toward the United States as their possible protectors as the war's flames raged nearer their territories, and explained away their neutrality by their complete helplessness.

This indecision, or probably physical inability to make a decision, produced some strange situations. Finland, long a friend of Great Britain and the United States, suddenly found herself in the war on Germany's side when in 1941 she saw in Hitler's attack on Russia her chance to win back—perhaps with interest—territory she lost to Russia who in 1939 was the aggressor against Finland. All this Finland did without much sympathy for the Nazi regime.

The problems of these four Baltic states could not, therefore, in 1944 be considered as internal diplomatic problems of the United Nations. Nor could they be ignored, since they were to many Americans moral problems that, in their very existence and certainly in their solution, brought the war aims of Soviet Russia into direct conflict with the principles of the Atlantic Charter. Those forces in the United States which thoroughly mistrusted Russia, and opposed American-Russian postwar collaboration, offered as their principal arguments these three issues, two of which involved Baltic problems: the Russian-Nazi pact, which resulted in the partition of Poland; the "incorporation" of the three Baltic states into the Soviet Union; and the Russo-Finnish war.

These were largely arguments stemming from American public opinion expressing its traditional sympathy for the underdog. This sympathy, however, conflicted with growing admiration of Russia's ever-increasing contribution toward Allied victory. Here was a moral conflict if ever there was one, a conflict not easy to solve.

Russia has recognized the existence of a Finnish problem, but she has flatly denied the existence of a Baltic states problem. So far as she was concerned, the latter problem was definitely solved in August 1940 when the Supreme Council of the Soviet Union accepted the "demand for incorporation" from the three Baltic republics, which until 1917 had been provinces of the Russian Empire. It was a problem involving geographic, ethnographic, political, and imperial difficulties, a problem whose origin can be found in the history of the Baltic peoples.

Their history is the recording of the long-enduring and unhappy experiences of small nations trying to establish and insure their independence in Eastern Europe, where the opposing expansionist forces of great powers never have been able to establish lasting boundaries. Along the eastern shores of the Baltic Sea, the "Mediterranean of Northern Europe," live 2,575,000 Lithuanians in 23,000 square miles of territory; 2,000,000 Latvians in 25,000 square miles; and 1,250,000 Estonians in 18,000 square miles.

They are neither Russians nor Germans: Lithuanians and Latvians are of Indo-European descent. Estonians are of Finnish or Ural-Altaic extraction; their language belongs to the Finno-

Ugrian family, and their kin are the Finns and the Hungarians. The Lithuanians are predominantly Catholic; the Latvians and Estonians are Protestant.

A branch of the Lithuanians, known as the Borussians or Prussians, became Germanized after their conquest by the Teutonic knights in the thirteenth century. In the fourteenth century other Lithuanian groups constituted a state three times the size of Poland, onto which Lithuania was linked by a dynastic marriage. The Lithuanians were annexed by Imperial Russia during the first partition of Poland. The Latvians and the Estonians, on the other hand, never did enjoy complete independence, living for centuries under German or Polish rule, with some pleasant "Swedish interludes." In 1721, as a result of the Russo-Swedish treaty, Estonia was annexed by Peter the Great into the Russian Empire. The Latvians, part of whom found their way into the Russian Empire with the Lithuanians, were definitely incorporated into Russia in 1795 during the third partition of Poland. And these three peoples remained under unbroken Russian rule until the 1917 Revolution.

The present war took back the independence that World War I gave these Baltic peoples. In the autumn of 1939 Russia signed formal treaties with Estonia, Latvia, and Lithuania permitting her to establish military bases in the republics. She was beginning to collect payment on the check given her in exchange for the non-aggression pact with Hitler, but Finland refused to give her similar bases. The Finns were better prepared to defend their country and did so when Russia attacked. But the Moscow peace treaty of March 1940, ending Finland's short-lived defense, gave Russia even more than she had asked for in the diplomatic negotiations of October 1939. Having obtained outer bastions for the defense of Leningrad and Moscow against the suspected intentions of Nazi Germany, Moscow was able to turn her attention back to the other Baltic states.

In their twenty years of independence, Russia had never forgotten them, and she still recalled her failure in the first years of the civil war (1918-19) to extend her rule over the new Baltic republics by supporting local Communist movements within their borders. The Soviet policy makers, when in 1920 they recognized the separate existence of the three small states in order to devote themselves entirely to establishing their own regime inside Russia, must have been convinced that the petit bourgeois regimes would not be likely to endure through the forthcoming world revolution.

Thus, when Hitler's aggression broke the armistice, Moscow evidently believed that the hour finally had struck for the achievement of all those objectives which the Russian Empire had pursued for centuries, some of which the Soviet Revolution had caused to be temporarily set aside. And when Vilhems Munters, Latvian Foreign Minister, was invited to Moscow to discuss the treaty on military bases, Stalin told him (according to Mr. Munters) that "that which was determined in 1920 cannot remain for eternity. Peter the Great saw to it that an outlet to the Baltic Sea was gained. We are now without an exit and the situation in which we are now cannot remain. We, therefore, wish to ensure ourself the use of ports, roads to these ports, and their defense." Thus did the strategic considerations of Peter the Great in 1721 become two centuries later a strategic necessity for Marshal Stalin.

Convinced by the fall of France that the zero hour of Nazi aggression against Russia was approaching, Stalin and his military advisers felt that their bases in the Baltic states were not sufficient; they wanted complete control of that territory. Consequently, in June 1940 Russian armies moved into Lithuania, Latvia, and Estonia. A month later elections were held with ballots listing only Communist Party candidates, and the three republics "voted" for incorporation into the Soviet Union. A year later these peoples became the first victims in the Nazi invasion of Russia. The successful defense of Leningrad and Moscow must have completely justified in the eyes of Soviet military leaders—if they ever felt the need for justification—their policy in the Baltic states.

As for Russia's attitude toward the postwar status of the Baltic countries, so long as Stalin felt uncertain about the postwar world, he considered it his foremost duty to assure Russia the most strategically advantageous boundaries. The Moscow Conference and Stalin's subsequent meeting with Roosevelt and Churchill must have alleviated somewhat his concern about Soviet security in the postwar world. Nevertheless, even then it seemed most unlikely that he would ever agree to restore the prewar status of these states.

To all those Americans who grieved over the disappearance of Latvia, Estonia, and Lithuania as the first infringement of the Atlantic Charter, Moscow replied that the "incorporation" elections must be considered as the plebiscite foreseen by the Atlantic Charter itself. And it began to look more and more improbable that Moscow would ever agree to have these elections confirmed after the war by a plebiscite conducted under United Nations' control, a procedure which might well be made obligatory for all territorial controversies.

London went further than Washington in accepting Moscow's viewpoint on the Baltic states. When Molotov asked the British in May 1942 to recognize their incorporation, Anthony Eden explained to the Soviet Commissar for Foreign Affairs that it was impossible for Britain to recognize territorial changes until after the war. But he offered Mr. Molotov a twenty-year alliance which Stalin immediately accepted. After it was signed, the names of Baltic diplomats in Britain were ingeniously secluded in an appendix to the official diplomatic lists.

However, their colleagues in the United States continued to enjoy full diplomatic privileges, while Washington's official circles insisted that it was incorrect to interpret their status in this country as the expression of an "anti-Soviet" attitude. It was due merely to the traditional caution of American foreign policy—the same caution that, during the fourteen years (1918-32) when the United States was following an outspoken anti-Soviet policy and refusing to recognize the new regime, made the United States also refuse to recognize Rumania's annexation of Russian Bessarabia.

As a matter of fact, the United States was one of the last great powers to recognize the independence of the Baltic states; this was in 1922, two years after Russia recognized their complete separation. On that occasion Charles Evans Hughes, as Secretary of State, declared: "The United States has consistently maintained that the disturbed condition of Russian affairs may not be made the occasion for the alienation of Russian territory, and this principle is not deemed to be infringed upon by the recognition at this time of the governments of Estonia, Latvia, and Lithuania which have been set up and maintained by the indigenous population."

The United States does not readily grant recognition, but once granted, she considers the recipient a full-fledged member of the international family, regardless of age and size. The Administration felt more than embarrassed, therefore, about recognizing the Baltic incorporations. Theoretically there was always a chance that Russia, in her anxiety to secure America's postwar co-operation, might accept the general application of the idea that all postwar plebiscites be held under United Nations' supervision and the Atlantic Charter principles of self-determination. But by the beginning of 1944 diplomatic circles here had come to the conclusion that there remained very little chance of modifying Moscow's viewpoint.

Finland offered a slightly different problem. At the Moscow Conference the Russians accepted a discussion of Finland's postwar status and even indicated their disposition to talk "reasonable peace terms" with any Finnish government which would be acceptable to Moscow as being independent of German influence. However, considerable difference of opinion developed in Helsinki and Moscow as to the meaning of "reasonable peace terms." The Finns, convinced of the moral integrity of their case, believed that reasonable terms should be based on Finland's 1939 borders, which had been recognized for nearly twenty years by the Soviet Union. Stalin and his advisers held that the 1940 borders accepted by Finland after her first defeat by the Red Army were reasonable bases for peace negotiations.

In the eyes of Washington, Finland's postwar status became a moral problem. Russia's 1939 attack inspired worldwide indignation against the Soviets and assured Finland of universal sympathy. This feeling was especially strong in the United States, for this country looked on Finland as a peace-loving member of the genuinely democratic and highly cultured Scandinavian community, a nation of hard-working people and fine athletes, with the reputation of being the most honest people in the world and the only nation to have paid the United States its war debt. And this paragon of countries now had become the victim of unqualified aggression.

This picture, as viewed from Washington, was absolutely correct. Moscow had another view of Finland and its perspective was not altogether false. For Moscow remembered Finland as the country in which during the civil war of 1918 the White Finns under General (now Field Marshal) Baron Carl Gustav von Mannerheim, a Swedish-Finn who served in the Russian Imperial Army, had defeated the Red Finns when the German contingent under General von der Holz landed in Finland. As the result of this German support, the Finns elected the German Prince Friedrich Karl of Hesse as king of Finland. It was only because of Germany's capitulation in November 1918 that he was unable to take possession of his throne and transform Finland into a military and economic outpost of the Reich.

Finland finally became a democratic republic, but the pro-fascist Lapua movement, which developed considerable strength during the depression of 1930, forced Parliament to declare the Finnish Communist Party illegal. That same year it helped elect the pro-German President Svinhufvud and in 1932 Lapua attempted to seize the government and establish a fascist regime. It failed, but its adherents, who were supporters of Field Marshal Mannerheim, remained free and continued to exert pro-German and pro-Nazi influence in certain sections of Finland's ruling classes, especially among high-ranking officers.

Russia first attempted to conquer Finland politically by establishing a pro-Soviet regime headed by Otto Kuusinen, a Finnish Communist who lived in Moscow. When this failed, she had to wage a hard, three-month winter campaign to break Finland's military resistance. Russia then obtained in 1940 the entire Karelian Isthmus with the fortifications of the Mannerheim Line, and Viborg, Finland's second largest city. Lake Ladoga became a Russian lake, and a large tract near Petsamo assured the Soviet of strategic control of this warm water Arctic coast port which she had ceded to Finland in 1920. Annexation of several small islands in the Gulf of Finland and a thirty-year lease on the port of Hangö were supposed to protect Russia against a German surprise attack through Finland. The Russo-Finnish treaty also gave Russia many economic advantages, such as duty-free transit to Norway.

Although the conquered nation accepted all these conditions and four hundred thousand Finns evacuated the ceded areas, they remained bitter over their defeat. Finland felt that she had been the victim of a grave injustice, that her lost war might be only the first step of a Russian conquest. The Finns lusted for revenge. They had never cared much for Russia and their dislike, growing steadily since 1809 when Sweden ceded their territory to Russia, was intensified by vain efforts to Russify them at the end of the nineteenth century. Now frightened by the Soviet aggression, the Finns hoped for help from Britain and France. And both were seriously considering coming to Finland's aid when she capitulated, leaving her only Germany to turn to.

The great majority of the Finns had as little sympathy for the Nazi regime as they did for the Soviet, but they had not forgotten that the Germans had saved them from Communism in 1918. And they knew that Nazi Germany could not tolerate the idea of further Russian expansion. Whether the Helsinki government signed a secret alliance with the Nazis has not yet been established. It is certain, however, that on the day Hitler attacked Russia, Germany became the natural ally of a great many Finns. Blinded by their hatred of Russia, they saw in Hitler's Germany not a totalitarian aggressor seeking to conquer the world, but a powerful avenger who would defeat and dismember their worst enemy.

The day after Hitler's legions crossed Russia's borders he spoke of German divisions which "in co-operation with the heroes of Finnish freedom, under their Marshal, are protecting Finnish soil." Even so Finland was not yet in the war. Her trade unions and Social Democrats, despite their eagerness to recover their nation's prewar borders, tried to prevent her from entering the war on Hitler's side. But soon German bombers were taking off from Finnish soil to bomb Kronstadt; German infantry divisions crossed the Finnish-Russian border, and the Finnish government declared a second war against Soviet Russia.

Since then the Finns have tried to convince the world, and perhaps themselves as well, that although they were fighting Russian troops simultaneously with and sometimes alongside Hitler's forces, they were not Hitler's ally. Finland and Hitler, they insisted, had a common enemy but no common aims, although many Finns fully realized that after the two wars with the Soviet Union, they could never again feel secure so long as Russia stood as a great power across their frontier. Moreover, the Finns denied that they were fighting a "second war"; to them the war that began on June 25, 1941, was merely the continuation of the war that began on November 20, 1939. The Moscow Peace Treaty of March 1940 was to them not a peace but an armistice.

They were still counting on the universal sympathy extended them in the first war and they believed, or tried to believe, that they continued to enjoy it in their second war. For to the Finns the first episode, or war, with Russia was the moral justification of the second.

Soviet Russia, on the other hand, found moral justification for her first Finnish war in the second one and in the related facts that Finland was now fighting on Hitler's side and that Mannerheim, as Commander-in-Chief of Finland's armies, had proclaimed the annexation of the Soviet Union's eastern Karelia. This stand was further supported by Germany's action compelling Finland, anxious as she was to emphasize the separate character of her war, to sever diplomatic relations with Britain.

London hoped for months that Washington's mediation would succeed in re-establishing peace between Finland and Russia and bring the former out of Hitler's camp. Meanwhile, the United States worked indefatigably to the end that, as early as August 1941, Constantine Oumansky, then Soviet ambassador to Washington, assured the State Department that his government "was prepared to negotiate a new treaty of peace with Finland, which would involve the making of territorial concessions to Finland." Finland's President informed the United States that "Finland in her fight for existence cannot enter any engagements that would denote imperiling her national security by the artificial suspension or annulment of military operations which are fully justified."

In that black autumn of 1941, when Hitler's armies were besieging Leningrad and threatening to capture Moscow, Russia was disposed to make concessions in order to alleviate her plight. But little Finland had confidence in Hitler's forthcoming victory. The State Department informed her that if she desired to maintain her long-standing friendship with the United States, she should give satisfactory evidence of her intentions to discontinue military operations against Russia. In reply Finland pointed out that

Russia was definitely a threat to her while Germany was not, whereupon she joined the Anti-Comintern bloc.

The day before Pearl Harbor, Britain abandoned her hopes of American mediation and declared war on Finland. From then on American-Finnish relations deteriorated steadily, although Finland was able to resist German pressure to declare war on the United States. In August 1942 the United States withdrew all consular representation from Finland and the following spring reduced the Helsinki legation to a "symbolic expression" by transferring legation families to Stockholm.

By now the tide of war was changing in favor of the Russians and Finland's desire to get out of the war grew stronger daily, while Russia's willingness to make concessions declined as her war machine stormed back successfully at her aggressors. At the Moscow Conference it became apparent that Russia would insist on the 1940 borders and it was understood that she might also ask for the port of Petsamo, strategically important as a base for German submarines harassing convoy routes to Russia.

But the Finns held firm in the hope that the "unconditional surrender" formula extended by the Moscow Conference to all of Hitler's satellites would not be applied to them, for they stubbornly refused to consider themselves a satellite country. They also continued to hope that America's friendship and her devotion to moral principles would help them defend what they considered to be their legitimate rights. And they steadfastly rejected any admission that they might have compromised their rights by chaining their country to the German chariot and staking everything —except their faith in America's sense of fair play and ethics— on a Hitlerian victory.

Restoration of the 1940 borders, they insisted, would strangle the economic life of eastern Finland and would seriously reduce the export of timber, one of Finland's main sources of wealth. Frightened by Russia's demands for a Finnish government completely independent of German influence, they were not less concerned about Finland's economic independence.

All this time Moscow obviously was in search of a Finnish "Beneš" whom she could trust to take over the leadership of this border nation. The Finnish Socialists had opposed siding with Hitler but Moscow's leaders were known to have no sympathy for Socialists. It was doubtful whether Moscow would accept as persona grata Väinö Tanner, leader of the Socialists, who had visited Berlin and conferred with Nazi leaders during the war. The most acceptable Finn appeared to be seventy-three-year-old J. K. Paasikivi, who negotiated both the Dorpat Peace Treaty of 1920 and the Moscow Treaty of 1940.

It was Paasikivi who went to Stockholm in February 1944 to establish contact with the Soviet envoy to Sweden, Mme. Alexandra Kollontai, when the deterioration of the German military situation on the northern front and the severe warning given Helsinki by Secretary Hull made even the most stubborn Finns realize that Hitler had lost the war and that they had to find the quickest way out of the tragic situation in which they found themselves, a tragedy due largely to the blindness of their political leaders.

Paasikivi could become Finland's "Beneš." But while Dr. Beneš could bring to his country liberation, restored independence, and promises of new prosperity, Dr. Paasikivi could offer to his compatriots nothing but sacrifices, hardships, and a very slight appeasement of their basic fears. This was the price which Finland was to be compelled to pay for having staked her fate on Hitler's victory. But the Finns refused to believe that it was fair to make them pay such a high price, and they looked with hope toward the United States, whose friendly advices they either did not want or were unable to follow in 1941 and 1942.

The stern warning given them by Secretary Hull was supposed to have opened their eyes and put an end to their illusions. The United States sincerely sympathized with their plight but considered them at least partly responsible for their troubles. America's sympathy could not, therefore, be translated into action. It was doubtful whether it could have been translated into active support even if Finland's case had been less reproachable. Apparently, the most that Finland could expect from the United States was her refusal to co-operate with the Soviet Union should the latter violate Finland's sovereignty and independence.

However, it was becoming obvious after five years of war that the sovereignty of a small nation had scarcely any chance of being restored to its prewar condition. It looked as though small nations would be sovereign and independent in the postwar world only to the extent to which the strategic interests and moral considerations of their great neighbors would permit. So long as Germany could be considered a potential threat to the postwar world, it was clear that Moscow would insist on her right to safeguard her security in the West in whatever way she thought best for her national defense. Military reasons were stronger than moral considerations.

V: Third or Fourth Republic?

France

Two important messages destined to become of historical significance were delivered on July 14, 1943, the one hundred and fifty-
fourth anniversary of the celebration of Bastille Day. In Washington President Roosevelt acclaimed "liberty, equality, fraternity" as
the creed of the Third French Republic. He hailed "immortal
France" which "has reaffirmed once again, in the most heroic circumstances, her greatness and her glory." He recalled that "the
fundamental principles which guide our democracies were evolved
from the American and the French revolutions."

On the same day in Algiers General de Gaulle acclaimed the
resurrection of France "amidst suffering, tears and misfortunes,"
and emphasized that reborn France will not return to "the regime
of the Third Republic which failed at the same time as its armies
failed." He declared that "France has already chosen a new road,"
a road leading to "the Fourth French Republic," which "will require that it be served and not that it be made use of by others."
He warned that "if Bastilles still exist [in France], they would do
well to open their doors of their own accord, for when the people
engage in a struggle with Bastilles, it is always the Bastilles which
are wrong in the end."

Thus both the President of the United States and the leader of
the Fighting French reminded us once more of the revolutionary
origins of the French Republic. As to the future of France, President Roosevelt, as an American, could not say more than that
"French sovereignty resides in the people of France," and give his
assurance that when "Frenchmen and their brothers-in-arms of
the United Nations have cleansed French soil of the enemy, the
French people will again give expression to their freedom of
erecting a government of their choice."

General de Gaulle, as a Frenchman—and a Frenchman who

considers himself not only a leader of Fighting France but as the most probable head of Liberated France—believed it was his right, perhaps his duty, to express his views on the future status of his country. "Frenchmen," he said, "want their affairs to be settled in an orderly fashion . . . they do not intend to pass from war to civil war."

However, we must remember that all French republics emerged from revolutions. The revolutionary origins of the First Republic (1791-99) are too well known to be commented upon here. The short-lived Second Republic (1848-51) which, through fear of the Socialists, opened the way to the Second Empire of Napoleon III, was preceded by a brief revolution of the Left Center and the Radical Party against the weak and corrupt monarchy of Louis-Philippe. The Third Republic was founded in 1871 after the explosion of the Paris Commune, which expressed the bitter exasperation of a defeated nation. It is quite likely, if not altogether certain, that the Fourth French Republic, which General de Gaulle expects to emerge after the liberation of France, also will draw its spiritual strength from the revolutionary tradition of the French nation. Some observers are even inclined to believe that the revolutionary cycle which will usher in the Fourth Republic had in reality begun as early as 1933 with the *Front Populaire*. This cycle was interrupted by the counter-revolution of Marshal Pétain and Pierre Laval.

Its leadership has now been taken over by General de Gaulle, or, to be more precise, by those political forces which now stand behind General de Gaulle and endeavor to use him for the realization of their social objectives. It is certainly surprising to see a French general, a graduate of St. Cyr Military College and the son of a professor at a Jesuit school, as the successor of the *Front Populaire* and the leader of a new social cycle of the French Revolution. It is not yet clear whether de Gaulle intends to assume the historical part imposed upon him by his political advisers and by circumstances, or whether he will try, when a liberated France accepts him as her leader, to follow some path more in accord with his military and ideological background.

In his Bastille Day speech, de Gaulle condemned the Third French Republic in terms which could be subscribed to not only

by Marshal Pétain but by all supporters of the Royalist *Action
Française*. He may have frightened those French politicians who,
without denying the numerous errors and weaknesses of the Third
Republic, still dream of its restoration as the best possible guarantee of the revival of French democracy. But he most certainly
wanted to reassure those who suspected him of a secret sympathy
for a personal if not semi-totalitarian regime along Bonapartist
lines. He therefore pledged that his France of tomorrow would
be a France of the Fourth Republic. He promised it would be a
republic in which the governors will govern, the officials will
refrain from trafficking in their offices, the magistrates will administer proper justice, and the soldiers will care only for their
country's defense. This republic, he promised, will abolish the
coalitions of interest and privileges which jeopardized the Third
Republic, caused the degradation of France, and opposed social
progress, and will strive to enable all Frenchmen to "live and
work in dignity and in social security." De Gaulle obviously was
anxious to assure for himself the leadership of the forthcoming
revolt.

Whatever the historical links and social origins of this revolt
may be, it is to be hoped that it will be directed only against
the Nazi invaders and against those Frenchmen who, because of
their weakness, their unscrupulous ambitions, or merely their
despicable material interests, have helped them to exploit an
enslaved France. It would be most unfortunate for the United
Nations and a real disaster for France if at the outbreak of their
great national anger against the foreign invaders and their own
Quislings, the French people should extend their resentment to
foreign friends who may have hurt the hypersensitive feelings of
a proud nation undergoing a tragic ordeal.

It is a most unhappy and disquieting situation that finds the
relations between those Frenchmen in exile who claim to speak for
their enslaved and silent country and the Allies and future liberators of France becoming ever more troubled and confused. It is
equally disturbing that since 1941 relations between the Fighting
French and the United States deteriorated to a much greater extent than between those same Frenchmen and Britain. The United
States and France were the only two great nations which had a

kind of sentimental approach to problems of foreign policy. Americans and Frenchmen had the same desire, often unconscious and both touching and irritating, to be loved by the peoples of other countries with which they had to deal. The Germans, even before Hitler's arrival to power, wanted to be feared. The British wanted to be respected. The Americans and the French wanted to be loved. Moreover, American-French relations were built up on the sentimental basis of an American debt to Lafayette, which the Americans, headed by General Pershing, tried to pay back in 1917. It was tragic that a sentimental misunderstanding should arise between two nations having a genuinely sentimental approach to their foreign relations while being extremely realistic in the defense of their material interests.

The weakening of American-French relations was induced mainly by diplomatic and military developments which placed the United States in a much less advantageous position than Britain in regard to Free France, although American sympathy for her was at least as strong as British sympathy. The United States, with the concurrence of the British, maintained relations with Vichy even after this country entered the war, while Britain built up and supported General de Gaulle.

American diplomatic documents published in October 1943 revealed that the United States government had been critical and suspicious of the Vichy regime since 1940, and that a diplomatic breach was near in November of that year, thirteen months before Pearl Harbor. Secretary Hull warned Vichy as early as June 17, 1940, that if the French fleet should fall into German hands, French relations with the United States would be fatally impaired and France would lose America's help in obtaining the restoration of her independence. President Roosevelt renewed the warning that October and added that if France helped Germany she would forfeit America's friendship and could no longer expect American influence to favor the postwar return of her overseas possessions.

After Pearl Harbor, suspicions of the Vichy regime became ever stronger, but as the American and British military chiefs began to plan their operations in North Africa, the United States was compelled to avoid Free France and to maintain her relations with

Vichy in order to prepare for the invasion and to insure its success. The original ground for antagonism between General de Gaulle and Washington was thus created. De Gaulle's unquestionably difficult personality contributed to its further growth.

The North African operation aggravated the conflict. The Fighting French, and with them many Americans, expected that General de Gaulle, the first French military leader to hoist the banner of resistance, would naturally be invited to participate in the liberation of North Africa. American agents in North Africa, however, pictured the whole region as extremely unfavorable to the de Gaulle movement. The Arabs and many French colonists, they reported, had developed even before the war strong anti-Semitic and pro-fascist trends which Nazi and Vichy propaganda nourished for thirty months. The high officials and commanding officers were devoted to Pétain; they hated the British and had little sympathy for the United States. Furthermore, de Gaulle was not an easy man to handle, so American policy makers decided to look for another French military leader. They believed they had discovered him in the person of General Henri Giraud, who repeated in this war the bold feat of escaping from a German fortress which had made him famous in World War I. He not only outranked de Gaulle but he also had had colonial experience in North Africa.

However, when Giraud was brought to Africa, it developed that his personal prestige was much lower with top-ranking French officers and administrators than the long-distance authority of Marshal Pétain. Admiral Darlan's timely arrival offered this solution: as Pétain's delegate, he could give orders which would be respected and executed by men for whom the old Marshal represented the supreme authority. The Americans realized they had no choice but to make a deal with Darlan. They reaped the military rewards of that deal and they also had to bear the burden of its moral responsibility and ensuing implications.

The outbursts of Free French indignation were echoed and re-echoed by American columnists, radio commentators, and editorial writers. The controversy over American policy in North Africa hardly needs to be recalled. But it must be noted that the controversy was greatly intensified by British criticism of American policy. The British agreed to the "Plan Giraud" but they could not approve the use of the outspoken anti-British Darlan. It is possible, moreover, that many Englishmen who still smarted from American criticism of the pre-Munich appeasement policy, availed themselves of the opportunity of criticizing the American policy of expediency which led to Darlan.

Those Englishmen who were opposed to American participation in European matters and who claimed for Britain the part of honest broker between the United States and Europe accused the Americans of complete incompetence in European affairs. Some of them went so far as to accuse the Americans of perfidious plans for deliberately breaking up the French Empire so as to justify later the disintegration of the British Empire. In return, certain Americans accused the British of having found in de Gaulle a tool for mischievous British postwar aims which included coveting French possessions in Africa as compensation for the loss of India. These heedless criticisms exchanged on both sides of the Atlantic helped to stir up French anger and suspicion. Expressed in the heat of a regrettable controversy, they were soon forgotten by both the British and the Americans. But in the wounded French hearts they left many seeds of corrosive suspicion. A Fighting French leader, perhaps as uncompromising as de Gaulle himself, declared, "French unity will be realized despite all American and British maneuvers to prevent it." And his bitter words found response in the hearts of many Frenchmen who supported Giraud.

Roosevelt and Churchill made a sincere attempt to unite the French at the Casablanca Conference in January 1943, when they brought together General de Gaulle and General Giraud. The generals shook hands in a Casablanca garden, and they repeated this gesture at the request of news photographers, but they parted without having reached the political agreement that was the principal aim of their meeting. If they could have met as two individuals, as two French soldiers, as two French patriots—which they are—they could easily have come to an understanding. General Giraud once criticized General de Gaulle's revolutionary theory of motorized divisions. But the two generals have spoken the same language all their lives. They both belong to the same French Army which served France but only tolerated the French Republic. Both refused to collaborate with the Germans. Both

escaped in different ways and at different times from their conquered country in order to fight the same fight of liberation. But
when they met at Casablanca, they were not free agents.

General Giraud was representing, to a certain extent against his
will, those Frenchmen who were anxious "to chase the Germans
out of France," but who were less anxious to restore the Republic
and French democracy. General de Gaulle was representing, also
to a certain extent against his will, those Frenchmen who hated
their conquerors as Germans and as Nazis and who wanted not only
to restore French democracy but to punish all who helped to assas-
sinate their republic. In the summer of 1942 French émigrés in
New York and London were still discussing the democratic loyalty
of General de Gaulle and taking exception to those reactionary
elements which had joined the Fighting French. De Gaulle's personality was completely transformed by the developments in
French North Africa, the tragic interlude of Darlan, and the deal
which General Giraud found himself obliged to conclude with
Darlan's aides. To his prestige as the living symbol of French
resistance, de Gaulle added his championship of French democracy; in direct opposition to all the malodorous financial-political
combinations which swarmed under the African sun, he stood up as
the guardian of French honesty, integrity, and purity. He became
the "Joan of Arc" of the French Republic.

When the two generals met, Giraud had under his command a
territory of great strategic importance, and could raise and equip,
with American and British aid, an army of 250,000 to 300,000 men.
Giraud pointed out that de Gaulle had only a limited armed
force, 20,000 to 25,000 men, at his disposal. However, he opposed
to Giraud's potential material power the actual moral strength of
the Fighting French, claiming to have with him all the forces of
resistance in France.

It was difficult to evaluate the exact number and composition of
the French resistance forces, which in the summer of 1942 became
strategically important. They gradually unified their scattered
efforts and established contacts with de Gaulle, whom they
originally mistrusted. Aware of the strength that the trade unions,
with their recently increased Communist elements, were giving
to the resistance movement, de Gaulle granted all possible guar-

antees to the resistance groups' representatives who maintained the liaison between France and London.

Developments in the North African campaign consecrated de Gaulle as the leader of French resistance. Nazi occupation of all French territory undoubtedly stimulated this resistance, which had in addition many new adherents from that part of France which had lived for thirty months under the Vichy regime. De Gaulle's Fighting French claimed that all the important resistance groups were now backing them.

Official quarters in Washington did not deny the importance of the French resistance forces, nor did they deny the ties existing between those forces and de Gaulle. They believed, however, that certain centrifugal currents had revealed themselves within the French resistance groups. Some elements, which were thought to constitute the majority, were anxious to see de Gaulle speed up the fight for liberation; other elements, impressed by military developments in Russia and disgusted by the financial-political collusions in North Africa, swung to the extreme left. The inclusion in the French National Council of Ferdinand Grenier, the French Communist leader who in the summer of 1942 escaped from France, indicated the growing strength of this leftist faction, for it was known that de Gaulle had hesitated for more than a year before he agreed to include Communists in his Council.

His political adversaries remarked, not without malice, that the inclusion of Communist elements in the Fighting French ranks might be debatable if de Gaulle insisted on the principle that he could not accept any Frenchmen who had collaborated with the Nazis under the Vichy regime. The French Communists did not collaborate with the Vichy regime, which persecuted them, but they had refused to participate in the French resistance movement until Hitler's armies crossed the Russian border.

Many foreign observers originally believed that the conflict between de Gaulle and Giraud was mainly a rivalry between two French generals, and that de Gaulle was too ambitious and too power-greedy to recognize the other's senior rank. Their conflict was not so much a clash of personalities as a serious conflict of principles. De Gaulle's political advisers always insisted that he remain adamant against proposals for a political compromise with the elements backing General Giraud, stressing that his greatest asset was his devotion to moral principles. A compromise, they said, might weaken his excellent moral position; intransigeance was held to be his best strategy. This weakened his diplomatic position not only in Washington but also in London. While the weakening of his international diplomatic position tended to increase his intransigeance.

There was nothing that de Gaulle resented more than being suspected by his compatriots of being a tool of British foreign policy. He was built up originally by the British Broadcasting Corporation through whose microphones he was able to reveal his program to the French people. He was also financed by the British treasury. Nevertheless, de Gaulle wanted to prove to his countrymen, and perhaps to himself, that he was not a British tool.

Contrary to common belief, de Gaulle never was very popular with the British Foreign Office. From the moment he arrived on British soil in June 1940, he manifested his characteristic uncompromising attitude and his almost mystic belief in his Joan of Arc mission. Officials of the Foreign Office assigned to establish liaison with de Gaulle often complained about the difficulties of dealing with the Fighting French leader.

Churchill himself, who signed a personal agreement with de Gaulle and who at the beginning greatly appreciated him as a talented military leader and as the personification of the fighting spirit of the French, once said that of all the crosses he had to bear "the Lorraine Cross [emblem of the Fighting French] was certainly the heaviest." De Gaulle's most influential friend in London was Anthony Eden. When Americans complained about de Gaulle's difficult ways, Eden used to smile and say, "Only Quislings have complacent characters."

While American leaders were becoming more and more disturbed and irritated by the growing antagonism of de Gaulle and his partisans, the British were not at all surprised by de Gaulle's anti-British feelings. British-French relations never had had the sentimental background of American-French relations. Britain was France's hereditary enemy for many centuries. The Entente Cordiale of 1907, which made possible the British-French alliance in World War I, was a *mariage de raison*. The two countries felt that they had to unite their efforts against the growing power of Germany, which was shaping up as their common enemy. However, their relationship did not exclude all kinds of friction. The period between the wars was filled with numerous controversies and conflicts. The British were, therefore, not in the least surprised when de Gaulle, following the traditional line of French nationalism and imperialism, entered into conflict with them in Syria, where the two nations had clashed several times before and after World War I.

Official London may have had no more love for de Gaulle than had official Washington, but it was Washington which sided with Giraud in the long and arduous negotiations over the administrative status to be given North Africa and to all other liberated French territories. Giraud visualized a military-controlled French Central Administration in North Africa to assure the administration of French colonies only. Washington approved this set-up, which would be under Giraud's military direction, since he in turn would be under the military control of American commanders in North Africa.

De Gaulle and his National Committee in London were definitely opposed to Giraud's conception. They wanted a large number of civilians—members of the French National Committee—to participate in the provisional administration, and they insisted on the inclusion of all those delegates who represented the French underground in London. In other words, they wanted those whom they considered the representatives of Metropolitan France to have a controlling voice in the provisional executive body which would eventually administer—if only temporarily—liberated continental France.

Giraud wanted to reduce the power of the executive group temporarily to colonial France, where it actually could be exercised, and to have it under his own military control. He offered to share with de Gaulle the political side of colonial administration. Giraud and especially his advisers had little sympathy for the representatives of the French underground organization, in which the Communists were reported to play a rather important part.

But de Gaulle was bound by his agreement with the French underground. He believed that he best served the interests of

France by including Communists in his organization, thus avoiding a split comparable to the lamentable conflict between Mikhailovich and the Partisans in Yugoslavia or to the clash between republican and more or less pro-royalist guerrillas in Greece. And above all else, de Gaulle wanted to eliminate all outspoken collaborators whom the Vichy regime, with the approval of the German-Italian Armistice Commission, had maintained in power in North Africa, and to restore the Third Republic, which in his opinion was the indispensable prerequisite to the creation of the Fourth Republic.

Backed by high civilian and military officials who had for many months been collaborating with Vichy, Giraud was not in a position to satisfy all of de Gaulle's demands during the negotiations in which the politically minded George Catroux, a de Gaullist, played the role of go-between. But the agreement reached in June 1943 in Algiers was a victory for de Gaulle. General Giraud was to be co-chairman with de Gaulle of the French Committee of National Liberation and was to maintain nominal command of the French Army, because American and British representatives in Algiers had insisted on that condition. However, the Committee was to be "the sole central French authority to direct the war effort in all its forms and in all places." De Gaulle obtained four of the seven places on the Liberation Committee for his supporters, and eight of the fourteen seats on the Commissioners Committee, which was to become the French provisional government.

In addition, de Gaulle was able to place his men in all key political departments—Foreign Affairs, Interior (liaison with the French underground), Labor (important because of the predominant part the trade unions played in the underground), Colonies (which in 1943 were the only free French territories), Information (which was to become the voice of a United Fighting France), and the Department of Co-ordination of Moslem Affairs (especially important because the Moslems constitute the majority in already liberated French territories).

Several high officials with an outspoken collaborationist record —for instance Marcel Peyrouton, Governor of Algeria, and General Charles Noguès, Resident-General of Morocco—were dismissed in order to meet de Gaulle's urge for purification. In December 1943

Peyrouton was arrested together with several other prominent collaborationists.

While Giraud maintained nominal command of the French Army, de Gaulle reserved for himself, along with the political command, the chance to assure for his political administration control of the Army. His position was enhanced by the political superiority of his associates over Giraud's group. Whatever might have been thought of the different elements in the de Gaullist movement, no one could deny their dynamic spirit and their natural advantage in that they were the first to raise the banner of French national revolt. His aides may have been divided by their different political conceptions and personal ambitions, but as a group they were determined and they knew what they wanted.

Giraud had practically no political experience and he was surrounded by even more heterogeneous elements than de Gaulle. Many of his aides were opportunists, some of whom left Vichy and went over to Giraud only because he was backed by Allied bayonets. As soon as they realized that de Gaulle was politically the stronger, they hurriedly crossed over to his side. A large number of Giraud's non-opportunist supporters, especially among the younger officers, were pushed toward de Gaulle by the too obvious support given by American officials to Giraud, and the favors showered upon him by Washington, which many Frenchmen felt to be "suspect" and certainly "interfering." For the French were warned that American equipment for their armies in North Africa was conditioned by the presence of Giraud at their command. While London hoped that the personalities of the two French generals would be finally absorbed by the French National Liberation Committee, Washington feared that the politically stronger de Gaulle would always run the show both in the Committee and in the Army. Washington shared the suspicions of those Frenchmen who for two years questioned de Gaulle's loyalty to the French Republic.

France has had some rather unfortunate experiences with those of her generals who tried to become national leaders. Napoleon, the greatest of them, left alarming liabilities. MacMahon, who failed in the transition period from the Second Empire to the

Third Republic (1871); Boulanger, who fell short of his political ambitions (1892), and finally Pétain successfully revealed the political incompetence of French generals. French Republicans, the bulwark of the nation, always have mistrusted their military leaders, and with some justification.

The drama of France in this war rose from the fact that at the crucial moment of her history, when the French needed more than ever a great civilian political leader such as they always have had at critical hours in their turbulent past, she had only two generals. And one of these—de Gaulle—was too much interested in politics and therefore subject to suspicion, while the other— Giraud—was completely lacking in any political sense and therefore without political value.

De Gaulle's popularity in France was built up very slowly, for when he emerged as a leader outside of France, he was practically unknown in his own country. As a political figure he was, and still is, an enigma. Gradually, his people came to know and accept him, first as a great French patriot and later as a symbol of their resistance. His opponents in exile tried to convince influential American circles that he would be destroyed the moment Washington and London publicly withdrew their support, because of their conviction that his Fourth Republic would not follow the democratic principles of the United Nations.

It is more than probable, however, that the resisting Frenchmen in occupied France who followed de Gaulle would be deeply shocked if they were to be told that his British and American supporters had erred and that he was to be eliminated because he was anti-democratic. Such action could create great political confusion and might throw many resisting Frenchmen to the extreme left, for those who were once disappointed in de Gaulle would never accept Giraud as a substitute leader for republican France. They would not question Giraud's patriotism and honesty, but neither would they forget that all his life he had been much closer than de Gaulle to the royalist *Action Française,* which had many adherents in the French Army but practically no voter support at election time.

The American preference for Giraud paradoxically weakened him and strengthened de Gaulle. The suspicions of many Frenchmen were raised by criticism of the Allied policy in North Africa. They definitely resented Allied interference in their domestic problems and American support for Giraud was interpreted in France, according to representatives of the underground, as an American-British attempt to dictate France's future. Contradictorily, de Gaulle, whom Nazi and Vichy propaganda pictured as a British agent, rose in popularity when the French learned that Giraud was invited to visit the United States and Britain in June 1943 while de Gaulle was left in Algiers.

De Gaulle became really popular with his compatriots when they learned he was resisting both the Americans and the British in the defense of what he believed to be France's national interests. He appealed to the national pride of Frenchmen; he represented to them the France which struggled to free herself not only from Hitler's yoke but from British and American influence as well.

The French could not and did not want to forget that until 1939 France was a great power. They realized they could not free themselves from Hitler without the victory of the United States, Britain, and the Soviet Union. But their hope in the victory of their powerful allies and their gratitude toward them was no greater than their bitterness over what they believed was only their temporary weakness, and no less than their resentment over the treatment accorded them by their allies, especially the United States and Britain. Soviet policy makers appeared to have been anxious to spare the French their wounded feelings. Moscow acted in the way most appropriate to win French sympathies. She always emphasized that the Soviet Union considered France a great power and de Gaulle the legitimate and trusted representative of a great ally. Moscow bestowed greater recognition on de Gaulle than he was able to obtain in the United States and also made the first move toward complete recognition of the French National Liberation Committee.

Washington, plainly dissatisfied with de Gaulle's supremacy over Giraud, was much more reserved than London in the diplomatic problem of recognizing the French Committee. The United States exerted pressure upon London and Moscow in order to coordinate both the dates and the degree of recognition by the three big powers. The dates were co-ordinated; the degree and style were not. After the close of the Quebec Conference Washington announced, "The United States . . . welcomes the establishment of the French Committee . . . subject to the military requirements of the Allied commanders." A very limited recognition.

London's action was also limited, but it was more generously worded: "His Majesty's Government . . . recognize the French Committee . . . as a body qualified to insure the conduct of the French effort in the war within the framework of inter-Allied co-operation." Moscow went much further, almost to the point of full recognition: "The Soviet Union recognizes the French Committee as representative of the state interests of the French Republic and as the leader of all French patriots fighting against the Hitlerite tyranny."

Washington's delaying action and the restraint it exerted upon London widened the rift between Washington and Algiers. The French began to suspect that Washington was contemplating a three-power directorate which would evolve its own blueprint for liberated Europe. They suspected Washington of planning the complete elimination of France in the Pacific as a result of American resentment over the capitulation of Indo-China which facilitated the Japanese conquest of the Southwest Pacific. This mistrust was later intensified by the Allied deal with the Badoglio regime in Italy and by the fight France put up for admission to the Mediterranean Commission, which was set up to determine Italy's future status along with all other Mediterranean problems. After the French obtained their voice in the Mediterranean Commission, they discovered that it had been decided at the Moscow Conference that the Mediterranean Commission would have only very limited objectives. The real political influence was to be exerted by the Committee for European Affairs, to be created by the Big Three in London. This meant another battle by the French in Algiers, this time for admission to the London Committee.

The French Committee in Algiers thereupon declared that "settlement of the fate of Germany and her allies after their defeat cannot be undertaken or successfully conducted without the participation of France," and disclosed that France would consider herself bound only by decisions in which she had participated.

When de Gaulle opened the First Political French Forum in Algiers in November 1943, he declared before the Provisional Consultative Assembly, which was to become France's provisional parliament, that "the voice of France is rising from the dungeon." Of the Assembly's eighty-four members, forty were representatives of resistance groups inside France, twelve represented resistance groups outside of France, twenty were members of the old French Chamber of Deputies, and twelve were sent by departmental councils in North Africa, West Africa, Martinique, and Guiana. Only forty-two of the eighty-four members of the Assembly arrived in time. The Assembly was not supposed to have any legislative or executive authority; its goal, as viewed by the Liberation Committee, was to express as far as circumstances permitted the feelings and desires of the French people.

It was before that Assembly that de Gaulle reminded France's allies that France was a great nation. He declared that it would be "first an injustice, and second, and especially, a mistake" not to recognize her dignity. He repeated the warning that France could not consider "any European settlement and any major world settlement made without France" as a good settlement. He claimed for France in the name of the National Liberation Committee the right to participate in the organization of the world to come. The rest of his speech was devoted to tracing the broad lines along which he proposed to build his "Fourth Republic."

By bringing to de Gaulle a kind of parliamentary expression of the French people's support, which he had been trying to win ever since he first raised the banner of resistance, the Consultative Assembly strengthened his moral and political prestige. It allowed him to realize in November 1943 what he was unable to achieve in his agreement with Giraud five months earlier. He established his political control of the French Committee by eliminating from it practically all of Giraud's supporters and even Giraud himself, who was compelled to resign as co-chairman and accept the reduced role of commander of the French military forces under de Gaulle's control, a post of which he was deprived early in 1944.

This was the victory of the intransigent patriots over what they termed the lukewarm supporters of French resistance. It was

what always happens in any European revolutionary movement—
the extremists win out over the moderates. Those who had forgotten or had failed to realize that the de Gaullist movement was
not only a fight for national liberation but also a revolutionary
movement, and who did not appreciate the full value of his announcement of the forthcoming Fourth Republic, now could understand its full scope. For with Giraud went two of his supporters
on the Committee, which was increased by seven new members,
four of whom represented the underground and all of whom accepted de Gaulle as their leader.

This was the victory of dynamic forces, capitalizing upon
France's exasperation and the diplomatic mistakes of her allies,
over elements perhaps no less patriotic but certainly much weaker
politically, because they were anxious to save what they believed
could be salvaged from the power of prewar France.

Representatives of the French underground, voicing the anger
of resisting groups, accentuated the unyielding character of the
French Committee for National Liberation at Algiers. Their hatred
for French collaborationists was greater than their hatred for their
Nazi conquerors and they insisted on the arrest of leading collaborationists in North Africa. They brought Pierre Pucheu, former
Minister of the Interior in Pétain's cabinet, to trial, and they saw
to it that the death sentence decreed by the underground was confirmed by the French court at Algiers and carried out.

The Algiers Committee approved the arrests, for it wanted to
make clear that the Fourth Republic would not be so generously
tolerant and so ready for compromise as the Third Republic. But
it opposed the trials before the hour of liberation in order to assure
adequate prosecution and defense. However, the underground
insisted on the immediate trial of Pucheu, claiming that if the
trial were delayed, the anger and impatience of the patriots in
France would break out in revolutionary explosion. The Committee agreed in its anxiety to channelize and to control French
national and revolutionary forces. Its ambition was that the new
French revolution be realized not after but before the liberation
and that it be directed by the Committee and General de Gaulle.

The General often has been criticized and scoffed at in the
United States for his Joan of Arc complex. His supreme political

achievement—history will determine whether the credit should be given to him or to his political advisers—was to achieve a synthesis of his Joan of Arc complex with the Jacobin principles of the French Republic. It can never be overemphasized that, for the nations of Europe, history is not a buried past but a living part of their national life. De Gaulle came from those French nationalist Catholic circles for whom the miracle of Joan of Arc was a living reality. He understood, too, that while the French Republic may have deceived many Frenchmen by her rotting fruit, her revolutionary roots were deeply planted in France's national soil. The Jacobins, to whom the French parliamentary orators liked to refer as *grands ancêtres*, were anxious to achieve bold reforms, but they were also ardent patriots. De Gaulle tried to unite the flaming patriotism of the mystic believers in Joan of Arc with the no less ardent patriotism of the free-thinking republican offspring of the Jacobins.

He realized that France had been successively deceived by the Third Republic, by the Pétain regime which succeeded the collapsed republican government, and, rightly or wrongly, by the allies of France. He realized that France needed a revolutionary faith for her renovation, and that his country was completing a new revolutionary circle. And he made his bid for leadership accordingly, indicating his goal as the Fourth Republic. De Gaulle believed that France, defeated by National Socialist Germany and betrayed by the gravediggers of the Third Republic who gathered around Pétain, would rise up in a revolutionary surge for the achievement of national and social objectives which neither the Third Republic nor Pétain's French State could achieve. He offered the Fourth Republic to his compatriots; and he offered it also as a new ally to the allies of the Third Republic.

He believed that his movement would be broad enough on both the national and social level to encompass even the French Communists, who had refused the seats he offered them on his Committee. They insisted that their delegates be appointed by the Central Committee of their party and not chosen by de Gaulle, who had declined to seat any of the twenty-seven Communist deputies imprisoned in North Africa for refusing to fight early in the present war. For them, the war had begun on June 22, 1941, when Hitler attacked Russia.

While de Gaulle knew that some day the Communists might become his rivals for leadership, he was aware that his Fourth Republic would face the much greater dangers of France's declining birth rate and the beginning of the disintegration of her colonial empire. The birth rate fell from 20.5 per thousand for the decade 1901-11 to 14.8 in 1936-38. The death rate in the latter period was 15.2, dangerously in excess of the birth rate. The prolonged absence from their homes of the two and a half million war prisoners and workers drained by Germany must have lowered even further the birth rate already affected by the undernourishment of French women. This then is the danger which threatens the French people in their very substance and which may imperil the future not only of the Fourth Republic but of the French nation itself.

To cope with this danger, postwar France will have to make radical changes in her social structure. The French middle classes, so anxious to maintain their social way of life for themselves and for the coming generations, were reluctant during the past decades to build up large families. Conditions must be altered to enable these classes to increase the number of their children without fear that their living standards would decline proportionately. The workers and even the farmers who have begun to share the social apprehensions of the middle classes should be given the same assurances for the provision of large families. The attraction of the industrial centers and the great cities with their numerous opportunities of comparatively easier jobs and better working conditions, along with the declining birth rate, depopulated the French countryside after the last war. It became dependent on Italian, Polish, and Czechoslovak immigrant farmhands.

Postwar France will have to face the major problem of how to replenish the alarming losses to her national substance caused by the last war and increased by the present conflict with all its social impact. On the success of the solution of this problem by the first French postwar generation will depend the future of the French people and the future of France herself.

And while France at home struggles for her survival as a nation, a less serious but more immediate danger of disintegration will loom on the remote horizons of her empire. It is a paradox of

French history that her people came to realize the full importance of their colonial empire at the very moment when that empire had begun to break up.

The French people were very slow to become empire-minded. Their colonies were virtually forced upon them by their missionaries, their army, their big business. Not until the 1930's did France begin to be aware of the real worth of her empire and of the necessity of defending it, whereupon she urgently increased her navy. However, it was only after the collapse of Metropolitan France that the French were able to appreciate the political and economic value of their empire. The Allied landing in North Africa, the transfer of de Gaulle's Committee from London to Algiers, and the establishment of the Consultative Assembly were consecutive stages in the intensification of the new "empire-consciousness."

Many French politicians, labor leaders, and private citizens, removed for the first time in their lives from familiar French soil, discovered how privileged they were to possess territories overseas which would contribute economically to the Allied war effort, and help to raise an army of half a million soldiers to assure the continuation of French national life. They were, indeed, not in exile in Algiers, which from the administrative viewpoint is an extension of Metropolitan France; they were not expatriated in the two French protectorates of Tunisia and Morocco, certainly not in the latter which bears the architectural and intellectual stamp of Marshal Lyautey's very personal and often quite successful administrative experience. These émigrés finally came to feel at home in their African colonial possessions.

Equally important, they began to realize the necessity of transforming their heterogeneous colonies into some kind of French Commonwealth. This certainly will not be an easy task, for their colonial possessions offer an extreme variety of racial elements and administrative levels. Only the three departments of Algiers, the colony of Senegal in French Equatorial Africa, and the Caribbean Islands of Martinique and Guadeloupe elected deputies to the French Parliament.

The French African Conference held in January 30, 1944 at Brazzaville was the first constructive attempt of the assumed leaders of the future Fourth Republic to assure for that republic the status of French Empire by finding a fair and lasting solution to colonial problems. Alarming signs had begun to multiply on different sectors of the French Colonial Empire: agitation among the Moslems in French North Africa; the clamor in mandated Syria and Lebanon for independence; uncertainty over the postwar fate of French possessions in the Pacific, especially Indo-China whose capitulation facilitated Japan's conquest of the Southwestern Pacific and forced the American Navy to become interested in her future.

Leaders of the future republic, seeking temporary but immediate solutions for the most urgent of their colonial problems, bestowed French citizenship upon the élite of Algeria's Moslem population in order to accelerate the integration of that territory into the French national community. They renewed and specified former French pledges to recognize the independence of Syria and the Lebanon in the postwar period. They revealed that the Fourth Republic would give a new political and economic status to Indo-China.

They must realize, however, that the Fourth Republic will not have, at least during its first decade, the international prestige of the defunct Third Republic. Even if the German danger is eliminated, the French international position will be greatly weakened. Russia, once France's ally, will be for her a potential protector rather than an ally, so far as the idea of alliance implies equality in partnership. Poland and the Balkan states, which between the two wars were integrated by French diplomacy into the French system of security, will belong to the new security system of governments friendly to the Soviet Union.

The Fourth Republic will depend, even more than did the Third, on Britain. And it is permissible to assume that this new regime will need England's support in blocking the centrifugal forces which threaten to disintegrate the French colonial empire. The fate of Syria and Lebanon, where British and French interests clashed so often in the past, probably will be determined by the necessity and possibility of establishing British-French co-operation in the Near East.

In the Far East, too, France will most likely need Britain's support to maintain her Pacific possessions. But here both the Soviet Union and the United States undoubtedly will have deciding voices after the termination of the war. It is highly probable that the United States will ask for naval bases not only in French Pacific possessions but also at Dakar and Casablanca.

France's allies have agreed that her postwar fate should be decided by the French people themselves. It is, indeed, the right of Frenchmen to determine whether they want to restore the Third Republic or build the Fourth Republic, and whether that Fourth Republic should or should not be headed by de Gaulle. The leaders of the Big Three, who refused to admit the French to the inner sanctum of their postwar deliberations, have emphasized that liberated France would be assured the opportunity of deciding whether she wants to become—with or without de Gaulle—the Fourth Republic.

But whether this Fourth Republic will be able to maintain the French Empire will not depend on its leaders alone. Some of the peoples living within this empire might and probably will voice their conflicting aspirations. And the Big Three of the United Nations will have to co-ordinate their opposing views on colonial regimes in order to decide whether France should maintain her colonial empire, and in what form it should be continued.

VI: Stable Northwest

Scandinavia and the Low Countries

THERE are very few problems of international importance in Northwestern Europe, which achieved both peace and internal stability. Its peoples were among the first to establish and maintain their national individualities. There are no boundary controversies within this area; the few minor problems along the Danish-German or Belgian-German borders cannot possibly endanger the peace. There are, also, no minority problems here, nor is the Northwest threatened by social turmoil. National and social life in this unusual corner of Europe have developed remarkably stable bases. The peoples of Northwestern Europe are happy in the knowledge that the downfall of Hitler's Reich will automatically restore their independence within their prewar boundaries.

Norway's only problem will be the punishment of Vidkun Quisling, whose name became in this war the hated symbol of treason, and of all those who followed him in his despicable collaboration with the Nazi conquerors. Their punishment—Knut Hamsun, Norway's greatest living writer, is unfortunately among them— will not endanger Norway's national unity. Certain Norwegians might have been confused when the Nazis, without declaring war, invaded their country in early April of 1941. But most of them immediately recovered their national conscience and unity in their loyalty to King Haakon and their resistance to the invader. The Norwegian monarchy in exile is one of the few prewar European regimes that will be welcomed on its return home by the vast majority of its people.

Social problems can hardly endanger the internal peace of this country. Undoubtedly Norway will resume the progressive social evolution which during the last few decades made such remarkable strides. Nor will her external problems be such as to endanger her independence. British-Norwegian ties, for example, have survived the corrosive test of exile. Some frictions have developed over British use of Norway's merchant navy, but it will not be hard to find a satisfactory solution. Even before the war the Norwegians looked to Britain as their most important customer and potential protector, and they are likely to continue to in the postwar years.

Some Norwegian circles cannot but resent with understandable envy the privileged status of their Swedish neighbors who were fortunate enough to maintain in this war the neutrality which all Scandinavia enjoyed during the First World War. Responsible Norwegians realize, however, that despite the strong feeling of Scandinavian solidarity developed between the two wars, Sweden was powerless to assist Norway except in humanitarian ways. With a population of 6,300,000 scattered over 173,347 square miles with dangerously exposed borders, Sweden could not have been of great military value as Norway's ally in 1941, any more than she could have helped Finland in 1939.

Scandinavian solidarity, it must be remembered, is not a diplomatic invention. It is a political reality created by geographical and racial ties and, to a certain extent, by economy. It appeared to have been dissipated when the four Scandinavian countries found themselves each pushed along different ways: Norway became a full-fledged member of the United Nations; Denmark was a "potential" member until August 1943, when the Nazis took over the whole administration and she became an "actual" member; Sweden remained neutral; Finland, a Baltic state admitted in September 1934 to the "political Scandinavian community," found herself fighting on Hitler's side, if not in Hitler's camp.

But it is most probable that Scandinavian solidarity, at least so far as the three truly Scandinavian countries are concerned, will survive the test of this war. And since it is a political reality, it is very likely to express itself with a new vigor as soon as the Scandinavian peoples recover the freedom to express their sovereign wills.

Denmark, too, will offer the peacemakers few difficult international problems. Invaded by Germany on the same morning as her fellow-victim to the north, Denmark capitulated after a few hours of confused and disorganized resistance. Her opposition to the occupying troops has not had the same fighting character as Norway's, but in spite of all their efforts to make Denmark the showplace of Hitler's New Order the Nazis never have been able to make the Danes accept their occupation. Sabotage and passive resistance developed apace while Denmark was permitted to maintain for propaganda purposes a fictitious independence in so far as her internal problems were concerned.

This fiction was ended in August 1943, after an outbreak of rioting that may have been deliberately provoked by the Nazis themselves. They were at that time seeking a pretext for tightening their control on the country which they feared might become one of the beachheads for the second front. Since then Denmark has been an "associate" nation, and it is very likely that, before the end of hostilities, internal developments might make her a full-fledged member of the United Nations.

King Christian X remained with his people and was compelled to submit to the occupation; but he never recognized it *de jure.* He became for the Danes the symbol of their resistance and the guardian of their violated independence. His popularity among his people is as great as that of his brother, Haakon VII, King of Norway, among the Norwegians. Some of his ministers may disappear from political life after Denmark's liberation, but his regime should emerge with new prestige, seemingly unthreatened by any social or domestic trouble.

Liberated Denmark will have to settle the status of Greenland, a Danish possession in which the United States has built air and radio bases. In the agreement with Henrik de Kauffmann, Danish Minister to Washington, the United States reiterated her recognition of Danish sovereignty over Greenland, and stipulated that the agreement was to stand "until the present dangers to the American continent have passed." Should the United States desire to maintain air bases in Greenland after the war, their status probably will be determined within the general agreement on American air and naval bases in the Pacific and Atlantic Oceans. And Denmark certainly would expect and be given adequate assurance that her political and economic rights in that territory would be safeguarded and respected.

The postwar status of Iceland, which has been an independent state since December 1, 1918, and which is legally united with Denmark only by recognition of their common king, will not present a difficult international problem. The Parliament of Iceland, which assumed control of Iceland's foreign affairs when Germany invaded Denmark, voted in May 1941 to cancel the monarchic union with Denmark and to establish a republican constitution. Two years later Iceland's Parliament provided by a vote of 45 to 7 for her full independence as a republic to be established on June 17, 1944. The Danes may resent the fact that the Icelanders chose to achieve their complete independence while they were very much occupied with and by the Nazis. But Denmark has long been reconciled to the idea that Iceland, which had embarked on the path to full independence, would eventually achieve that goal.

An argument might conceivably develop between Britain and the United States over which sphere of economic, if not political, influence the independent Republic of Iceland would come under after the war. Iceland's Minister to Washington has explained that his country looks to the United States as her most important big neighbor, but at the United Nations Relief and Rehabilitation Conference at Atlantic City Iceland was included in the European Committee. It is fairly certain, however, that if British-American collaboration in the postwar world should ever become compromised, it would not be over the issue of the influence zone—should such zones ever be established—into which the North Atlantic Republic of Iceland should fall.

In Holland we find a splendid example of political and social stability. Queen Wilhelmina's exiled regime is certain to find a hearty welcome upon its return from London to a liberated Holland—a nation without a boundary problem and whose internal peace is free of all signs of acute social disturbance. Holland, too, will have to punish her collaborationists, but their number is small. After Quisling failed to bring them any substantial support in Norway, the Germans renounced the use of the little group of Adrien Mussert's Dutch Nazis. Unable to break the resistance of the defeated but unconquered Dutchmen, the Nazis even tried to seduce them by promising to restore Holland's independence "after Hitler's victory."

Holland's principal postwar problem will be to maintain her economic ties with the Dutch East and West Indies. Her prewar prosperity, which gave her people the highest standard of living in all Europe, was to a very large extent due to the efficient and sound exploitation of her extremely rich overseas possessions. To restore one she must restore the other. Before the war the sixty-seven million East Indian natives did not manifest any special desire to be free of Dutch rule. And it is questionable whether Japanese occupation has been able to develop among them any violent antagonism to the white man. But the fate of the Dutch East Indies is not specifically a Dutch problem. The postwar status of the Dutch East Indies will be determined by the general status of European colonies in Eastern Asia. The Dutch East Indies will not be the first of those colonies to claim their complete independence. But should the other peoples of Asia be able to assure themselves political and economic freedom, then the East Indians probably will not fail to point out that their ancient culture entitles them to the same privileges. The Dutch boast of one of the best records in the history of colonial empires, and they have done their utmost to safeguard the rights to the riches of these tropical islands which they have developed and exploited for centuries.

Future plans for this section of the Dutch Empire may be glimpsed in a message Queen Wilhelmina sent to her people in Holland and in the East and West Indies in December 1942. She said she visualized for them in the postwar period a life directed toward a commonwealth of independent peoples, free to conduct their own internal affairs but ready to render mutual assistance in external matters. The Dutch, through generations of excellent tradesmen and bankers, have developed a remarkable capacity for adaptation to new situations. This capacity, combined with their paradoxically innate stubbornness, encourages them to envisage with confidence the drastically revised status of their overseas possessions. They are disposed to grant every political right to the natives in order to safeguard the economic advantages which they have assured themselves through centuries of daring enterprise and hard work.

The Belgians also have a colonial problem, but theirs is even less acute than the problems facing the Dutch. The Belgian Congo in Central Africa, a colony which King Leopold II created at his own peril and practically imposed upon an unwilling Belgium, is rich in copper, uranium ore, tin, gold, and diamonds, and is one of the foremost producers of palm oil, cocoa, cotton, ivory, and rubber. Even before the war the Belgian Administration was applying the "open door" policy to the Congo, and its postwar economic status will unquestionably be determined by the general economic status of colonies. But its political status can hardly become an urgent problem, for the Congo's Negro population has not yet attained the intellectual and social maturity to excite the claims of independence now stirring the minds and hearts of the Asiatic peoples.

Both Belgium and Holland have looked and will continue to look to Britain, herself the world's greatest colonial empire, for the protection of their outlying interests. And they realize that if France recovers her prewar empire, she, too, will be a firm ally for the combined defense of European colonial developments throughout the world.

At home Belgium has no boundary problems. Whether or not the German-speaking districts of Eupen-Malmédy, which she annexed in 1919, will remain with her is not a matter serious enough to shatter the peace of Western Europe. Nor does her social peace appear to be endangered. At the outbreak of the war the Communists had 9 of the 207 seats in Belgium's Parliament. They have increased their following somewhat under Nazi occupation, but it is hardly probable that they will be able to claim here as important a place as do their ideological brothers in France.

However, Belgium is the only one of all the Northwestern European countries which might conceivably face a constitutional problem after the war. King Leopold's surrender as Commander-in-Chief of the Belgian Army, after a twenty-one-day campaign against overwhelming German forces, has been badly misunderstood in Allied countries. In 1940 public opinion was inclined to accept at face value the accusation of Premier Paul Reynaud, who on the eve of France's collapse tried to make Leopold the scapegoat for the French catastrophe. The great majority of Belgians, including those who had disapproved of his prewar foreign policy, understood and appreciated the King's decision to stay with them and to share their ordeal by occupation. He considered himself a prisoner of war and sternly rejected all offers to collaborate, even when many Europeans, among whom were some of his friends and advisers, believed that nothing could prevent Hitler's victory and world domination.

Leopold's prestige began to decline at home with the announcement of his marriage in 1941 to a Flemish commoner, the daughter of a Flemish politician. The French-speaking Walloons always had resented the influence exerted upon their King by his Flemish friends and advisers. Now they feared his new wife might increase the opposition's favor with the crown.

The long-standing differences between the Flemings and the Walloons had been seriously aggravated during the First World War when most of the Belgian collaborationists with the Germans were recruited from among the extremist Flemings. As a national group, the Flemings have always wanted to live peacefully with the Walloons in Belgium. However, extreme Flemish nationalists, who at one time held seventeen seats in Parliament, kept urging administrative changes of a federative character which were unacceptable to the Walloons. With their higher birth rate, the Flemings already had exceeded the number of Walloons who, until the last war, were supreme in the Belgian government through electoral laws favoring their higher social circles. They consequently suspected the extreme Flemish aspirations of concealing the potential threat of a Flemish superiority, both in numbers and in government control.

In the period between the two wars, Belgium had gradually corrected many of the injustices in the linguistic rights afforded the Flemings. However, this period of peace was envenomed by discussions about the amnesty which Flemish politicians were urging for their extremist members who had been imprisoned for collaborating with the enemy during the First World War. It was further disturbed by Belgium's adoption in 1936 of a new foreign policy of "independence." It was undertaken by the Crown to satisfy the Flemings, who were disposed to defend their country but opposed a permanent military alliance with France. The Walloons wanted to see Belgium tied even more closely to Britain and France and they sharply criticized Leopold's new program.

In reality it was because of France's weakness and Britain's unpreparedness that Belgium—and all the other small countries of Europe—were compelled to revise their foreign policies. King Leopold believed his was a realistic policy of independence, for he was fully aware of the trend toward appeasement among the Western powers and he used all his diplomacy in an effort to achieve constructive co-operation between the Axis and the Western democracies. His purpose was solely to prevent his country from becoming once more the battlefield of Europe, but at the same time he sought to prepare Belgium against the coming German aggression. And to obtain Flemish support for his important rearmament measures, he had to take his country out of the French-British orbit.

In return for disentangling Belgium from these military alliances, a step which the Flemings believed would automatically free their country from the dangers of a new war, Flemish members of Parliament voted for every national defense measure. But the new policy left the Walloons unconvinced that they could avoid being drawn into war, and equally certain that they would need both Britain and France.

Belgium's new independence naturally brought her closer to Holland, but not as close as King Leopold and his advisers had hoped. For the Dutch, whose peace had been unbroken since Napoleonic days, entertained the happy illusion that their neutrality had become an institution. While welcoming Belgium's new policy, they were not anxious to commit themselves to a close military alliance with their neighbor. As late as May 1939, when the shadows of the new European war were already distinct against the troubled horizon, high-ranking Dutch military experts publicly declared that it would be a mistake for Holland to enter into a military alliance with Belgium. Should Germany invade Holland, they argued, Belgium would necessarily be a victim of the same aggression, and the two countries then would find themselves fighting side by side. But so long as there was a chance that Germany would restrict herself to the route of her 1914 thrust across Belgium, they believed that Holland should gamble on it and refuse to expose herself to reprisals for military commitments.

Hitler succeeded in uniting Belgium and Holland by attacking the two nations simultaneously. The unconquered countries continued to fight Nazi occupation at home and contributed substantially through their colonies and other resources to the Allied war effort. It seems very likely now that in the postwar world these two countries will consolidate their co-operation. Their governments in exile are endeavoring to study and develop economic bases for such co-operation.

These two nations have always been of primary strategic importance to Britain and she can be expected to favor any program designed to bring them together. Her self-appointed guardianship of the Low Countries arises from the historical and military fact that any European power which has access to them holds a gun pointed directly at England's heart. William Pitt's England fought Napoleon who tried to maintain French control of that annexed territory. The England of Winston Churchill, who took over British leadership on the day the Nazis invaded the Low Countries, cannot now allow Germany to control Belgium and Holland.

Since Britain is directly interested in the restoration of Belgian and Dutch independence, it is not beyond belief that, having committed herself to their defense, she may try to impose upon them postwar diplomatic and military obligations designed to insure automatic co-ordination of the Low Countries' defenses. However, she may have broader views, such as the unification of the whole of Northwestern Europe. For Britain knows that in the political and social stability of this region she will find the best possible material for the construction of a regional security which would be the cornerstone of—or, at the very worst, a substitute for—that great hope of all peace-loving and economically satisfied nations, international collective security.

Field Marshal Jan Christiaan Smuts, considered by many diplomats as the most influential person after Churchill in the British Empire, expressed this trend of British political thought when in November 1943 he extended to the smaller democracies of Western Europe an invitation to join the British Commonwealth. Smuts believes, as do many other British and non-British statesmen, that "neutrality is obsolete, is dead." He hopes that the small democracies of Western Europe have learned that by themselves they would have been lost, and may be lost again. Why then should they not join the British Commonwealth with which they have so much in common: outlook, way of life, ideals, political and spiritual substance.

Smuts explained with almost brutal frankness that the disappearance of three nations from the ranks of the five great powers of Europe—France, Italy, and Germany—would leave Britain in the postwar world in the position of an unequal partner squeezed between the United States with her immeasurable power, and the Soviet Union, "the new Colossus in Europe." Against the possibility that Churchill's conception of the British-American cornerstone might fail and Eden's hope of collective security might prove once more impossible of realization, Smuts would like to see Great Britain strengthen her European position in order to protect herself from the danger of being crushed between her partners. In his opinion, the best means to this end would be the attachment of the small Western European democracies to the British Commonwealth. He did not mention, but he certainly could not have overlooked, the fact that the addition of Holland and Belgium and their overseas possessions would strengthen not only Great Britain's European position but also the world position of the British Empire.

However, Smuts' invitation was not received enthusiastically in the exiled political circles of Holland and Belgium. The Low Countries are naturally anxious to strengthen their ties with Great Britain and some of their statesmen are prepared to see their countries voluntarily sacrifice a portion of their sovereignty in exchange for a greater security. But before envisaging the possibility of tying their fate to that of the British Empire, they would like a clearer view of the paths along which this empire will move in the postwar period. They want also to try first to consolidate their position by organizing their own region as completely as they can.

The five Northwestern countries, Norway, Sweden, Denmark, Holland, and Belgium (the latter representing also the interests of Luxembourg which she was united with by an economic union), attempted in 1930 to build an economic regional solidarity through the Oslo Convention. They undertook thereby not to increase their customs duties or to establish new duties without informing the others and offering them an opportunity to present their objections. In 1932 Belgium, Luxembourg, and Holland tried to advance a step further by reducing their custom duties by 10 per cent every year over a five-year period. But Britain made this impossible by insisting on her right to benefit by those reductions, in virtue of the commercial treaties which assured her position as the "most favored nation." The Oslo Convention remained thereafter more of a symbol than a practical reality. It was, nevertheless, an inspiring symbol of the struggle to allay economic antagonisms between nations, and as such was spiritually related to the American economic policy of reciprocal trade treaties.

If Britain is seriously considering the postwar possibility of leaning on small organized European countries to increase her potentialities as leader of a Western European bloc in the face of the growing powers of the United States and the Soviet Union, the small democracies of Western Europe would like to see the Oslo Convention become an inspiration for a sound economic base on which a politically and socially stable Northwestern Europe could be built.

VII: The Controversy Around a Hyphen

Czechoslovakia

THE minority problem has plagued Europe for centuries and it will unquestionably be one of the major obstacles to her peace after this war. It is the crux of the postwar settlement of Central Europe's difficulties, for inseparably intermingled minorities readily become crushing burdens on the shoulders of the smaller and the younger nations. People who have lived for centuries under foreign domination find it extremely difficult to co-ordinate their historical claims based on past glory with new and implacable realities. Their economic weakness and social immaturity make them easy prey for the never-satisfied aspirations of great powers. This, in brief, was the history of the small nations that emerged in Central and Southeastern Europe after the First World War. It was the history of Poland, Hungary, Rumania, and Yugoslavia. It was also to a certain extent the tragic history of Czechoslovakia, whose postwar status is uncertain even after a United Nations victory.

The very name of this brave country indicates that it was the union of two national entities with the potential minority problem inherent in such a union, although it took twenty years for the hyphen to appear officially between the Czechs and the Slovaks. It was on October 28, 1918, that members of the Czech National Committee meeting in Prague began their new nation's declaration of independence with the hopeful words, "The independent Czechoslovak state has come into being." Two days later the Slovak National Council affirmed that the "Slovak nation is a part of the Czechoslovak nation, one with it in language and in the history of its civilization."

Six million Czechs and two and a half million Slovaks were jubilant. Separated for a thousand years—the Czechs ruled by Austria, the Slovaks by Hungary—they were finally about to build their independent state together in freedom. The capitulation of the

115

Hapsburg Austro-Hungarian Empire to the terms of Woodrow Wilson's Fourteen Points was a victory for democracy. A short-lived victory, though, for in 1938 Britain and France capitulated at Munich to Adolf Hitler and the national home of the Czechs and the Slovaks was broken asunder.

Deprived by Germany of her western Sudeten-German provinces, mutilated Czechoslovakia was dismembered into a pseudo-federation of three small states—Czech, Slovak, and Carpatho-Ukrainian—which were then united by a Nazi-made hyphen under the new name of Czecho-Slovakia. In March 1939 the terrorized Prague cabinet gave way before Hitler's new outburst of threats. Nazi columns rolled into defenseless Prague and the so-called "Second Republic" of Czecho-Slovakia ceased to exist. The Czechs were arbitrarily placed in the Nazi protectorate of Bohemia and Moravia, and the Slovaks were granted the status of "independent" Slovakia, becoming thereby Hitler's first puppet state. Part of the Slovak territories were given to Hungary together with the Carpathian Ukraine, which then appeared likely to be useful as the nucleus for the Nazi dream—never to be realized—of a Great Ukrainian puppet state.

Paradoxically, the outbreak of World War II brought new hope to the Czechs and Slovaks. A National Czechoslovak (without the hyphen) Committee was created in London. It later became the Czechoslovak Government-in-Exile, but only after fighting for complete recognition by the Allied powers while the Czechs and many Slovaks in their homeland were courageously battling the Nazi invaders.

Certain of the exiled Slovaks did not approve the makeup of the Czechoslovak government in which the Czechs held seven of the eleven portfolios. While the Slovaks wanted to be liberated from the Nazis and to live together with their Czech cousins, they did not want to live in a centralized, pre-Munich Czechoslovakia which was led, if not dominated, by the Czechs. Their goal was a federated, hyphenated Czecho-Slovakia without the Nazis. The Czechs declared that they were fighting Hitler and would never recognize any changes made by the Nazis; the hyphen was of Hitler's making and, therefore, unacceptable. Many Slovaks also shared this viewpoint, but this did not remove the existence of dissension on a postwar problem while the war was still raging. Fortunately, the Czech-Slovak conflict did not reach the tragic proportions of the civil war and massacre of the Serb-Croat rift in Yugoslavia. But basically the conflict here developed from the same causes as in Yugoslavia: the conflict of two different mentalities in two peoples closely related racially but separated for centuries by foreign domination and, as a result of living in different economic and cultural environments, having developed fundamentally different viewpoints.

Historically Czechoslovakia's conflict originated in two medieval states—Bohemia and Hungary—which arose in the tenth century from the ruins of the Moravian Empire left by the conquering Magyars. The unconquered Slavs in Bohemia became the Czech nation. The Slovaks in eastern Moravia, vanquished by the Magyars, were separated from the Czechs for nine centuries, and in the Hungarian feudal state were never given an opportunity to develop their own culture and political institutions. In the fifteenth century, because of Bohemia's political and military prestige, the Czech language became the written language of cultivated Slovaks. By the end of the sixteenth century—the period of the Reformation which strongly influenced the Protestant Hussite movement in Bohemia—Czech Bohemia and Slovakia were very close culturally and psychologically.

In the seventeenth and eighteenth centuries, however, Prague began to lose her political and cultural prestige. Separate political and social institutions in Austrian-dominated Bohemia and Magyar-dominated Slovakia tended to separate the Slovaks from the Czechs. Their linguistic unity was broken and the Czechs, who remembered the Hussite opposition to the Catholic Church, began to absorb the liberal ideas of Western Europe. But in Slovakia, meanwhile, the Catholic Church strengthened its position and soon began to work for the substitution of a language based on local dialect for the written Czech then in use. And written Slovak was introduced in the 1840's as a demonstration of national Slovak opposition to the Magyar language, which had begun to replace Latin as the official tongue of Hungary.

In the twentieth century the Slovaks found themselves much weaker economically and socially than the Czechs, and the older

Slovak generations felt somewhat estranged from the Czechs and resented their cultural superiority. But the younger generation now began to look hopefully toward Prague where Thomas Masaryk, by blood and temperament as much Slovak as Czech, since his mother was a Slovak, was leading the fight for the independent existence of the united Czechs and Slovaks. The First World War intensified these hopes. The Czechs developed their "Maffia," an underground resistance organization which prepared the revolt at home while Czech politicians escaped abroad to win Allied sympathy for their cause. Czech and Slovak legions were formed in France, Russia, and Italy. Support for an independent Czechoslovakia grew apace and was advanced considerably by the adoption in June 1918 of the so-called Pittsburgh Agreement at a meeting of American Slovaks and Czechs with Masaryk. This convention, held in the heart of the Czech and Slovak settlements of this country, approved the union of these two people into one nation under one government.

Later, when Czechoslovakia had been established in the family of nations, the Slovak Clerical (Catholic) Party, headed by Father Andreas Hlinka, accused the Czechs of misinterpreting the Pittsburgh Agreement so as to establish a Czech-dominated centralized republic. Father Hlinka demanded autonomy for Slovakia within the Czechoslovak state frame, an autonomy which he told his followers was promised them in Pittsburgh. The Czechs denied that the word autonomy was even mentioned in that agreement and quoted in rebuttal this passage on the future administrative status as accepted at that convention: "Slovakia shall have her own administrative system, her own diet, and her own courts. The Slovak language shall be the official language in the schools, in the public offices, and in public affairs generally. The Czechoslovak state shall be a republic, and its constitution a democratic one."

The Slovaks were, perhaps, right in claiming that the Pittsburgh Agreement was not carried out to the letter, but the Czechs countered that it was not a treaty but simply the proclamation of a program; and that moreover it was made by representatives of Czechs and Slovaks in America who could not speak for the Czech and Slovak national organizations in Bohemia and Slovakia. As to Masaryk, the Pittsburgh declaration merely stated that the deliberations took place in the presence of the chairman of the Czechoslovak National Council; there was no mention whatever of his approval of any of its specific points.

It was this controversy, this demonstration of the devastating destructive power of a minority problem (the Slovak autonomists numbered only 30 to 35 per cent of the Slovaks) that gave Hitler the opportunity to dismember Czechoslovakia. Not that Father Hlinka had any sympathy for the former Hungarian rulers who had sent him to jail because of his nationalist activities. He claimed autonomy for Slovakia only because of his disappointment in the centralized regime of the free-thinking Czechs. But a few other Slovaks, such as Bela Tuka and Alexander Mach, pushed their opposition to Prague so far as to adopt a pro-Hungarian attitude. They belonged to that small group of embittered Slovak intellectuals who were chagrined at not receiving the positions in their new country to which they believed they were entitled. They contested the seniority rights of their Czech cousins while recognizing the feudal privilege of Hungarian landlords to go about "booting" the Slovak peasants.

The majority of the Slovaks—the Socialists, the Democrats, and even the conservative Agrarians—co-operated fully and loyally with the Prague government. Dr. Milan Hodza, leader of the Agrarians, became Prime Minister in 1935 through the political arrangement whereby Dr. Edward Beneš' election to the Presidency was assured. He resigned with President Beneš after the Munich capitulation, which resulted in the Slovaks realizing their long sought autonomy in the hyphenated country. Final dismemberment of this democracy gave them even more totalitarian autonomy with the "independence" of Slovakia guaranteed by Hitler for twenty-five years. Monsignor Josef Tiso, who succeeded to Father Hlinka's political leadership, was elected President of Slovakia and Tuka became his Prime Minister. Slovakia joined the Axis officially in November 1940, and soon followed her Axis masters into the war, sending four Slovak divisions to the Russian front along with other satellite cannon fodder.

Not even the Slovak autonomists were happy about this war into which they had been sandbagged to fight for their illusory independence. They comforted themselves with the thought that if

Hitler should lose, they might still be saved by the Slovak representatives in the Czechoslovak government in London. For there were still four Slovak ministers seated in Dr. Beneš eleven-man cabinet. His diplomatic representatives to the United States, Colonel Vladimir Hurban, Ambassador to Washington, and Dr. Jan Papanek, chief of the Czechoslovak Information Center in New York, were both Slovaks. While they loyally supported Beneš, two other Slovak leaders abroad, Dr. Milan Hodza, and Dr. Stefan Ossusky, for twenty years Czechoslovakia's Minister to Paris, emerged as leaders of the non-separatist Slovak opposition. Dr. Ossusky published in London a pamphlet severely criticizing the conduct of Czechoslovak affairs since Munich and charging Beneš with running his government in exile along dictatorial lines. Dr. Hodza accused him of insisting on the old centralistic policy and of committing Czechoslovakia's future to the foreign policy of Soviet Russia.

Beneš did not allow himself to be disturbed by these criticisms; he was sure of himself and he felt that he was fighting for the right. His whole life was identified with the democratic government of Czechoslovakia and his biography is practically a history of the Czechoslovak state. He entered political life in 1908 with a graduate dissertation at the University of Dijon on "The Austrian Problem and the Czechoslovak Question." It was his underground work in the First World War that prepared for the creation of Czechoslovakia. He served it as Foreign Minister and later as President until its death, and during his political life realized two remarkable achievements. As the representative of a numerically unimportant party he nevertheless succeeded for twenty years in directing his country's foreign policy. And as representative of a small country, he managed for those twenty years to remain one of the outstanding European leaders at Geneva, where his advice and opinion often determined the decisions of both great and small nations.

As leader of the Little Entente, comprising Czechoslovakia, Rumania, and Yugoslavia, Beneš used all his diplomatic abilities and political shrewdness to organize and maintain strong opposition to the restoration of the Hapsburgs and to the Hungarian revisionist aspirations. For many years he was considered Enemy No. 1 in

Austrian legitimist circles and in the Hungarian capital. He did not have many friends, either, in the Warsaw of Colonel Beck's semi-Fascist "Colonels'" government. And, curiously enough, his allies in Belgrade and Bucharest were not always able to hide their resentment over what they called "Beneš' professorial superiority." Rumania and Yugoslavia both were envious of the diplomatic position he had gained for his country. For to the Western democracies Beneš was, after Masaryk, the great leader of what has been considered the only genuine democracy in Danubian Europe.

It was only natural that his ability and confident authority should breed numerous adversaries at home as well as abroad. His opponents taxed him with having created an ideological front between democratic France and the Soviet Union, with Czechoslovakia as the ideological go-between. He was, indeed, the first statesman to urge the coalition of the Western democracies with Russia as a defense against the Nazi menace, which he at first underestimated in his deep concentration on the two lesser dangers of the Hapsburg restoration and Hungarian revision. He also was the first European leader to voice the foreign policy slogan "fight for democracy," which he offered in opposition to the so-called realistic conceptions of diplomacy.

In his long career, Beneš committed many political and diplomatic errors. He occasionally overestimated his potentialities, though he was not a dreamer. If he became a passionate partisan of an ideological democratic front in foreign relations, it was because he believed so intensely not only in democratic principles but also in the material strength of the democratic powers. The most tragic period of his life came in the months between October 1938 and March 1939. His resignation after Munich from Czechoslovakia's Presidency marked the end of a democratic, independent, and prosperous Czechoslovakia.

He must have lived thereafter through months of terrible doubt, asking himself perhaps whether his rightist opponents among the Czechs had not been correct when they urged a more conciliatory attitude toward the Sudeten Germans, closer co-operation with Colonel Beck's Polish government, and a gradual divorce from ailing France. For it was the decline of France coupled with the weakness of England that bought Hitler's temporary peace at the cost of Czechoslovakia. But after Hitler's entrance into Prague, Beneš knew that whatever or how bad his tactical errors might have been, he had been basically right: no compromise could have saved Czechoslovakia.

This belief must have greatly strengthened his confidence in himself, and when World War II came he resumed the part he had played in the earlier war with an ardor not affected by twenty-five years of political battle. Before the war was a year old, the British government had recognized Dr. Beneš as head of the provisional government of Czechoslovakia and a year later he obtained from Anthony Eden full recognition of his government in exile. That same month the United States, which had never recognized *de jure* any modification of Czechoslovakia's status either at Munich or afterwards, accepted his cabinet as a provisional government. It took him a year more to obtain Washington's complete recognition. In October 1942, on the twenty-fourth anniversary of the Czechoslovak proclamation of independence, President Roosevelt cabled his wishes to "Dr. Eduard Beneš, President of Czechoslovakia." There was no "temporary" in his title nor was there a hyphen in Czechoslovakia.

Beneš presented the British and American acceptances, and recognition of his government by Russia and all the other United Nations, as the answer to his political enemies, especially those among the Slovaks who indicted him with having illegally restored himself as President of the Republic and Commander-in-Chief of the armed forces abroad. He signed an agreement with the Polish Government-in-Exile in November 1940, and a more specific declaration in January 1942 dealing with Polish-Czechoslovak federation in the future. But when Polish-Russian relations began to deteriorate and Russia indicated plainly her dislike of all plans for Eastern European federations, Beneš extricated himself from these commitments on the ground that Poland must first settle all her problems with Russia. Faithful to his long-tried diplomatic technique, he apparently had decided to play once again the part of go-between, convinced that it is the most advantageous role for the leader of a small nation. Only France, his greatest asset in pre-Munich Europe, was now replaced by Russia.

Still faithful to his lifelong political history, he declared that he favored Slovakia's autonomy but refused to commit himself on her postwar status until the end of the war. His Czechoslovakia has been and always will be spelled without the hyphen. To him that punctuation mark will always symbolize the weapon Hitler has used to destroy Czechoslovakia's democracy.

As to his old apprehensions—the restoration of the Hapsburgs and Hungarian revisionism, which had a temporary triumph in this war—he knew that Russia would take care of those problems in postwar Europe. During his visit to the United States in 1943 Beneš remarked that "the Hapsburgs were a problem for Washington and New York, but not for Europe." Also, he did not become alarmed by Slovak propaganda in the United States. He was convinced that in postwar Czechoslovakia, even without the hyphen, the Slovaks of Slovakia would find fair and satisfactory solutions of their legitimate aspirations. And some of the Slovaks, he believed, would then do well to humble themselves to make the Czechs forget and forgive their part in their country's dismemberment and their collaboration with the enemy. He considered the irreconcilable "Slovak League" in the United States, which tried to persuade Washington to recognize Hitler's separate Slovakia, as having excluded its members from Czechoslovak national life and that as American citizens they had no right to determine Czechoslovakia's internal postwar status.

Dr. Beneš was the last of the United Nations representatives to be invited to Washington, and his regime was the last of that coalition's membership—tiny Luxembourg excluded—to have her legations raised to the rank of embassies. His adversaries here did not fail to interpret these delays as a manifestation of Washington's coolness toward the man who was considered in many political circles as the main obstacle to the realization of their postwar plans. Hapsburg and Hungarian propaganda in the United States depicted Beneš as the principal stumbling block to satisfactory solution of Danubian Europe's problems, accusing him of preparing a complete revision of the prewar Little Entente and of taking over representation of the Soviet Union's interests in Central Europe.

The Poles, already unhappy over their troubles with Russia, and, in their worry about the future, more than ever angry with their old adversary, echoed these accusations. They insisted that it was only because of Beneš that they were unable to establish the Polish-Czechoslovak Federation which, they asserted, was earnestly desired by many Czechs and practically all Slovaks. Political leaders of the Catholic Church viewed Beneš with suspicion because of his lifelong activity as a Free Mason, an adversary of the Church's political action, and advocate since 1933 of an alliance with the Soviet Union. They did not consider the presence of Monsignor Jan Shramek, leader of the Czech Catholic Party, as Prime Minister in the Beneš cabinet, a sufficient pledge of his political honor and good intentions.

This veteran of propaganda warfare, who turned the murder of Lidice into one of the greatest propaganda successes of this war, met the concentrated fire of all his adversaries calmly. Beneš reiterated his position against the proposed federation—that as long as Moscow was against it, he did not believe it would serve either Czech or Polish interests—but to prove his good will he agreed to the British suggestion to delay signing the Soviet-Czech treaty until after the Moscow Conference. And he accepted a clause in this treaty providing for the eventual admission of Poland.

In defending his position toward Poland, Beneš was able to point out that while Great Britain and Free France and all the other United Nations had repudiated the Munich settlement and the resultant changes in Czechoslovakia's borders, it had been impossible to obtain similar action from Poland. But the Poles also had a counter-argument. They were obliged to be uncompromising about the former Czech province of Teschen, which they seized in March 1939 during Hitler's partition, so long as they intended to make no compromises about their eastern boundary dispute with Russia. However, the quarrel over Teschen's mixed Czech and Polish population is only a modern expression of ancient Czech-Polish misunderstandings. The province once belonged to the crown of Bohemia. The Poles took it over when the Austro-Hungarian Empire collapsed. The Czechs did not recognize the Polish claim to Teschen, which was allotted to them by the Ambassadors' Conference, and they seized it in 1920 when the Poles were defending Warsaw against Russia. Hitler generously allowed the Poles to take it back because he knew that six months later he would snatch it for himself, together with the greater part of Poland.

On the eve of Munich the Polish government of Colonel Beck ignored Prague's plea for help, in the name of Slavic solidarity, against the common Teutonic aggressor, just as in 1278 the King of Poland ignored the pathetic appeal of Premysl Ottokar II, King of Bohemia, who wrote to his kinsman and neighbor, "If we should be defeated in the present conflict . . . the greed of the Germans . . . would be after your lands, too. We are for you . . . a protective outpost, and if we are unable to hold out, you must face the danger that threatens you, for the Germans' omnivorous greed would not be satisfied with conquering us, but your domains would be subjected to unbearable hardships."

The reading of European history is very disheartening; it shows how little European nations have learned during the last seven centuries. There is hope, however, that after this war both the Czechs and the Poles will understand that their Teutonic neighbor has been their main danger for the past seven hundred years. They may then achieve the collaboration which they could not establish in the period between the two wars. They may even be allowed by Moscow to realize their dream of federation. Then the minor but irritating problem of Teschen, where the Poles claimed a 110,000 minority while Czech statistics recognized only 80,000 Poles, will disappear.

Liberated Czechoslovakia will face other and more important minority problems. There will be the problem of the five hundred thousand Carpatho-Ruthenians. Intellectually, culturally, and economically much weaker than the Czechs and the Slovaks, they have been living in almost medieval conditions. Only ten hours by sleeping car from the twentieth-century Prague station on Woodrow Wilson Place, the poor and illiterate Ruthenian peasants live with agricultural tools and political conceptions that date back to the seventeenth century. Hesitating between the Ukrainian and Russian languages and unable to determine their national individualities, the Carpathian Ruthenians enjoyed an illusory autonomy under Hitler's watchful eye from October 1938 to March 1939, when he gave them to Hungary as advance payment for her cautious participation in his future aggressions.

Russia, busy reconquering the Western Ukraine and western White Russia, did not claim Carpathian Ruthenia, although she was not certain whether the Ruthenians, who had been somewhat dissatisfied in unhyphenated Czechoslovakia, might not be attracted to the victorious Soviet. This might prove true especially if the Soviet Union and Czechoslovakia had a common boundary. In this connection it is interesting to recall that the Soviet-Czechoslovak mutual assistance and postwar pact did not discuss the problem of Czechoslovakia's postwar boundaries but merely guaranteed her territorial integrity. Moscow has indicated that the new frontiers of Czechoslovakia and the Soviet Union will "touch over a considerable length." This would be possible only if Czechoslovakia recovers Carpathian Ruthenia and the Russians retain that section of eastern Poland which they took over in 1939.

Czechoslovakia will also face the problem of the Hungarian minority. Czech figures admit to seven hundred thousand Hungarians; Budapest claims one million since it considers approximately three hundred thousand Magyarized Slovaks as Hungarians. Hungary unquestionably will be required to restore to Czechoslovakia her Slovak territory, but it is not clear how the Hungarian minority problem will be solved nor how good a neighbor relationship can be established between these two nations so long as Hungary retains her feudal system. This alone made her a socially foreign body in the heart of prewar Danubian Europe.

But the most difficult of the minority problems here is the one which was used by Hitler to destroy Czechoslovakia: the 3,230,000 Germans who lived in the Sudeten area before Munich. The long struggle between Czech and German elements in Bohemia led the Germans to congregate pretty much along her western border although many also scattered to the north and south. Very few districts could boast of a completely homogeneous population. Although the Germans were the majority in the Sudetenland, only 122 out of 227 districts had an absolute German majority. Any kind of autonomous arrangement approved by Prague for this section would immediately create hundreds of Czech Ulsters.

Thus the government of a restored Czechoslovakia will have to meet the same difficulties that it tried so desperately and unsuccessfully to solve on the eve of Munich. Bohemia is historically, geographically, and economically an entity; it can scarcely be divided and live. Moreover, the strategic importance of this little country has once more been established in this war, although it was Bismarck who first affirmed that "He who is master of Bohemia is master of Europe."

Many planners of postwar Europe advocate a complete exchange of population as a radical solution for these minority problems. This may, perhaps, be the best answer to the Hungarian minority question. It may also solve the Sudeten German problem although it will be much harder to realize. There is, of course, the theoretical solution of the Swiss Federation applied to the minorities. But that federation was realized long before the crystallization of modern European nationalism. There is, finally, the hope that after their experience under the Nazi heel, the Sudeten Germans may be glad to return to democratic Czechoslovakia. It appears, however, that the Sudeten German problem, and probably most of the other minority problems in that part of Europe, can hardly be solved without the solution first of a much more difficult problem—that of the Germans in Europe.

VIII: Prelude to Postwar Chaos

Yugoslavia

YUGOSLAVIA can claim the sad privilege of having served as the testing ground for the many racial, political, and social conflicts which may ravage postwar Europe. The chaotic situation in this literally war-torn country may indeed be the prelude to postwar chaos, and it is all the more tragic because of the enormous debt of gratitude the United Nations owe her. For it was Yugoslavia that stirred the hearts of all free and freedom-loving men when in April 1941 a group of patriotic Belgrade officers led their people in a revolt against the signing of a pact with the Axis.

Yugoslavia again stirred the world's imagination a few months later when her defeated but unconquered patriots, headed by a Serbian colonel, Draja Mikhailovich, chose to die on their feet rather than live on their knees. The United Nations' applause soon turned to consternation at the sight of Yugoslavia's patriots split by national and social issues and fighting each other with all the hatred and fury that should have been concentrated on their enemy.

The Chetniks, Serbian guerrillas led by Mikhailovich, were first on the scene and to them went practically all the honor and glory of standing up against the Axis forces. Then the mysterious Croatian Communist Josip "Tito" Broz appeared suddenly as the leader of the left-wing Yugoslav Partisans—patriots and guerrillas even as the Chetniks, but supported by Moscow and called Partisans after the Russian guerrillas. The tragic conflict between the Partisans and Mikhailovich's Serbian Chetniks, developed during 1942 and 1943 into the proportions of a full-scale civil war. Their conflict became the more alarming because behind the fighting silhouettes of the Chetniks and Partisans rose the impressive shadows of Britain and Russia, both traditionally interested in the Balkans.

The two patriot armies became divided originally because of differences in their ethnographical composition, their conflicting ideologies, and their diametrically opposed conceptions of the proper strategy for their type of warfare. This domestic disagreement became even more confusing as the result of the barrages of propaganda laid down by both sides, and elaborated by their foreign sympathizers with what appeared to be slight regard for the facts.

In the Balkans, more than in any other region of the world, history is part of the living present. It is impossible, therefore, to understand Yugoslavia's tragedy without a knowledge of the turbulent background of those unfortunate southern Slavs who attempted after the last war to amalgamate into a single nation peoples who had been divided for generations.

The kingdom of the Serbs, the Croats, and the Slovenes arose out of the First World War through the Wilsonian principles of self-determination. It translated into the truth of reality the old, old dream of the southern Slavs, but it failed to dispel the historic sources of the nightmares which tortured Yugoslavia throughout the Second World War.

Separated for centuries by Turkish and Austro-Hungarian rulers, the Serbs, Croats, and Slovenes were disunited, not only by religion (the Serbs followed the Greek Orthodox Church while the Croats and Slovenes became Roman Catholic) but also by two entirely different civilizations. Although the Croats and the Serbs are of the same race and speak the same language, in exactly the same way that the United States and Great Britain both speak English, they have developed different ways of life. Slovenes, whose language differs slightly from the Serbo-Croat, have shared the way of life of their Croat neighbors.

The Serbs evolved as a nation under the influence of Orthodox Byzantium and under the Turkish yoke, from which they freed themselves only after an arduous struggle. Their past made them tough, rough, freedom-loving, and willing to fight. The Croats, however, lived under the influence of Catholic Rome and the Hapsburgs. They tried, though unsuccessfully, to establish their independence by compromises and conspiracies. Their past, replete with deceptions and disillusionments, rendered them suspicious and embittered. Although both were essentially peasant peoples, their élite groups differed greatly. The Serbian élite consisted of soldiers and lyric poets, brought up in the spirit of the French Revolution. The Croatian leadership was composed of bourgeois and artists, educated in the principles of Central Europe and looking at France through spectacles made in Vienna or Munich. And each group considered itself superior to the other.

However, at the dawn of the nineteenth century these peoples began to be aware of their racial community and their common national aims, which finally overshadowed their cultural differences. Again it was Napoleon, who had aroused so many of Europe's national aspirations, who laid the cornerstone of Yugoslavia. In 1809 he brought together the Slovenians and the Dalmatians in the ephemerous "Illryian Provinces." At the same time Napoleon manifested a sympathetic interest in Karageorge (Black George), the ruthless leader of the Serbian peasants who revolted against their Turkish masters. Consequently, the nineteenth century did for the southern Slavs what the seventeenth century did for the French and the eighteenth century for the Germans. It made them aware of their national unity. Unfortunately, this awareness was achieved so late, after many centuries spent under completely different social, moral, and political regimes, that to this delay can be attributed most, if not all, of Yugoslavia's present fratricidal struggles.

The Serbs led in the fight for emancipation of the southern Slavs, fighting with their rifles, their knives, and their hands. They fought in the mountains and in the forests and they won their freedom and independence. It was a piecemeal victory, but by the end of the nineteenth century they could boast of a free and independent Serbia that was to champion the liberation of all the southern Slavs in the first decade of this century.

Inspired by the Serbian success, the Croats fought—but they fought in the municipal councils and in the lobbies of the Austro-Hungarian Parliament—for their political and linguistic rights. So also did the million and a half Slovenes who, because they were not numerically important enough to represent a threat against

Austria-Hungary's Empire, were accorded more privileges than the Croats, the Czechs, or the Poles.

The Croatian and Slovenian struggles were for the most part political, but from time to time groups of nationalistic-minded youths broke out into action. Occasionally their local demonstrations threatened to develop into local revolts, but they were quickly quenched by firing squads composed of Austrian or Hungarian gendarmes who executed their leaders.

The older Croats, especially among the bourgeoisie, also wanted autonomy, but they found consolation in the fact that they had access to Hungary's and Austria's ruling classes. Without abandoning their claims of better treatment for their people, the Croat nobility and bourgeoisie tried to make the best of their regime. Not so the intellectuals and the peasants, who furnished the bulk of the malcontents. The latter groups felt that the Croats were entitled to at least the same degree of independence as that won by the less civilized Serbs. And they believed that the best way to achieve their objective was to join forces with the Serbs and thus gain the support that remote but powerful Russia was giving her Slavic kin in the Balkans.

While the Croatian intellectuals did not include as large a percentage of pro-Russians and "Slavophiles" as did the Slovenians, nevertheless two outstanding Croats of the nineteenth century—Bishop Strossmayer and the great poet Ivo Masuranich—were not only ardent supporters of the "Yugoslav" idea but also definitely pro-Russian. It is most significant that Bishop Strossmayer, the Croats' great Catholic leader, did not consider their differences as to creeds a serious handicap to the union of southern Slavs.

Croatian sympathy for the Serbs reached climactic proportions with the latter's success in the two Balkan wars which were the preludes to the First World War. It was a young Serbian patriot, Gavrilo Princip, a subject of the Hapsburg Empire, who formally opened that war in 1914 by assassinating Austria-Hungary's Crown Prince in Sarajevo. The Serbs, who had been living under the Hapsburg rule in Bosnia, Herzegovina, and Banat, hurried to join their free brothers in independent Serbia.

After evacuating their country under pressure of the enemy's overwhelming forces, the Serbs with the aid of the Allies established themselves on the Salonika front, where they were joined by many Croat and Slovene volunteers. Among the Croats were such men as Monsignor Stepinatz, the present Bishop of Zagreb, and Ivo Shubashich, the present *Ban* or Viceroy of Croatia, who went into exile after Yugoslavia's collapse and maintained the Yugoslav line. They were all fighting for the realization of the agreement on union which the greatly respected Dalmatian-Croat patriot, Dr. Ante Trumbich, had signed in 1917 with Nikola Pashich, Serbia's grand old man.

The National Assembly of Croat Representatives meeting in Zagreb approved this agreement in December 1918 and enthusiastically voted for the union of the Croats and Serbs under the dynasty of Karageorge. The Slovenes gave their equally enthusiastic approval a few days later. All signs pointed to a lasting and happy union. Within a few years, however, the partners came to realize that none of them was really contented.

Self-determination was a constructive force among Europe's nations of the last century. It helped achieve those national unities which in previous centuries were imposed by fire and sword. But in the first decade of this century, this same principle became a disruptive force. Peoples who had lived their separate lives for centuries became suddenly aware of their specific individualities as peoples and felt constrained to burst to confining ties of their new nationalities in order to give fuller expression to their own characteristics.

Louis XIV and Richelieu imposed unity upon the Alsatians, the Burgundians, and the southern Frenchmen by force. Wilhelm I and Bismarck, by means of the Prussian saber, unified the German-speaking people, a unification Hitler tried to achieve in his own brutal way. But when peoples are united by voluntary acceptance of the idea of union, as the Serbs, Croats, and Slovenes were, the spirit of compromise, not force, is essential. The basic difficulty in this instance was that the two principal partners were not psychologically prepared to compromise.

The Serbs, as men of action and iron will, despise those who compromise. They believe that when a man is in an advantageous position, he must—if he is not a fool—take all possible advantage of his position. They considered themselves to be in a very advantageous position in 1918 and they would have hated themselves if they had not exploited it to the fullest. They believed, moreover, that they were morally entitled to the advantage of their position. Had they not paid the heaviest toll in blood, sweat, and tears? Had they not lost in casualties almost one-third of their population?

The Croats, while not minimizing the Serbs' casualties, had such an exalted idea of their own intellectual superiority that they expected the Serbs to be highly appreciative of the precious gift of union which the Croats had so generously offered them. And they were surprised and deeply chagrined to discover that their intellectual superiority was merely a source of growing irritation to the Serbs. The Croats, in turn, were irritated by the Serbs—by their superiority as soldiers and men of action, by the conflict of their completely different ways of life. Friction was unavoidable and politicians on both sides did all they could to intensify the ill-feeling.

The situation was sharply aggravated by the fact that the war had robbed Serbia of the intellectual manhood she had just begun to build up at the end of the nineteenth century. The Serbs had no trained administrative personnel and they had to send to Croatia their sergeants and gendarmes who behaved there as though they were in a conquered country. The Croats were deeply disillusioned and hurt. French psychoanalysts use the term *Bovarisme* from Gustave Flaubert's famous novel *Madame Bovary*, to describe the state of mind of a woman who, married to her intellectual inferior, suffers from a frustration that gradually develops into a persecution mania. The Croats suffered from *Bovarisme* on a national scale. They were sentimentally disappointed in their romantic dreams and the recriminations started at a similarly romantic level.

They accused the Serbs of not giving them their proper proportion of commanding officers and diplomatic positions. The Serbs tartly replied that those Croats whose backgrounds justified such high positions had served in the army or diplomatic service of Austria-Hungary and therefore could not be trusted to serve Yugoslavia. Displeased by the ever-increasing taxes, the Croats charged the Serbs with robbing them to glorify Belgrade and to enrich Serbian politicians. There was some basis for this charge. The corruption had been incidental to the Austrian administration, under which the Croats lived. This was, however, an inheritance from the Turkish regime, and continued in Belgrade's routine. Bribery was accepted as a quasi-legal means of speeding government action. However, it is only fair to note that after Belgrade's palatial ministries were built and the no less palatial private homes of Serbian ministers completed, the bulk of the remaining Croatian funds and taxes was expended in the national interests. But the Croats objected to the Europeanization of southern Serbia at the expense of the Croatian provinces which, being the richest areas of the country, furnished the greater share of the taxes.

On the other hand, the Croats refused to admit that their industry had greatly benefited by the union, which gave Croatian products all of Yugoslavia as a protected market ringed by high tariff walls. Nor were they ready to understand that World War I had left all European states with most difficult economic and financial problems, and inherited by the newly born nations. The Croats regretted the good old days, economically speaking, of the Austrian regime and they refused to be satisfied with what Yugoslavia was able to achieve in cultural and economic fields.

But with whom could the Croats live? From whom could they expect help? The answer was clear to Ante Pavelich, future Quisling of "independent Croatia," and his Ustashi, a gang of rebellious peasants originally stemming from the romantic but poverty-stricken province of Lika. They went into exile and sold their hatred of the Serbs to the foreign powers who used it for their own interests. They obtained in Italy and Hungary the guns which made King Alexander the first casualty of World War II.

For Stefan Radich, leader of the Croat Peasant Party, which represented about 80 per cent of the Croat peasantry, the problem was more complicated. The Serbian politicians were too shrewd for him, outwitting him whenever he attempted to make a deal with them, and the King was even shrewder than his ministers, whom he used as pawns. But Radich was too patriotic and too Slav-minded to do business with the enemies of the Slavs. So he went to Moscow to see what kind of arrangements he might make with Russia. He could not find at that unsettled period of history a common social language between his Croat peasant group and the Soviet statesmen. Belgrade had steadfastly refused to recognize the Soviet government, influenced as it was by White Russian refugees and inspired by gratitude to Czar Nicholas II who had brought Russia into the First World War to defend Serbia. Radich had no alternative but to persist in his opposition to the centralist tendencies of the Belgrade government, which he did for four years with all the bitterness of a frustrated politician conscious of his own weakness.

The weaker Radich felt, the stronger and more passionate became his oral attacks on the government. Passions flared higher and higher, and in June 1928 a Serbian fanatic who believed, along with many others, that Radich was a traitor to the cause of the southern Slavs had recourse to the supreme remedy in the explosive tradition of the Balkans. Radich, his nephew, and another Croat deputy were shot in the Parliament at Belgrade. This tragedy rocked Croatia with indignation and horror and for several months it appeared as though the smoldering revolt would break out and sweep through the kingdom. King Alexander saved the situation by destroying his kingdom with his own pen. By royal decree on January 6, 1929, he abolished the Kingdom of the Serbs, the Croats, and the Slovenes, disbanded its turbulent parliament, and created in its place the Kingdom of Yugoslavia with Alexander as "trustee dictator."

Alexander was undoubtedly an intelligent man who believed that history had assigned to him the mission of unifying the southern Slavs. Unfortunately, his faith in this mission was stronger than his critical judgment. Although he was a very shrewd statesman and a keen analyst of men and events, he made two fatal miscalculations. He split with the Serbian Radical Party, which had traditionally supported the nationalist policy of the Karageorge dynasty, and he entertained the belief that it would be possible to abolish merely by royal decree the ethnographic boundaries within his heterogeneous state, substituting for them the *banovinas* (governments) as administrative units.

Bereft of trustworthy advisers by his own doing, Alexander surrounded himself with obedient soldiers and politicians who had

no real support among the people. While their king was working
passionately to establish his idea of what Yugoslavia could and
should become, the Serbian gendarmerie and functionaries in
Croatia and Slovenia strove as diligently to tear it down. Alexander
never failed to have several Croat ministers at hand to fill out his
many cabinets, but they were either opportunists who would have
served any regime, or men convinced that no sacrifice was too
high for the preservation of the unity and prosperity of their country. In both cases, they were seldom representative of any forces
or opinions other than their own. This was not true, for example,
of the vigorous leaders of that time, like Dr. Vlatko Matchek, an
honest but stubborn politician who succeeded Radich and inherited his following. Because of an interview too frankly given to a
foreign correspondent, Matchek came under police surveillance,
but his political power continued unchecked.

King Alexander was assassinated in October 1934 at Marseille.
Prince Paul, his cousin, who succeeded him as regent, did not have
the military background of Alexander who had fought in the
Balkan wars and in the First World War. Paul's frail health did
not permit him to follow the military traditions of Karageorge. He
preferred ancient paintings to modern war maps and the French
Impressionists were more familiar to him than the instructors of
France's St. Cyr Military Academy, where his uncle Peter I, his
father, and the cousin he succeeded were trained. Prince Paul
was an honest man but a weakling who was strongly and regret-
tably influenced by two women, his wife and his mother-in-law.

His wife, Princess Olga of Greece, was extremely unpopular
among the Serbs who accused her of inspiring her husband to
dangerous ambitions. His mother-in-law, the Grand Duchess
Helena of Russia, maintained friendly relations with Marshal
Hermann Goering and she endeavored for years to convince
Prince Paul that Hitler was the only man who could save Europe
from Communism.

He sometimes responded to these appeals even though he was
by background perhaps the most pro-British of all Europe's rulers.
He had been brought up at Oxford and was the brother-in-law of
the late Duke of Kent and a friend of King George VI, but he in-

terpreted British and French policy toward Hitler as an expression of the irremediable weakness of the Western democracies.

One of his first political acts was to bring into power Dr. Milan Stoyadinovich, Belgrade banker and economist. The two men played the policy of balance between the Axis and the democracies in the naïve belief that they could save their country by being more of an appeaser than the appeasers in Paris and London.

Stoyadinovich was the best poker player in Belgrade and he thought he could transfer this ability to international politics and bluff both Hitler and Mussolini by pitting one against the other. He also believed himself able to bluff Matchek and the Croats by persuading them to sign an agreement which would strengthen his government both abroad and at home without compromising the position of the Serbs in Yugoslavia. But Stoyadinovich discovered that he could not bluff either Hitler or Matchek. The Nazi Fuehrer used Stoyadinovich to destroy the Little Entente. Matchek preferred a coalition with the United Serbian Opposition to an agreement with Stoyadinovich.

Prince Paul finally realized the double failure of his Prime Minister and dismissed him in February 1939. The war brought Stoyadinovich, exiled in Greece by Prince Paul, to the island of Mauritius as "His Majesty's guest"—the British honorary title for political prisoner. The same war sent Prince Paul as "His Majesty's guest" to the British colony of Tanganyika.

When the Serbs and the Croats began to quarrel, the Slovenes found themselves in an excellent position. They were needed desperately by the Serbs who wanted to prove that while they could not come to terms with the Croats, they could co-operate with the Slovenes. The latter's political strength at this time was about equally divided between two parties—the National Radicals, whose supporters lived in the cities, and the Catholic or Clerical Party, whose followers ruled the countryside. In no other country of Europe was the Catholic Party so well organized as here. It controlled the press, education, the co-operative societies, and the banks. The peasant who wanted to obtain a mortgage had to be on good terms with the parish priest. The party's leader was Father Anton Korochets, a veteran fighter for Slovene rights in the Austrian Parliament, who became under Prince Paul the power behind the throne.

Father Korochets, an anti-Semite and hater of the Free Masons, French, and Czechs, tried to convince Prince Paul, who considered Franco to be "Europe's greatest statesman," that a Yugoslavia friendly to the Vatican could become one of the main pillars of the new moral order along with Spain. He systematically placed obstacles in the path of the realization of the Serb-Croat agreement, without realizing that he was playing into the hands of Yugoslavia's enemies. He died a few months before his country was invaded and was spared the knowledge of the catastrophe his policy helped to bring upon Yugoslavia, a catastrophe in which the hardest blows of all fell upon the Slovenes.

On August 27, 1939, when Hitler's guns and Stukas were already poised to release their fury upon Europe, Matchek tricked his allies of the United Serbian Opposition by reversing his earlier position and signing a pact with Cvetkovich's Belgrade government, of which Father Korochets was the real head. Matchek justified his reversal with the argument that if his allies had had the same opportunity, they would not have hesitated to betray him in the same manner. Moreover, he had a legitimate patriotic reason for his political double cross: the approaching war.

In May and again in July of that fateful summer, Mussolini's emissaries had asked Matchek not to conclude any agreement with the Serbs, but to wait rather for the coming war between Germany and the Anglo-French-Polish bloc. This war, they told him, would enable him to obtain better conditions from the Serbs or to come to terms with Italy which was prepared to guarantee Croatia her historic frontiers. Matchek stood firm against the Italians and joined forces instead with Cvetkovich's regime in order to prove to the world the solidarity of the Yugoslavs in the face of the forthcoming world war. He was convinced that Prince Paul's policy would spare Yugoslavia from war and preserve her independence, and for almost two years his hopes appeared to be borne out until, in February 1941, Hitler forced a crisis on Yugoslavia by pressure on her to sign the Tripartite Pact concluded by Germany, Italy, and Japan.

Hitler wanted Yugoslavia first to enter his diplomatic axis; his next step would have been to force her into his camp of military satellites where the Fuehrer had already installed Hungary, Rumania, and Bulgaria. The Nazi pressure was too much for Prince Paul and he sent his Prime Minister and his Foreign Minister to Vienna where, on March 25, 1941, they signed away their country's independence and became members of the Axis. But not for long. Two days later a group of Serbian officers and writers seized Belgrade in a *coup d'état*. They dismissed Prince Paul, arrested his ministers, and acclaimed as King the Regent's eighteen-year-old nephew, Peter, who under normal circumstances would have ascended to his father's throne the following September. They remained true to the tradition of Czar Lazar, who on the eve of the Battle of Kossovo in which he was crushed by the Turks in 1389, told those who advised a policy of appeasement instead of battle that he chose to lose his "kingdom on the earth" in order to save his "kingdom in the sky."

In this crisis the Serbs were guided by their national instinct to sacrifice the present for the future. The Croats also hated totalitarian governments; they too were courageous, but for nine centuries they had not fought under their own flag. For centuries all their energies had been concentrated exclusively on the problem of obtaining home rule. They had gained not autonomy but a series of delusions and deceptions in Yugoslavia. Should they now lift their eyes from the domestic scene and rise up, like the Serbs, to fight as one man for this Yugoslavia? What could they expect in the future from the Serbs who had overthrown Prince Paul to whom the Croats were indebted for the agreement recognizing their right to a large advance toward autonomy?

As a Croat, Matchek was cognizant of the confused state of mind of his countrymen, although as a convinced democrat, he unquestionably hated the thought of his country joining the Axis, even on paper. And later, those of his followers who went into exile insisted that even though Matchek had preferred life in the occupied country to exile, he did not approve of the Tripartite Pact. At that time, however, he knew the Croats hated the idea of a war in which their plains would become the chief battlefield. Matchek, therefore, was fortunate in having the opportunity to take refuge in the authority of the Serbian Minister of War and the Chief of the General Staff who, together with the Foreign Minister—all Serbs—insisted on signing the Axis agreement because of their unpreparedness. Even more important evidence to support Matchek's position was his belief that the Regent had assurances through Lord Halifax, with whom he was in correspondence, that the British would "understand Prince Paul's difficult and delicate position."

Nevertheless, the Serbs reproached Matchek because he did not resign from the Cvetkovich government when it signed the Tripartite Pact, and he made General Simovich's government lose eight precious days in negotiations with the new Belgrade cabinet over its attitude toward the Serb-Croat agreement of August 1939. Thus he contributed, argued the Serbs, to the failure of Yugoslavia's mobilization, and helped to speed her collapse after five days of desperate fighting against overwhelming odds.

Then came the division of the spoils between the Axis and its greedy satellites. Italy obtained Dalmatia and shared Slovenia with Germany. Hungary received the Serbian province of Banat while the Bulgars took Macedonia and part of eastern Serbia. In Croatia the Italians produced in true Viennese comic style a puppet kingdom with an Italian prince who never dared take possession of his throne. The invaders entrusted the role of Croatian Quisling to Ante Pavelich, who was responsible for the assassination of King Alexander.

The peasant leader Matchek refused to co-operate with Pavelich, but he did not want to let the Croat Quisling take all the credit for the establishment of an independent Croatia. He went to Zagreb in order to maintain his contacts and to preserve the prestige of the Croat Peasant Party, meanwhile delegating Dr. Jurai Krnievich as his representative in General Simovich's government in exile. Matchek believed his prestige with the peasantry was so great that neither the Axis nor Pavelich could safely prosecute him. While he did not have the Serbian fighting temperament, he was disposed to risk resistance in Gandhi's passive style.

When King Peter and General Simovich's cabinet fled into exile, the General originally had planned to reorganize his government on a strictly military basis. He was a patriotic officer without much political experience; in his *coup d'état* he had been the focus rather than the inspiration of the Serbs' righteous indignation. General Simovich and practically all the other officers had little sympathy for the Croats, and continued to blame them for the delayed mobilization and the subsequent military disaster. However, as a high general staff officer, Simovich could not ignore the fact that others shared the responsibility. He knew from his own military experience that the Stoyadinovich-Korochets appeasement policy and Belgrade's corruption had left the army unprepared for Hitler's military machine, so unprepared as to be unable to make the best use of Yugoslavia's mountainous terrain and the excellent defensive possibilities of its rugged hills. So he permitted the Croats to fight with their Serbian colleagues because this domestic quarreling helped justify the necessity for a military government from which all politicians could be excluded. And he probably would have been able to carry out his plans if news of the Ustashi atrocities had not reached London.

They occurred in Bosnia where, with Serbs and Croats living side by side, national passions were bound to clash. It is certain now that the Axis deliberately provoked the Croats to slaughter the Serbs in order to make union between these two people impossible. The full extent of the atrocities is a matter of sharp controversy. The Serbs asserted that between 250,000 and 600,000 men, women, and children were tortured and killed by the Ustashi. The Croats at home and abroad insisted as firmly that the number barely reached 25,000, although some later admitted much higher totals.

Reports of these mass murders created a revolution in Yugoslav political quarters in London. The Croats were confused; the Serbs were indignant. Serbian politicians who had learned of Simovich's plans to eliminate them from the government capitalized on the massacres to eliminate Simovich himself. If they could have had their way, they would have turned out with him all the Croats whom they considered at best as half-repentant or potential collaborationists. But this they could not achieve because of Washington and London. To maintain a certain Yugoslav face even in exile, they kept the Croats in the government, ousting only Simovich. They reserved the Premiership for Slobodan Jovanovich, the Serbian writer commonly known as "Serbia's conscience," and gave the War Ministry in absentia to Draja Mikhailovich, the Chetnik commander who had emerged as "Serbia's soul" and her greatest propaganda asset in the first large-scale revolt against Nazi tyranny.

Fighting in the wildernesses of Yugoslavia's mountains, Mikhailovich had become one of the epic figures of the war. This forty-seven-year-old general staff officer was born in the heart of old Serbia, the son of a colonel in the Serbian Army. Hitler's invasion found him in Herzegovina serving as assistant chief of the general staff in the coastal area. He withdrew his detachments through Pech and Novi Pazar to the wooded mountains of Sanjak. Many other soldiers found refuge in these mountains where Serb peasants had fought for generations for their freedom.

The Serbs were punished severely for daring to oppose Hitler's plans and so upset his timetable. Fury burned high in the men hidden in the mountains when they heard of the suffering of their families in the Nazi-occupied villages and cities. They determined to fight their conquerors with guerrilla warfare just as their fathers had fought the Turks, the Bulgars, and the Austrians. But with this distinction: whereas their fathers were led by small shopkeepers, village teachers, and country priests, they were led by an experienced, trained, wily general staff officer.

The free world admired their courage and hailed Mikhailovich as a patriot, a democrat, a great hero. By the fall of 1942 he had become a legend, "democracy's superman," the personification of heroic resistance everywhere to the Nazi invaders. And only a month later he was being as vehemently described as a reactionary whose primary, if not sole, aim was the restoration of a nationalist, Serbia-dominated Yugoslavia in which Serbia's ruling classes would have special privileges. His courage was questioned, his inaction criticized. He was charged with co-operating secretly with General Milan Nedich, the Serbian Quisling in Belgrade, and of having secret contacts with the Axis occupants.

These accusations came from the other group of fighting Yugoslav patriots, the Partisans, whose propaganda was given voice by a secret radio station, "Free Yugoslavia," located on Russian soil. "Free Yugoslavia's" communiqués were published by Soviet newspapers and in Communist papers abroad, and as the Partisans' military successes continued, they appeared as well in the British and American press. A fierce propaganda fight soon developed abroad between supporters of these two groups.

The Yugoslav government in London, which, in order to boost its own prestige, gave to Mikhailovich the portfolio of Minister of War, was obligated to defend him, which it did vigorously. Its officials accused the Partisans of being led by Communists more anxious to establish a Soviet regime in Yugoslavia than to defend their country's national interests. The Partisans argued back that they were the only genuine democrats in Yugoslavia and that they offered the only hope of uniting the conflicting elements to assure them a new and better world after the war. This propaganda quarrel would not have been of primary importance if it had not reflected the physical battles waged in Yugoslavia between the Chetniks and Partisans.

It is always difficult to establish liaison between fighting units in a guerrilla war. It proved even more difficult to establish such liaison in this country divided on fundamental issues long before the war began, especially since their prewar disunity was aggravated by the variation in treatment accorded the Croats and the Serbs by the occupying forces. Croatia, having been granted the dubious privilege of an independent puppet state, was able to have war prisoners released immediately. Her Quisling government declared war upon the United Nations and contributed four divisions to the Axis armies. Serbia was reduced to the more honorable but infinitely more uncomfortable status of an occupied country. True, the Germans did succeed in finding a group of Serbs who betrayed the traditions of their people by accepting the despicable role of Quislings. But this did not change dismembered Serbia's position. And finally, the Ustashi massacres in Bosnia and Herzegovina incensed rather than allayed the natural Serbo-Croat antagonism, although the Croatian people could not be held responsible for the crimes of a minority of no more than 15 per cent of its population.

Mikhailovich's forces consisted principally of disbanded soldiers until their ranks were increased by peasants climbing to

the hills from neighboring villages, and later by Serbian intellectuals who fled the enemy-controlled cities.

In Croatia and Slovenia the bourgeoisie and the intellectuals together opposed the enemy by passive resistance, with the exception of the collaborationist minority. The most aggressive elements
here were the Communists who were more numerous in these
semi-industrialized provinces than in agricultural Serbia. To their
ranks came large groups who were happy to join any organization
fighting the hated invaders.

The Serbian Communists, who naturally participated in this
struggle from the beginning, were exalted by the idea that by
attacking Russia, Hitler had given them a new and powerful
ally. Peasants carried pictures of Joseph Stalin beside that of their
young king and they were convinced that their "little Peter" would
marry Stalin's daughter Svetlana and that President Roosevelt
would be one of the wedding guests.

In the dark winter of 1942 relations between the Chetniks
and the Partisans first began to be seriously strained. The Chetniks,
as well as the other guerrilla groups, had benefited by the confusion resulting from the blitz conquest of Yugoslavia. The Nazis
pushed on headlong across Yugoslavia into Greece, their minds
already preoccupied with the forthcoming campaign against Russia. They had no time to rid the sparsely populated mountain
regions of the patriotic bands. Instead, they were compelled to
limit themselves to controlling the populous centers and main
railway lines and junctions.

As a trained military man, Mikhailovich soon became aware
of his limited possibilities and decided to withdraw to mountain
hideouts inaccessible to punishing expeditions. From there he
planned to continue to sabotage the Nazis whenever possible,
meanwhile expanding his organization to a potential army of two
hundred thousand or three hundred thousand fighting men, ready
to strike the enemy's rear flank when Allied forces landed in
Yugoslavia. He revealed his strategy to Josip "Tito" Broz, the
Partisan commander, explaining that he insisted on reserving his
men as a nucleus for the future liberation army, and to that end
would avoid all engagements which could achieve only temporary

success, and for which he felt the civilian population had to pay too high a price.

Tito categorically rejected any such proposal. This fifty-five-year-old Croat railway worker and Communist Party member received political and military training in the Soviet Union. On the basis of the revolutionary tactics he had thus learned and practiced, he favored immediate, direct action regardless of the cost in lives or other strategic considerations. Tito maintained that the Nazi murders of innocent hostages would only incense the population against the occupying troops and would result in a revolt which, even if crushed, would embarrass the Germans who lacked sufficient policing troops in the Balkans. It was only natural that Moscow give her moral, if not material, support to the Partisans regardless of any ideological affinities. For Partisan military action, sporadic as it was, served the Soviet Union's interests; it obliged the Nazis to reinforce their Yugoslav garrisons and thus reduced the number of troops available for use on the Russian front. Consequently, the conflict between the Chetniks and the Partisans became the original second front issue translated realistically into Yugoslav terms. The Partisans practically created the Balkan sector of the second front in Yugoslavia.

Certain Serbian peasants who sympathized with Mikhailovich and who were terrorized by Nazi punitive expeditions and also by some private plunderings, for which the Partisan leadership undoubtedly was not responsible, revolted finally against Tito's followers. This group began to kill the Partisans, in the misguided belief that they had to commit these murders to save their own lives. The Partisans immediately accused Mikhailovich of sinister designs, of secretly working with the collaborationists and with the Axis leaders. This charge was based on the fact that some of the Chetnik groups had bartered Italian prisoners for Italian gasoline and munitions. They defended their actions by explaining that in guerrilla warfare it is impossible to keep prisoners. Moreover, they were receiving from London considerable amounts of Italian currency enabling them to buy from demoralized Italians their munitions and supplies.

At this critical point the Yugoslav government in London made a fateful diplomatic error by following unwise British advice. While on his way to Washington in May 1942, Molotov was disposed to sign an alliance with the Yugoslav regime in exile. The British government, which had just signed a twenty-year pact with the Soviet Union, viewed its alliance as the nucleus of a general postwar agreement and was not anxious for minor members of the United Nations to have separate agreements with the Soviet Union. The Yugoslav cabinet accepted the British view. By the time Molotov returned to Moscow the exiled Yugoslavs had changed their minds, but it was too late—Moscow had cooled to the idea of an alliance. This step naturally led to increased attacks by the Communist press against Mikhailovich. Soviet-Yugoslav relations deteriorated further and a few months later Moscow formally voiced its displeasure over the Chetnik-Partisan clashes. Since then the Yugoslav Cabinet was moved to Cairo and reshuffled several times. Diplomatic relations with Moscow were maintained. But the rift between Mikhailovich and Tito continued to widen.

There were practically no Croats among the warriors of Mikhailovich, although his propaganda claimed that several young intellectuals from prominent Croat and Slovene families were with him. Many of the fighters in his forces were Serbs from Bosnia and Herzegovina whose families were massacred by the Ustashi. Although the Partisans operated mostly in Croatia and Slovenia, they claimed to have numerous Serbs in their ranks, insisting in their propaganda that the Serbs constituted 58 per cent of their total number. It was not clear, however, whether those Serbs were in overwhelming majority from the Croatian provinces (Bosnia, Lika, etc.) or whether they came from old Serbia. At any rate, the Partisan statement revealed that many Serbs from Bosnia had apparently overcome their feelings of "revenge" and had united with the Croats for the sake of their country's liberation.

The question of the ideological adherence of the Croats and Slovenes fighting in Tito's "People's Liberation Army" became of considerable importance. Supporters of the Partisans, especially those abroad, protested vehemently against labeling all the Partisans as Communists. The rank and file membership certainly was not all Communist, but many leaders, despite widespread insistence to the contrary, appeared to belong to the Communist Party. Serbian nationalists and Slovene clericals in exile grew concerned about the moral support and publicity given by the Soviet press and radio to the Partisans.

Although many Serbs are traditionally friendly toward Russia, their nationalist group—and Mikhailovich undoubtedly must be numbered among this faction—is afraid of, and sternly opposed to, a Soviet or even a Soviet-inspired type of government. The Croat nationalists of Dr. Matchek are perhaps even more fearful of such an eventuality since they are more prosperous than the Serbs and therefore more anxious to maintain their way of life. However, many Croat nationalists in exile took a much more sympathetic— and later even an enthusiastic—attitude toward the Partisans than did the Serbian nationalists. The reasons for their attitude were both political and psychological.

The Serbs had a choice between the Partisans and the Chetniks, but the Croats knew that the fighting elements of their own resistance were practically all in the Partisan ranks and that Mikhailovich's Serbs had little if any use for them. While the Croat Peasant Party did not favor a Soviet regime in Yugoslavia, they might well have preferred it to a Serbian-dominated Yugoslavia in which, they feared, one of the first Serbian actions would be a Croatian blood bath to revenge the Ustashi massacres. Furthermore, the Croats in exile were unhappy over the fact that both the patriotic uprising in Belgrade of March 1941 and Mikhailovich's early guerrilla fighting were Serbian activities. They tried to explain their hesitancy and confusion at the outbreak of war by the lack of a basic Serbo-Croat understanding on constitutional problems. The Partisan movement, therefore, offered them an opportunity to contest the Serbs' apparent monopoly of patriotism. In so doing, those Croats who opposed Communism took great pains to point out that there was no communistic danger in the Partisan movement but that it was, rather, a genuinely democratic force and the only possible means of restoring Yugoslavia. While admitting the leadership of two Croats—Tito, the military head, and Ivan Ribar, spokesman for the "National Liberation Authority," the Partisan political body established in Bihac in November 1942— they insisted that the Serbs maintained a majority in the political council. The first Allied newspaperman to visit occupied Yugoslavia was Daniel DeLuce, an Associated Press correspondent, who arrived in September 1943. He reported that he saw no traces of terror or plundering, that Catholic priests were working side by side with the Communists, and that Partisans denied that Tito had instituted a Soviet government in Partisan territory.

DeLuce learned also from a Partisan officer with whom he discussed the political situation that Tito's men were in conflict with Matchek, too. While the Partisans recognized that he had refused to collaborate with the Ustashi Fuehrer, they reproached him for refusing to co-ordinate his peasant organization with their government, and went so far as to accuse him of secretly supporting Pavelich. The Partisans thus found themselves opposed not only to Mikhailovich but to the Croatian peasant leader whose democratic faith was supposedly beyond question and who, as late as 1941, had the active support of 75 per cent of the Croats.

At the beginning of 1944 Yugoslavia was in the throes of an ideological triangle—Tito, Matchek, and Mikhailovich—in which the Serbs and the Croats were fighting out their old grudges, the Serbs, moreover, being divided within their ranks by an ideological rift that caused their left wing to side with the Croats in the Partisan forces. As to the Slovenes, who were especially anxious to see the restoration of Yugoslavia as the only possible means for their own national existence, they were divided, but the majority of them apparently supported Tito. Whatever the real political face of the Partisans, and whatever their ultimate political objectives, all unbiased foreign observers recognized that since late in 1942 their military action had been much more important than Mikhailovich's. Mikhailovich asserted that at the hour of liberation he could raise an important army. In 1944, however, he had only 20,000 fighters—according to British sources—while according to the same sources the Partisan forces exceeded 200,000. Geographically they were in a better position than the Chetniks to benefit from the collapse of Italy. But both sides exaggerated the importance of their actual strength, and both were claiming the capture of the same territory, accusing each other of all kinds of treachery.

King Peter's government vainly expressed its regrets over this

unfortunate schism but revealed itself completely helpless to end
the fratricidal strife. The British were greatly embarrassed in their
military planning by this civil war. They also knew more than anyone else about the real situation inside Yugoslavia. Their liaison officers were with both the Chetniks and the Partisans. Late in 1941
they had sent an intelligence mission to establish radio liaison between the Yugoslav regime in exile and Mikhailovich, who was thus
enabled to become Minister of War. British control over these
radio communications proved to be a psychological error. The British wounded his nationalistic pride and, on the other hand, roused
Soviet suspicion. Frictions developed immediately. His relations
with the British, consequently, were not especially smooth or
pleasant. They discovered very soon that Mikhailovich refused to
be treated as a subordinate officer and that he insisted on his own
wait-and-strike strategy, with which they could not agree. He demanded greater military aid than could be furnished him.

Disappointed in Mikhailovich, the British became interested in
the increasingly more important military action of the Partisans.
Their radio propaganda to Yugoslavia recognized the Partisan
campaigns as well as Mikhailovich's, and in the summer of 1943
they assigned liaison officers, including Churchill's personal friend,
Lieutenant-Colonel William Deakin, and Brigadier General Fitz-
roy MacLean, to Tito's forces. Although the British were ideologically closer to the Serbian nationalists than to the Partisans,
they must have taken into consideration the strategic importance
of the latter's fighting and the fact that the Partisans operated
mainly in Slovenia and Dalmatia in the Adriatic sector, very
near to the area in which Britain's chief Mediterranean forces
were stationed and where their principal postwar interests were
located. The British were anxious also to prove to Moscow that
friends of the Soviet Union were automatically their friends.
They realized that such evidence was essential for the political
agreement without which any major military action in the Balkans
could not be undertaken.

With the support of Washington, British diplomacy, therefore,
concentrated all its efforts on co-ordinating the two Yugoslav factions. When they realized that it was absolutely impossible to
establish an agreement between the Serbs and Croats in Lon-

don, they permitted the Yugoslav government to constitute a purely technical cabinet headed by a Serbian diplomat, Bozidar Purich, an old friend of Anthony Eden. But they simultaneously suggested the elimination of Serbian nationalist officers who had surrounded young King Peter. The British Broadcasting Corporation began to pay such tribute to the Partisans' military undertakings that "Free Yugoslavia" proudly quoted the flattering comments. And, of course, Mikhailovich's "Democratic Yugoslav News Agency" multiplied at once its protests to BBC. This Chetnik press service began to broadcast in August 1943 over a station that called itself "Woods and Mountains of Yugoslavia."

The British continued to go even further in spite of these protests. They helped the Soviet Union organize broadcasts to the Balkans from Cairo. They did not miss a single opportunity to prove to Moscow that they intended to co-operate with it in the Balkans. They suggested to King Peter that he ask Mikhailovich to avoid battle with the Partisans and Peter did request him not to fight the Partisans unless their attacks made such action inevitable. But neither King Peter's request nor all the efforts of the British, who since 1942 had presented three ultimatums to Mikhailovich, were able to achieve success. The rival press services continued to bandy accusations, and the assassination by the Partisans of General Djurakovich, Mikhailovich's delegate in Montenegro, marked a high point in the conflict. But British efforts apparently did bear fruit in Moscow. There they were able to convince the Soviet leaders of the integrity of British strategic objectives in Yugoslavia. They were able to submit to the Moscow Conference a perfect record on their policy toward Yugoslavia, which Moscow always has considered her potential zone of influence.

America's policy in the Yugoslav conflict led to much less direct involvement. The United States considered the regime in exile as the legitimate Yugoslav trustee government. In October 1943 President Roosevelt turned over four American Liberator bombers to Mikhailovich's men. The Partisan radio taxed Roosevelt with having given the bombers to the "wrong side," and both factions demanded that the Allies choose between them. Partisan sympathizers abroad assured the Allies that should their forces land in Yugoslavia to support Mikhailovich, Partisan guns would be turned against them. The Chetniks promised guerrilla war against any British and Americans who came to help the Partisans.

The battle waged furiously in charges and countercharges after the Teheran Conference when the Partisan radio announced the formation of a Yugoslav People's Government in Jaice, Bosnia, with Marshal Tito as military leader and Ivan Ribar as Prime Minister. Both men were Croats but the Serbs had several representatives in the government.

Richard K. Law, Britain's Undersecretary of State, explained to the House of Commons in December 1943 that the greater part of British military assistance was then going to the Partisans because they were more active than any other group in Yugoslavia. Secretary of State Hull made the American attitude clear the next day when he declared that his government would aid the Partisans as well as the Chetniks on the principle that the Allied policy was to help any group in Yugoslavia that was effectively fighting the Germans. It was the intention of the United States, he states, to assist all resistance groups from the point of view of their "military effectiveness" without discussing political differences while the fighting was in progress. Yugoslavia's postwar status, he declared, was to be left for her people to decide.

Foreign Secretary Eden repeated Mr. Law's statement, emphasizing that Britain did not want to impose any government upon the Yugoslavs, who would be able to determine freely after the war the manner in which they wish to be ruled. Late in February 1944 Prime Minister Churchill made the attitude of the British government still more clear. Having reiterated the former British criticism of Mikhailovich, Churchill unreservedly praised Marshal Tito, to whom his son Randolph carried the Prime Minister's autographed picture. Apparently in his eyes national conceptions had superseded the original communistic elements, and Tito's army had become "a national and unifying movement."

While Churchill renewed the British promises to give all possible aid to Marshal Tito, he emphasized, however, that Britain could not disassociate herself from King Peter. Churchill wanted to put all the blame on Mikhailovich and then on the Yugoslav government in Cairo; but he wanted at the same time to save King Peter's theoretical chance to come to an agreement with

Marshal Tito, despite the fact that Tito and his government desired such an agreement even less than did the young king and his Serbian advisers in Cairo.

As to the Soviet government, it officially recognized King Peter's regime in Cairo, as did all other United Nations. However, it had been supporting the Partisans from the beginning, and when Tito announced his new government in Bosnia, the Soviet government disclosed that it would send a military mission to Tito. While Tito was praised in Moscow for assisting "in the struggle of the peoples of Yugoslavia against Hitlerite Germany," Mikhailovich was reprimanded for having "damaged the struggle." This is why Mikhailovich "could not but meet a negative attitude from the U.S.R.R." The postwar status of Yugoslavia was diplomatically ignored in Moscow.

Thus at the beginning of 1944 the United Nations' Big Three, after discussing the Balkan problems in Moscow and at Teheran, had indicated the basic outline of their policy toward Yugoslavia. They had reached a strategic agreement on military action in the Balkans to further soften "Europe's soft under-belly," a program requiring action by Partisan troops rather than the strategic delay proposed by Mikhailovich. As to the political or constitutional issue, both London and Washington desired to delay their solution until the liberated people of Yugoslavia were able to express their will. They considered themselves morally obligated to Peter's regime, which, under strong moral pressure from these two capitals, brought Yugoslavia into the war. But Moscow made no secret of her sympathy for the regime of Marshal Tito.

British sympathies toward Tito have been interpreted in Washington diplomatic circles as a possible shrewd diplomatic maneuver. Its eventual aim might have been to safeguard British interests in the western Balkans, should the Balkans be divided after the war into two spheres of influence, reserving the eastern part along the coast of the Black Sea for the Soviet Union, and the Mediterranean shores for the British.

Many Allied statesmen, aware of the conflict between the hard realities of "military effectiveness" and their moral commitments toward King Peter, felt almost as embarrassed and unhappy as

Peter himself—who must have realized in Cairo the tragedy of his country and of his personal position. There is an ironic twist in his situation—the fact that he is perhaps the most Yugoslav of all his Yugoslav politicians in exile. Those elderly men passed the greater part of their lives in pre-First World War Serbia or in the former Slavic provinces of the Austro-Hungarian Empire. Peter, on the contrary, was born and brought up in Yugoslavia. He is assuredly a Serb, and as a descendant of Karageorge, the founder of his dynasty, he must take pride in his ancestral roots. But since he was destined to be King of the Croats and Slovenes as well, his education was along Yugoslav rather than Serbian lines. However, the nationalist Serbs, for whom their modern history is identified with his dynasty, are his main supporters. For all other Yugoslavs his dynasty has been merely a "political solution."

Peter knew his was the hardest political mission ever assigned a European ruler. Nor was his burden made easier by the men who surrounded him. It appeared, furthermore, to be made almost unbearable by those who stayed at home and continued to fight the enemy. And in the final analysis, his country's problems will not be solved by exiled politicians. They will have to be solved by those who suffered in Yugoslavia under the Nazi yoke.

In the interest of their own survival, both the Serbs and the Croats will have to muster the necessary strength to overcome their grievances and their mutual resentments. The Partisans claim to have found a new social formula which will make possible a common life for the Serbs, the Croats, and the Slovenes who would be the biggest losers if Yugoslavia should disappear. However, at the beginning of 1944 many Serbs still refused, for nationalistic or ideological reasons, to recognize the Partisan movement, headed by a Croat of Communist faith, as their national movement.

The Partisans claimed that tomorrow belonged to them and scorned Mikhailovich and those politicians who hoped to use him to restore a Serbian-dominated Yugoslavia as being "men of the past." Undoubtedly Mikhailovich did come from Serbia's past, but for many Serbs it was a living past still able to inspire Serbian hearts. He was for them the personification of their ardent nationalism which survived centuries of Turkish and Teutonic oppression. Because of their social aspirations and their faith in a better world, the Partisans might have more dynamism than Mikhailovich's warriors who were fighting for their freedom and for the preservation of their nationalism. But that nationalism, forged during long centuries of oppression, and revitalized by Hitler's attempt to crush it, was so strong that many Serbs from Old Serbia were determined to fight for what they believed to be their sacred rights. On the other hand, the Croats and the Slovenes were determined not to accept the restoration of a Serbian-dominated Yugoslavia.

A very real civil war threatened Yugoslavia at the very hour of her liberation from the foreign yoke. In this civil war the already endangered unity of the Serbs and the Croats may be destroyed for generations to come. Then Hitler, though defeated by the United Nations, would be able to boast of having won the "Battle of Yugoslavia." The political vacuum created in Southeastern Europe by the disappearance of Yugoslavia would oblige European statesmen to look for new solutions, which might or might not prove successful. And the social chaos originated in Yugoslavia might expand beyond her broken boundaries.

IX: A Shaky Throne
and Permanent Aspirations

Greece

THE Greek people paid a very high price in blood, sweat, and tears for their membership in the United Nations. They have continued to pay a high price for their place in the ranks of the Allies. Their six months' fight against the overwhelming forces of the Italians added a new chapter to their heroic history. It was the blow which first shattered the morale of Fascist Italy, revealing to the Italians and to the rest of the world the fundamental weakness of the Italian Army which had been camouflaged by the pompous parades of Fascism.

Greek resistance served the United Nations' cause tremendously by upsetting Hitler's timetable and forcing him to delay for six or eight weeks his attack on Russia—a diversion that may have been of great importance contributing to the failure of his drive on Moscow. Once conquered, the Greeks could sadly yet proudly claim a high place in the ranks of martyr nations in Nazified Europe.

Living in a country which in normal times had to import 50 per cent of her food because only 15 per cent of her soil can be cultivated, the Greeks were soon brought by the occupation to the very edge of starvation. In the first winter one thousand people died daily in the Athens area alone. Ninety-two per cent of the students at the University of Athens developed tuberculosis from malnutrition. Their ordeal was further aggravated by inflation. Prices in depreciated Greek drachmas skyrocketed to a level reached only in Germany and Austria after the last war.

It is to the everlasting credit of the Greeks that despite such unbelievable hardships they furnished such an insignificant percentage of collaborationists. The practically nonexistent Greek

Nazi Party headed by Spyros Botsaris, was ignored even by the Axis occupants, who found it impossible to use men without any backing in their own country. General George Tsolakoglou, who after the capitulation of the Greek Army in April 1941 tried to establish a Pétain-style puppet government, failed to win any support and resigned after the Allied landings in North Africa. Those few Greeks whom the Axis compelled to collaborate tried to justify their attitude by the "Communistic danger" which, they said, would threaten Greece if Hitler were defeated. They were despised and ignored by their countrymen who courageously developed a most efficient resistance to the occupation forces.

While the Greeks at home were deprived of their liberties, their regime in exile was to remain the guardian of their national independence. It soon became apparent, however, that a serious political schism was developing between the resistance forces at home and the regime in exile. The causes are to be found in the turbulent history of the Greek people between the two World Wars, when they could not agree among themselves whether they wanted a republic or a monarchy. An essential consideration in an examination of Greek problems is the fact that the Greek dynasty is of foreign origin. It was imposed upon Greece in 1863 as a means of ending the almost continuous struggle between rival military factions. The British government, anxious to re-establish order in this important way station on Britain's imperial lifeline through the Mediterranean, designated a Danish prince as King of Greece. To make him acceptable, the British offered the Greeks a premium with their new monarch—the seven Ionian islands which had been under British protection since 1815.

The Greeks accepted the islands and the young Danish-German Prince William George of Schleswig-Holstein-Sonderborg-Glucksburg, who became George I, King of the Hellenes. He managed to retain this title for fifty years, although his exceptionally long reign was not a particularly happy one. It was filled with bitter domestic fights and devastating Balkan wars. George escaped political assassins in 1898 only to die at their hands in 1913.

His successors inherited the most unstable throne in modern Europe. George's son Constantine was in almost continual difficulties with Eleutheros Venizelos, the great Cretan patriot and pro-Ally leader who as Prime Minister fought tirelessly to expand his nation's strength and territory. He did his best to bring Greece into the First World War despite King Constantine's pro-German feelings. After his government fell twice during 1915, he established a provisional government in Salonika which was definitely pro-Ally. In 1916 he compelled Constantine to join the Allies, and in 1917 the King was compelled by them to abdicate. In 1920, after the death of his son Alexander, a national plebiscite recalled him despite Allied opposition. The revolution that followed the disastrous war against Turkey in 1921 obliged Constantine to leave Greece in 1922 and he died in exile in Italy.

His eldest son, George II, was driven from Greece a year later by the revolt of the republican army and navy officers. In the 1924 plebiscite proposed by Venizelos, 758,742 voters acclaimed the republic while only 352,322 voted for a monarchy. Another plebiscite thirteen years later called George back to Greece from England by a 98 per cent vote, but the authenticity of this poll has always been contested by the republican opposition.

Weary of these unceasing fights, the Greeks believed that a constitutional monarchy would bring order out of the chaos compounded of political feuds, revolts, and grave financial crises. King George returned with the best British-inspired constitutional intentions and promises. Yet less than a year later the Greeks found themselves living under a semi-fascist, military dictatorship.

The 1936 elections revealed that it was not easy to apply the English-style parliamentary regime to Greece. The Royalists who, to judge from the plebiscite, should have had the overwhelming majority, won only 125 seats. Their principal opposition, the Venizelist Liberals who were paying only lip service to the monarchy, obtained 135 seats. General John Metaxas, whose group held only 9 seats, and the Communists with their 14 seats thus became the arbiters of the Greek political situation through their power to produce a majority coalition vote.

Death further complicated the Greek position. Marshal Kondyles, who was responsible for the return of the King, and Venizelos both died early in 1936, leaving General Metaxas, then Vice Premier, alone on the political stage and virtually without a rival. This helped him to forget that the number of his supporters was out of proportion to his vast ambitions. He formed a new government and succeeded in having Parliament adjourned for five months. Four months later, under threat of a general strike by the Communist Party, he obtained the King's signature to the dissolution of Parliament and the suspension of the constitution. The dictatorial regime established in this way survived the 1941 invasion and even the death of Metaxas during the last weeks of Greece's heroic resistance. In September 1941 King George appointed Emmanuel Tsouderos, an Athenian banker and apostate from the Venizelist Party, to liquidate the dictatorship. Holdovers from the General's government were dismissed and the regime itself abolished within a month, whereupon Tsouderos pledged himself to re-establish the parliamentary constitution.

Panayotis Kanellopoulos, a young leader of the Greek underground resistance who had escaped to Cairo, was instrumental in persuading Tsouderos to this step. Kanellopoulos organized a Union Party in 1936 with the slogan "Disciplined Freedom," but he was unable to win a single seat in Parliament. When he protested against Metaxas' dictatorship, he was exiled to a small island. When Italy attacked Greece he returned to join the army as a private. After the occupation he participated in the underground movement, escaping early in 1942 to Egypt where he represented the Greek organizations which had united in resisting the Axis. He brought word of the growing insistence of the Greeks upon restoration of their constitutional liberties simultaneously with their liberation from the Axis yoke.

Kanellopoulos became Vice Premier in the Tsouderos government and his adherence to the regime in exile was interpreted as a guarantee of the sincerity of the promises made by the cabinet. Tsouderos had, indeed, repeatedly stressed that his government would resign as soon as it returns to Athens, leaving the Greek people free to express their sovereign will. But in March 1943 Kanellopoulos resigned because of a partly personal, partly political conflict between the two factions in the Greek military forces stationed in the Near East. His resignation coincided with the transfer of the Greek regime in exile from London to Cairo, and precipitated the reorganization of the Tsouderos cabinet.

The numerous and prosperous Greek colonies in Egypt were

definitely Venizelist. In addition, many of the Greeks escaping to
Egypt were from Crete, Venizelos' home, and they were traditionally anti-Royalist. King George found himself compelled to
introduce into the government five Venizelists, including Sophocles
Venizelos, son of the old leader, and George Roussos, former Greek
envoy to the United States. Some of them had more or less accepted the monarchy while others remained intransigent in their
republican opposition. But for patriotic reasons they were all disposed to back the royal regime in exile as the "trustee of Greek
sovereignty." It was pressure from this sector that led King George
to pledge, in a broadcast from Cairo in July 1943, free elections
for a constituent assembly convention within six months of
Greece's liberation, and an understanding that he would respect
the assembly's decisions about the future political establishment,
including the problem of the monarchy. This pledge was considered sufficient until a group of political leaders of the organized Greek underground arrived in Cairo a month later.

The head of this delegation, Emmanuel Tsirimokos, son of the
former speaker of the Chamber, immediately attacked the royal
government. He recalled all the grievances the republicans held
against King George and especially against the dictatorship, and
accused governmental agents who had been sent from Cairo to
Greece of "ignoring, misrepresenting, and even persecuting" the
liberation movement. He concluded his lengthy report by urging
the King not to return to Greece before the plebiscite he had promised had been held. Tsirimokos declared he spoke in the name of
EAM, the National Liberation Front, which was the most powerful
of the underground movements, and also in behalf of EDES
(Greek National Democratic Army) and EKKA (Greek National
and Social Liberation Army), two less important resistance groups.

The estrangement between the Greek people and their monarchy
in exile so bluntly revealed by this incident, became a matter of
great concern because the nucleus of the underground resistance
consisted of the most aggressive anti-Metaxist and anti-Royalist
elements. EAM and its fighting unit, the Liberation Army known
as ELAS, succeeded in bringing together the majority of the democratic elements in their country. But it did not appear that the
Communists were able to assume the same leadership here as in

the Yugoslav Partisan armies. EAM declared a political truce for
the duration and organized their operations by dividing Greece
into five military districts—Thrace, Macedonia, Central Greece,
Peloponnesus, and Epirus, with a separate guerrilla unit in Crete.
Military activities were co-ordinated throughout the districts, but
they did not impose a specific political program on their adherents,
agreeing simply on two broad objectives: "Resistance against occupation and the liberation of Greece from the invaders, and the safe-
guarding of the people's supremacy after liberation has been
effected."

EDES consisted of more conservative elements but it was not
definitely Royalist. Its leader, Colonel Zervas, was a political
protégé of General Plastiras, who lived in exile in France because
of his anti-Royalist feelings, but Zervas was not a man of such firm
political convictions. It was, therefore, not impossible that, as a
leader of conservative elements, he might join forces with the
Royalists.

The resistance movement included a third and less important
element, EKKA, politically midway between ELAS and EDES.
It did not become involved in the clash of the latter two organizations, which had all the appearances of having been provoked by
a misunderstanding that probably originated with, and certainly
was exploited by German agents. The spokesmen for these underground organizations were supported in their attacks on the King
by a prominent leader of the Agrarian Party who spoke not only
for his own organization but for all the political parties in existence
until 1936—the Liberals, National Democrats, Democrats, Progres-
sives, and Popularists. Then the underground delegates addressed
a joint letter to Tsouderos urging "for the sake of national unity"
a statement promising that the "King would not return to Greece
before the people express their will on the type of government."
According to the delegates, this memorandum was approved by
the cabinet in which the Venizelists then had a majority.

The King found himself in a difficult position with his government and the delegates definitely opposed to him, and with Greek
soldiers in the Near East manifesting hostile intentions toward
him. He appealed to Roosevelt and Churchill who were then con-
ferring in Quebec. Churchill answered him publicly in his Quebec

address by devoting a significant passage to Greece and Yugo-slavia. He sent a message of encouragement not only to the peoples of these two countries but also to their kings "who have never faltered in their duties and whom we hope to see restored to their thrones by the free choice of their liberated peoples." Churchill's private answer to King George was said to be even more encouraging.

The President's answer is reported to have put a much greater emphasis on the sovereign will of the Greek people in the selec-tion of their postwar regime, although it was reported that Churchill had done his best to induce Roosevelt to share his viewpoint. The President was more anxious than the Prime Minister to avoid any impression that he might wish to influence in advance the Greeks' free expression of choice. And of course the United States has never had the same interest in Greece as the British. It has been traditional British policy to make allies of small mari-time nations. The Greek revolution against the Turks in 1821 was inspired by Russia, who had coveted Constantinople and the Straits of Bosphorus since the eighteenth century. But it was by the Convention of London that Greece was declared an inde-pendent kingdom in 1832 under the protection of Great Britain, France, and Russia. Since then Britain has closely watched all de-velopments of Greek foreign and domestic policies.

The British have a weakness for "traditional solutions." They were satisfied with their original candidate King George I, and his grandson George II proved during his years in power and in his two periods in exile that he was Britain's faithful friend. It was only natural that the British should give him their fullest support. They believe that after this war they will have a chance to give Greece a premium with George II—as they did with George I—in the form of the twelve Dodecanese Islands which Italy obtained after the last war despite the fact that their population is pre-dominantly Greek.

In the fall of 1943 British Intelligence received reports from their agents in Greece that while 25 per cent of the Greeks were definitely against King George and only 10 per cent were un-reservedly loyal to him, 65 per cent were disposed to accept him with satisfactory constitutional guarantees. American Intelligence

sources were of the opinion that their British colleagues were correct only in their evaluation of the King's unreserved supporters.
They argued that the Metaxas regime had been opposed by approximately 90 per cent of the Greeks. When Italy attacked Greece,
all her people united in their patriotic resistance. Once their
country was conquered, however, they resumed their grievances
against the Metaxas regime and against the King, whom they held
responsible. They indicted him for not having replaced the
dictatorship with a national coalition government when Greece
was attacked; for having liquidated the Metaxas regime only in
exile, and then gradually and reluctantly; and for having allowed
the monarchy to become identified with the dictatorship.

Nevertheless, the British were determined to support King
George and the constitutional monarchy as the best preventive
against political extremes leading to social chaos. In this connection, while welcoming help from the Communists for the Greek
liberation movement, the British could not help but fear the sharp
reaction that might result among the nationalist bourgeois elements
if the Communist strength were increased. Another consideration
was the British belief that it would be extremely difficult, perhaps
impossible, to protect their stake in this Mediterranean outpost
if the rest of the peninsula should come within the Soviet sphere
of influence. Such a division, they feared, would lead inevitably
to a Russian-British conflict. Preferable to that would be a federation of Balkan peoples under the joint protection of Britain,
Russia, and, if possible, the United States. Certainly it would be
welcomed by a majority of the Balkan peoples who are still striv-
ing to realize their old dream of "the Balkans for the Balkan
peoples" after centuries of power politics. But so long as this type
of federation seemed impossible of realization, the British alternative was to consolidate and maintain her influence in Greece.

Consequently, Cairo and London were disturbed to learn in
October 1943 of a clash between the ELAS and the EDES. Leaders of ELAS apparently had come to believe that Colonel Zervas
of the EDES had signed an armistice with the Germans to permit
distribution of food in Epirus by the Red Cross. Actually Zervas
refused to sign the armistice after consulting the British, but the
ELAS leadership continued to believe that he had betrayed the

cause of liberation. The situation was not improved by independent action of ELAS branches in the Peloponnese, stronghold of the conservatives and Royalists. It is highly probable that the Peloponnese branches actually felt closer to Zervas' units than to their own central committee.

The possible political implications of guerrilla clashes in Greece appeared to be less dangerous than those which threatened Yugoslavia because the Soviet Union, which had from the beginning of the Yugoslav conflict openly supported Tito's Partisans and criticized Mikhailovich, refrained from taking sides in Greece. The Soviet press at home and Soviet broadcasts to Greece had high words of praise for ELAS but they completely ignored the controversy over the monarchy.

Not until January 1944 did Moscow publicly express for the first time her interest in the internal affairs of Greece. An article in the Soviet magazine *War and the Working Class,* signed by Dimitri Vlahov, accused the Greek Government-in-Exile of developing in the homeland a situation similar to that existing in Yugoslavia. It charged official Greek circles in Cairo with "dividing the Greek people by portraying the resistance of the EAM Partisans as German-inspired" and with having "paralyzed the Greek resistance by sponsoring the idea that active struggle should be suspended until the Allies land in Greece." Colonel Zervas was portrayed as a Greek Mikhailovich, and the two leaders were said to be in contact with each other and to have established a common line of "secretly negotiating with the conquerors and of openly attacking the real patriots."

The Greeks in Cairo were perturbed not only by this breach of Soviet non-interference in Greece's internal affairs but by the man who made this first public Soviet attack on their exiled government. Vlahov is a Bulgarian Macedonian, and Greek guerrillas, whether rightist or leftist, are not accustomed to receive either condemnation or praise from a Bulgarian, especially a Bulgarian Macedonian. The Bulgarian Macedonians have never abandoned their claims to the Macedonian territories taken over by Greece, and they were among the most brutal elements in the Bulgarian occupation forces which terrorized and expelled the Greeks from northern Thrace.

The Greeks—and foreign diplomatic circles shared their suspicions—wondered whether the main objective of this Russian attack was to create a favorable impression in Bulgaria and thus strengthen the Bulgars in their belief that if they abandoned Hitler before it was too late, Russia might take them under her protective wing. Many Bulgars were dreaming of a Soviet-sponsored federation of Southern Slavs in which—with Moscow's backing—they might find a privileged place, and through which—with Russian support—they might even obtain the outlet to the Aegean Sea which they had failed to achieve for themselves.

The clash between the Greek guerrilla forces did not have the same origin, importance, or consequences as the Yugoslav conflict. But the increasing acuteness of the Yugoslav crisis in the winter of 1943-44 greatly impressed King George of Greece and his British friends. The British were most anxious to prevent the extension of the Yugoslav conflict to Greece. Consequently, they decided to be less intransigent in their support of King George who, as he himself must have realized, was not personally popular even among the Greek Royalists who accepted him as a symbol but did not like him as a man.

Early in November 1943 Churchill told the House of Commons that Britain had no commitments to King George but would support him as the constitutional head of the Greek state until the people of Greece could express their will. This statement did not represent a new element in the Greek picture; it was merely reaffirmation of the status quo. But it revealed that Britain had shifted her emphasis—Churchill underscored not so much his support of the King as the fact that Britain was not committed to him.

A month later King George made an important but ambiguous statement. While not specifically pledging himself not to return to Greece in compliance with the request of the underground representatives, he gave his people to understand that he was prepared to delay his return until they decided on the form of government they wanted and invited him back. The political troubles of King Peter, his neighbor both in Yugoslavia and in exile in Cairo, unquestionably influenced the King's resolution. Moreover, there was some question whether he really was anxious to go back to the land where he knew he never had been, and hardly could be, popular. The King was unyielding about his return only so long as the British—or more specifically Churchill—wanted him to be. And their change in position was conditioned principally by a desire, at the beginning of 1944, to have the best possible conditions for military action in the Balkans. This, of course, necessitated satisfying the political demands of the Balkan people.

Moreover, the British began to realize that the re-establishment of King George in Athens after the war was becoming ever more doubtful, whereas the problem of maintaining their influence in postwar Greece was the permanent concern of Britain's foreign policy. Hence, London felt that it would be wiser to soften her adamant position in support of King George, or rather in attempting to impose him upon the people of Greece. This change in policy was viewed with particular bitterness by the Prime Minister, who on so many occasions had gone on record in support of King George. Churchill's grievances against Greece, which had refused to accept the plans he had evolved for her postwar status, found full expression in his report on the war of February 22, 1944, when he described Greece as "the saddest case of all." His bitter words about the clashes between rival Greek factions came surprisingly at the very moment when the Greeks realized the necessity of establishing a united national front.

At the beginning of 1944 leaders of all former political parties in Greece informed Cairo that they were prepared to co-operate for the duration with the government in exile. The leftist EAM, leading the underground resistance, voiced the same disposition. The majority of Greeks realized that the monarchy had little chance of surviving the war and that King George had ceased to be an acute political problem. After having spent many years in directing their main attention to the King problem, they now were able to concentrate on the problems of their foreign policy, made more urgently real by the approaching end of the war.

Though disunited at home, all Greeks present a united face to the external world in regard to their national aspirations. Regardless of their political or social creeds, they all have the same national objective: the reunion of the Greek peoples, who during the Middle Ages were divided between Turkey and the Venetian Republic.

After Italy's surrender, the Greek government immediately revived its claims to the Dodecanese Islands on the basis of common ethnography, language, and religion. Count Carlo Sforza, who as Italy's Foreign Minister in 1920 defended his country's presence in the Dodecanese by her permanent interests there, was eager in 1943, as a political émigré about to return to his defeated but half-liberated country, to recognize Greece's claims as fully justified.

The Turkish government also has informed Tsouderos that it would have no objection to the cession to Greece of these islands, which belonged to Turkey until 1921. It would be satisfied with Greek neutralization of the islands which lie so close to Turkey's shores. The Turks might object if the British should establish a naval and air base in the Dodecanese Islands, but their return to Greece certainly would not constitute any diplomatic problem.

The Greeks, therefore, look with a general feeling of confidence to their future in postwar Europe. They believe that this time they will have a chance to obtain the final realization of their national aspirations and definitely consolidate themselves as the most homogeneous nation in the Balkans.

They may have cause for concern, however, when they look to the north. The project of a Southern Slav federation, which would naturally come under the Soviet Union's influence and which some day might even become a new Union Republic, disturbs them. Some of them hope that Britain will be able to defend them against the extension of Moscow's influence, by means of a Balkan Slav federation, along the entire Balkan peninsula. But while none of them questions Britain's intentions, many wonder whether she will be in a position to defend her traditional Balkan interests if Moscow's influence, stretching out beyond defeated Rumania, should extend from the Bulgarian shores of the Black Sea to the Yugoslav shores of the Adriatic.

X: *The Uncertain Southeast*

Danubian Europe

S OUTHEASTERN Europe has been the classic arena for power politics. And, in addition, for centuries there has been in this part of Europe the discreet but pressing, invisible but permanent, influence of the great power of the Vatican.

Russia had appeared there as protector and liberator of her kin. Great Britain, protecting her vital communication line in the Mediterranean, anxiously watched Russia's moves and opposed her policy by supporting the Turks, oppressors of the Balkan Slavs and Greeks. Austria-Hungary appeared later on the Balkan scene. Only after the defeat by Prussia in 1866, when the West was closed to it, did the Hapsburg Empire allow its Hungarian statesmen to turn their expansion policy to the East, where the inchoate Balkan states were stubbornly fighting for semi-independence, augmented by Russian assistance. The clash of Austrian and Russian interests led to World War I.

France took an active interest in the Balkans only at the turn of the century, ready to finance these states as she was financing Russia, though on a smaller scale. Appearing with this material assistance added to her intellectual prestige, she was bound to find many friends. And after World War I she tried to capitalize on those friendships by building up an eastern defense system which, together with Poland, was to replace a faltering Russia.

The small Balkan states attempted their own solutions by creating two Ententes. The Little Entente (Yugoslavia, Czechoslovakia, and Rumania) was designed chiefly as a defensive group aimed at preventing the restoration of the Hapsburgs and balking Hungarian revisionist schemes. But the so-called Balkan Entente (Yugoslavia, Greece, Rumania, and Turkey) was a positive grouping and was well on its way to becoming the first constructive regional organization, the first significant step toward healthy federation within the European continent. Both Ententes were destroyed by Hitler. It is most uncertain whether it will be possible to restore them once Hitler disappears. Yugoslavia, torn by war and internal strife, may not recover her prewar position. Rumania joined the Axis and may be exposed to the Soviet Union's especially severe treatment in reprisal for her recapture of Bessarabia and occupation of Ukrainian provinces.

Thus Bulgaria and Hungary, against whom the prewar Balkan and Little Ententes have been created as defensive organizations, have suffered less than all other Southeastern European countries, despite the fact that like Rumania, both Bulgaria and Hungary have backed the losing side.

Hungary, country of eternal paradoxes, managed to create for herself a situation of extreme paradox within the Nazi camp. Hungarian propagandists in neutral and Allied nations—and the Budapest government anxiously supported them as a form of life insurance in the event of a Hitler defeat—claimed that Hungary had been Hitler's victim rather than his ally. Yet, more than any other country in Europe, she has benefited by Germany's New Order.

Hungary took an active part in the war with Russia and declared war on England and the United States. But in order to safeguard at least a part of her territorial aggrandizement (obtained through the partition of Czechoslovakia and the dismemberment of Yugoslavia), Hungary would like to be the first Axis satellite to crash the gate of the United Nations.

Paradoxical Hungary, a kingdom without a king, a nation without a navy, has for Chief of State an Admiral. She joined the Axis, but her Social Democratic Party was not dissolved. Her government includes the most outspoken anti-Semites, but often these same men have "non-Aryan" grandmothers. She has a Nazi-sponsored candidate for the regency—a Hapsburg archduke. She does not claim any Russian territory, but has sent soldiers to die in the streets of Stalingrad. She would like to annex Slovak and Rumanian territory, but both countries are her allies within the Axis. Her Foreign Minister, General Joseph Gomboes, was the first European statesman to visit Hitler. The term "Axis" was coined in the capital of Hungary. Nevertheless, Hungarian propagandists assert that Hungary's main intention, purpose, and ambition has always been to desert the Axis as soon as possible and before anyone else.

It is not easy to understand such a nation. It is particularly difficult for the diplomat who does not speak the language and who, by the nature of his mission, has to live in a superior social strata as remote from the Hungarian people as Czarist Russia's aristocracy was from the Russian masses. For the Allied statesmen who have to rely on the dispatches of their agents, Hungary is an exciting enigma which must be solved because of her crucial position in the Danubian valley.

Should the Hungarian foundation of the Axis structure fall, Axis control over Southeastern Europe would become gravely compromised, if not seriously threatened. Admiral Nicholas Horthy, Hungary's Regent, holds in his hands the keystone. A deal with this Danubian Admiral might consequently become strategically more important than the similar deal in Algiers in 1942 with the late French Admiral Darlan. There is undoubtedly the possibility of such a deal. But could it be made actual? What price would the United Nations have to pay for it? What would be the advantages and disadvantages of such a deal?

In 1943 reports from Hungary indicated the growing discontent of the population with the war in which the Horthy regime had allowed the country to become involved. The Hungarians were shocked by their losses in Russia and were losing faith in Hitler's victory. The increasing number of Hungarians arrested for "sabotage, Communism, and opposition to the friendly spirit between the Hungarian and German armies" revealed the growing anti-war feeling and defeatism in the country. There was also growing resistance to Nazi pressure in the Hungarian Church and in conservative circles. This resistance, however, expressed itself only on the level of internal affairs. The Hungarian conservatives would have liked to replace German Nazism by the "Szeged idea," a Magyar combination of Fascism and Nazism. As for the Catholic Church, it fiercely opposed the "racial marriage" legislation.

The Hungarian propagandists in this country—especially Tibor von Eckhardt who was sent here to defend Hungarian interests

—tried to convince the Allied authorities that the nucleus of the resistance to Nazism was to be found in the Small Landowners Party. This party, however, replaced its leader, von Eckhardt, with Tildy, a Protestant minister who maintained in the Parliament a quasi-liberal opposition to the Horthy government but who none the less "indorsed the government's views on all questions of the army and Hungary's military contribution to the fight against Bolshevism." As for the Peasant Union, its president expressed admiration for the German Reich.

Nevertheless, there could be no doubt that the Hungarians were growing war-weary. It is necessary to bear in mind, moreover, that even those Hungarians who sympathize with Fascism dislike the Germans. They supported Hitler because he was granting them the realization of their territorial aspirations. The day they definitely lose faith in Hitler's victory they will be ready to stop fighting. In order to prevent this, Hitler occupied Hungary in March 1944.

The Hungarians may passionately disagree among themselves on political and social issues, but they find themselves spontaneously united in the defense of their vital national interests. For the defense of those interests they mobilized their church, both Catholic and Protestant; their aristocracy, intermarried with British and American society; their bankers and industrialists, who have excellent international connections; their Jews, whose civil rights were greatly reduced but who were not persecuted as in other Axis-controlled countries; and their emigrated Hungarians, mainly in the United States.

Admiral Nicholas Horthy, Hungary's Regent, and his propaganda minister, Istvan Antal, paid particular attention to the American-Hungarians, whom they wanted to use as defenders of the Hungarian cause. A 100-kilowatt transmitter was built for special broadcasts to Hungarians in America. Many Hungarians in this country were so anxious to save their old country in postwar Europe that they were even prepared to work for a deal with Horthy. Others, however, although they were in disagreement among themselves on many social and political issues, strongly opposed any deal with the regime that brought their country into Hitler's camp. Any deal with Admiral Horthy, which incidentally would be impossible to realize until the United Nations' armies land in Southeastern Europe, would arouse the indignation of the democratic Hungarians in this country. This indignation would be shared by all other democratic elements. And what is much more important, it might have disastrous repercussions in Hungary.

Charles Rassay, leader of the Hungarian liberals, marked in the Hungarian Parliament that it was "the extremists of the right and not the liberals who paved the way for revolutions like that of October 1918." The Hungarian liberals and farmers have certainly not forgotten the terrible experience of the Communist revolution of Bela Kun. The most violent opponents of the Horthy regime, however, are to be found among the workers and the landless farmhands, who are now very accessible to communistic propaganda. One of the most popular songs in present-day Hungary begins with the words, "There will be a flower-rich spring and Father Stalin will come to us. . . ." A deal with Admiral Horthy, unless previously approved for strategic reasons by the Soviet Union, might direct Hungarian discontent into some form of Communism.

It is most unlikely that Moscow would ever approve of a deal with Horthy. The Soviet Union, which became Hungary's neighbor after the second partition of Czechoslovakia in March 1939, will never forget that Hungary influenced the Austro-Hungarian foreign policy, which is at the origin of every conflict between Austria-Hungary and Russia. Defeated in 1866 by Prussia, Austria found her way to the West closed, and let herself be drawn by her Hungarian associate into the aggressive policy of the Balkans. Few people are aware of this underlying Russian-Hungarian animosity. But it must be taken into consideration if further conflict in the Danubian valley is to be avoided.

Hungarian hopes were stimulated by the declaration on Austria issued at the Moscow Conference by the Secretaries of State of the United States, Russia, and Great Britain. If the Soviet Union accepted the idea of Austrian independence in postwar Europe, the Hungarians believed there was no reason to oppose the existence of an independent Hungary. Some Hungarians went so far as to believe that the Soviet Union, opposed to any federations along her western border, might accept the restoration of the

Hapsburgs in Austria and Hungary as the best possible combination to block both the danger of a new German expansion in Danubian Europe and the establishment of an Eastern European federation which might eventually be used as a *cordon sanitaire* against the Soviet Union. Such ideas have indeed been fostered in Austrian legitimist circles and supported in rather influential Vatican circles, where for many years Archduke Otto, pretender to the nonexistent throne of Austria-Hungary, has been considered a potential political factor in the realization of Catholic Federation plans.

Vatican foreign policy is not easy to analyze: its agents and supporters are too discreet, its opponents are too passionate. But an understanding of the basic lines of it foreign policy is of the greatest importance at this hour when Vatican political circles and their sympathizers throughout the world are trying to assure to the Holy See a prominent part in the shaping of the postwar world.

The aftermath of World War I dealt two great blows to the Vatican. Bolshevism threatened the eastern outposts of the Catholic Church in Poland and Galician Ukraine. The disappearance of the Austro-Hungarian Empire with the "Apostolic" Hapsburgs weakened the Vatican's position in Central Europe. Pope Pius XI, who in 1919 as Apostolic Nuncio in Warsaw saw the Communist threat to Catholic Poland, concentrated his efforts on the erection of a political and spiritual bulwark against Communism. The aged Cardinal Gasparri, his Secretary of State, helped him in the work of trying to restore the great Catholic power on the Danube. He found an intelligent and discreet ally in Monsignor Ignace K. Seipel, Chancellor of the Austrian republic, who patiently laid the foundation for a new Holy Roman Empire. Monsignor Seipel, however, died in 1932, just a year before Hitler's rise to power.

In the first years after World War I, the two main obstacles to the realization of the Vatican's plans in Central Europe were Czechoslovakia and Yugoslavia. Faithful to its tradition of compromise so long as the basic principles of the Catholic Church were not endangered, the Vatican maintained diplomatic contacts with both countries. However it did not have any sympathy for either of these states. In Yugoslavia the Greek Orthodox Serbs ruled over the Catholic Croats and Slovenes. In Czechoslovakia the Hussite and free-thinking Czechs administered over the passionately Catholic Slovaks. The diplomatically adroit Czechs managed to avoid any open conflict with the Vatican. But in Yugoslavia, where passions become more easily exasperated under the Balkan sun, the proposal of the Concordat with the Vatican in 1937 provoked the Serbs to open revolt. While the Vatican was persevering in the improvement of its positions in Czechoslovakia and Yugoslavia, two more redoubtable enemies appeared in Europe: Fascism in Italy and Nazism in Germany.

The Vatican was, and still is, willing to encourage a people fighting for their autonomy or independence—as, for example, the support given to the Croats and the Poles in the nineteenth century, and to the Flemings in the twentieth century. However, it has a tendency to combat triumphant, overbearing nationalism. A conflict between the Vatican and the totalitarian super-nationalistic regimes was unavoidable. The Catholic Church became one of the most important factors of resistance to the Nazi rule. The Vatican backed this resistance throughout the war as far as it could without compromising its neutrality. With the defeat of the Axis in sight, Vatican policy became more active, although it was temporarily dimmed by the Nazi occupation of Rome.

The present war opened great new possibilities to Vatican statesmen. Pope Pius XII, who as Cardinal Pacelli was Secretary of State succeeding Cardinal Gasparri, pursued the policy of Pius XI, with the difference that he may have a chance to realize the grandiose political dreams of his predecessor. Pius XI dreamed of a Catholic Federation stretching from the Baltic to the Adriatic Sea. Cardinal Gasparri's idea was for union of all the Catholic German countries—Austria, Bavaria, the Rhineland. This plan continues to seduce those who believe in the possibility of dismembering Germany; but, reputedly, hardly anyone in Vatican circles believes in its feasibility. Therefore, the Vatican politicians have tried to sponsor two other Catholic Federation projects.

The first project foresees the restoration of Austria-Hungary, under the Hapsburgs if possible, but not necessarily. A restored Austria-Hungary would form a federation with Poland in the north and with Italy in the south. It would constitute a strong official bulwark against the German danger, and an "unofficial" one against Communism. Should the restoration of Austria-Hungary meet with too great resistance from the Catholic Slovaks, Croats, and Slovenes who have suffered under the Austrian and Hungarian administration, the Vatican would support a less ambitious plan, namely, a federation between the Poles and the Czechs and Slovaks. The Croats and the Slovenes, probably unable to come to an agreement with the Serbs, would be invited to join the federation, and the Poles would later bring in the Hungarians, with whom they have always been on good terms. Austria, coming last, would have to accept the status of the federation, and Hapsburg ghosts would no longer intimidate the Slavs.

Vatican political circles are anxious to win the support of all Catholic Slavs. The Polish Primate, Cardinal Hlond, has been permitted to tell from the Vatican the truth about the sufferings of his compatriots. The Vatican radio, so far as it is possible, assures the Poles that their independence will be restored. The puppet Slovakia with its clerical Premier Josef Tiso (who succeeded Father Hlinka) necessarily enjoys the support of the Vatican. The puppet Croatia was not recognized *de jure,* but there is a Vatican emissary in Zagreb; and a counselor of the Croat Legation in Rome maintains liaison with the Vatican. On New Year's Day of 1943 the Pope sent a message of greeting to the terrorist Ante Pavelich, head of the Ustashi regime.

Catholic priests in Slovenia have been secretly instructed to assure their flocks that the 1,200,000 Slovenes of Yugoslavia and the 500,000 Slovenes of Italy will be united after the war, but they are unable to specify whether they will be united in Yugoslavia, in Italy, or somewhere else. The Vatican hopes also to find supporters for their federation plans among the Agrarian parties in Poland, Czechoslovakia, Hungary, and Croatia.

Undeniably there is strong resistance to such plans in many countries and even among Catholic leaders. Dr. Beneš, who concluded a pact with the Soviet Union on the British-Soviet pattern, is definitely opposed to Vatican combinations; neither does his

Catholic Premier, Monsignor Jan Shramek, support them. Certain Polish, Croat, and Slovene Catholic prelates view them with little enthusiasm, fearing that such plans will fail to protect them in the long run against the German or Italian danger, but will expose them immediately to Moscow's ire.

For twenty-five years the Vatican and the Kremlin have been considered irreconcilable adversaries, two ideological and moral poles of our stormy, revolutionary world. It is true that in certain Catholic circles, particularly since Germany's attack on Russia, there has been a tendency to consider Nazism as a more redoubtable enemy than Communism. Communism, those Catholics reasoned, creates a religious vacuum. Nazism, with its worship of race, imposes a religious ersatz. The vacuum is obvious; the ersatz may be accepted. Consequently, the ersatz is more dangerous than the vacuum.

Despite this ideological differentiation favored by certain Catholics, Nazism and Fascism have been considered by the Vatican, at least until 1943, as politically more acceptable than Communism. There were two important reasons for this. Nazism and Fascism were political regimes accepted by, or imposed upon, millions of Catholics, while there were practically no Catholics under Communist rule. Nazism and Fascism were ideologically opposed to the Vatican, but, aware of the Vatican's moral power, they were willing to sign a political agreement with the Holy See. They needed such an agreement as evidence of their moral respectability.

The Vatican has always been prepared to make every necessary political compromise, so long as such compromises would assure certain advantages for the Catholic Church and the welfare of the Catholic peoples. Moreover, in the eyes of Vatican policy framers, those compromises have been of a strictly temporary character. For the Vatican, with its centuries of political experience, Nazism and Fascism are incidents which can last for only an historical moment.

Communism, too, is considered but an incident of the same time value. But there were no political reasons for an agreement with the Soviet rulers who, furthermore, never cared to obtain from the Holy See any evidence of a moral, if restricted, respectability.

Thus for twenty-five years animosity developed between the Vatican and the Kremlin, animosity which was accentuated on the Vatican side.

The Kremlin's rulers were not directly interested in Vatican policy, as there were few Catholics in the Soviet Union. As to Vatican influence in Western Europe, they had a natural tendency to underrate it. However, the Vatican had personal experience in 1919 with expansionist Communism. But many things have changed in Europe since 1919. The Bavarian Communists, who in that year threatened the present Pope Pius XII, then Apostolic Nuncio in Bavaria, with a pistol, have been replaced by Nazi Stormtroopers. And Stalin, who has liquidated the obsolete Communist International and recognized the Greek Orthodox Church in Russia, has no more bitter adversaries than those who have believed in Leon Trotsky's "permanent" world revolution.

Thus rumors began to circulate in Europe that Soviet accord with the Vatican might be next on the international diplomatic schedule. The first rumors of a forthcoming agreement between the Vatican and the Kremlin were registered on February 1943 in Switzerland—a report that a Soviet diplomatic delegation was expected at the Vatican, which was immediately denied by the Vatican's Secretariat of State. Lately, those rumors have been repeatedly revived in different European circles, only to be met with skepticism in both responsible Vatican and American quarters.

There is no doubt that such agreement would not be easy to realize. Nevertheless, there are certain interesting diplomatic rumors concerning Stalin's Moscow and papal Rome. The same air in which these rumors abound also carries a number of official broadcasts. "Papal words do not pass unheeded" is the theme of many of the Vatican's broadcasts. And in April 1943 Radio Vatican inaugurated its transmission in Russian to the Soviet Union.

Recalling the Pope's interest in Russia and the hope of extending Roman Catholic influence into the Soviet Union, these Vatican broadcasts were presumably motivated by the desire of the Holy See to remind the world of the existence of the Russian Catholic Church (generally known as the Catholic Church of Eastern Rite, or Uniate), and of the Holy See's efforts "to facilitate the return of Russia to the unity of the one true fold." Despite all Vatican efforts in this direction, its success has been rather meager. In Czarist Russia the Catholic Church had very few converts, and those mostly from among the ladies of higher Russian nobility who lived in Rome or Florence. The Catholic Church, however, had what it believed to be a very valuable outpost among the Ukrainians of Eastern Galicia who, before 1918, lived under the Hapsburgs and since then under the Poles, and who are members of the Eastern Catholic Church which the Vatican hoped would one day become the bridge between the Orthodox and Catholic Churches.

Their aged Bishop Sheptizky, whom the Galician Ukrainians have always recognized as their spiritual leader and who remained in former Polish Galicia under the Nazi occupation, has issued an appeal to the Orthodox Church to unite with the Catholics. It has been reported, on the other hand, that the Germans brought Catholic priests of both Latin and Eastern rites into occupied Ukraine. As the Vatican certainly does not want to see Catholic action developed in the Soviet Union under the Nazi sign, the Vatican's Russian broadcasts, it must be assumed, give to Russian listeners the genuine Vatican line without any Nazi coloring.

On the other hand, Vatican statesmen undoubtedly came to the conclusion that it might be wise to sound out, without making any advances, the possibilities for an agreement with the great power which is expected to play a major role in shaping postwar Europe and which, moreover, rules 2,500,000 Catholics in Poland's eastern provinces. Poland has always been very close to the Vatican's heart, and Vatican leaders never miss an opportunity to defend Polish interests. An accord with the Soviet Union might appear to them as the best means for the defense of those interests.

It is not altogether clear what advantages would accrue to Moscow through such an agreement. It does not look as if the Soviet leaders were eager to improve their moral and spiritual standing with the Catholics in Allied lands and in Danubian Europe. Vatican policy makers might believe, however, that it is a good idea to try to obtain Stalin's assent to a Central European Catholic Federation on the grounds that it would be directed exclusively against the revival of German imperialistic might. But this would be as difficult a diplomatic mission as it would be for Stalin to obtain the Vatican's approval of his plans in Eastern Europe. Finally, the Vatican's permanent interest in Russian problems is indicated by the fact that the Pope is personally directing the important Eastern Congregation, with the French Cardinal Eugène Tisserand as Secretary.

The head of the Vatican Information Bureau, on the other hand, is a Russian aristocrat, Alexander Evreinov. An old-time convert, he served after 1921 as the Nuncio's secretary in Paris. He failed to win converts there among even those Russian émigrés most opposed to the Soviet regime. He has very little or no chance to convert the Russian peasants and workmen who fight and die for their country.

The Vatican's Russian broadcasts, which Evreinov supervises and which one week recall "the Vatican's disapproval of Marxism and state worship," and another week extend the "Pope's love to all races without any consideration of their political and religious conceptions," are nevertheless extremely interesting. They indicate that while the Pope maintains, as always, the integrity of Catholic doctrine, the Vatican's diplomatic door may be opened to the Soviet Union if she should ever choose to advance in that direction.

It is far from certain, however, whether a Vatican-Kremlin agreement would help Otto of Hapsburg to return to the throne of his ancestors, or whether it would forever block his road to Vienna and Budapest. It is not likely that Stalin, who has manifested a thorough knowledge of Russian history, has forgotten the Austrian-Russian diplomatic battle in the Balkans. In 1943 the overwhelming majority of political observers believed that Otto belonged in the "dusty archives of European medieval history." The Austrian Battalion, which the United States War Department authorized Otto to recruit in 1942, was dissolved after it proved a total failure and inadvertently caused a protest which united to a remarkable, harmonious degree the hitherto squabbling foreign-born groups in the countries formed from Austria-Hungary after the last war. Archduke Otto, however, continued to be received by Roosevelt and Churchill, and he was convinced that he had not yet irrevocably lost his chance. Indeed, in these days of political confusion and incredible political contradictions, no diplomatic situation can be dismissed in advance as impossible or absurd. And no political pretender can be "buried alive." While he yet lives there is hope.

When in 1918 the United States, through Woodrow Wilson, recognized the right of self-determination for the Slavic peoples, it undercut the foundation of the Hapsburg Empire. In 1943, after twenty-five years, the United States, though still an ally of the bulk of the Slavic peoples, listened to influential groups who wished it to play a leading part in the restoration of that same Hapsburg Empire. This might assuredly become one of the more bitter paradoxes of our time. To grasp the implicit tragedy of it, it is necessary to remember that the destruction of the Hapsburg regime came from within, and was generated by the Slavs living under the Hapsburgs. Restoration can come about by that same disruptive force which is currently playing havoc with the Slavic people, and which Hitler adroitly exploited. Should the Serbs and Croats not end their strife, and should the Czechs and Slovaks not settle their differences, they might pave the way for Hapsburg restoration, a regime under which they suffered for generations and against which they are deeply, essentially united.

The Vatican may be greatly interested in the postwar status of Austria and Hungary which, at one time, constituted the "Apostolic Empire," but there is little reason for it to be concerned with Greek Orthodox Rumania, Hitler's most unfortunate satellite. Great Britain and France guaranteed Rumania's integrity in 1939. After France's fall, Rumania, weakened by a decade of political and social turmoil, found herself exposed to the simultaneous pressure of the Soviet Union and Nazi Germany.

In June 1940 Soviet Russia occupied Bessarabia, a Russian province from 1812 to 1918, and northern Bukovina, which had been part of the Hapsburg Empire. King Carol, who had succeeded his son Michael and who had declared a year before that Rumania would defend her frontiers at any cost, capitulated to Germany after he had surrendered to the Soviet Union. In August 1940, under Axis pressure, he ceded northern Transylvania to Hungary.

In September, southern Dobruja was given up to Bulgaria—but King Carol was already in exile and his son Michael was once more on Rumania's unstable throne.

The terror unleashed by the Rumanian Iron Guard Fascists was brought to an end by the German military, interested only in maintaining order in this oil-producing country. General Ion Antonescu became Germany's "stooge" in Rumania. He obediently brought his country into the Axis camp, and on June 22, 1941, Rumanian soldiers were sent to the Russian front. Rumania nominally recovered Bukovina and Bessarabia, but her soldiers were sent to die in the mountains of Caucasia and on the Volga's shores.

In 1943 the Rumanians felt themselves trapped in the burning Axis camp. Their army had been sacrificed to the magnificent Russian war machine; its bewildered remnants would be dispersed at the hour of Rumanian collapse. Stripped by the Axis and by her own corrupt pro-fascist regime, Rumania found herself on the point of distintegration. Shortages of food and clothing (the Rumanian press complained about disinterment of freshly buried bodies which were robbed of their burial garments), inflation and evil political practices daily accelerated the process of decomposition. And Rumania had few friends or defenders abroad. In despair over the fate of the country, the Antonescu regime, by means of a union with the Catholic Church, contrived to bring the orthodox Rumanians under the mighty protection of the Vatican. But the Vatican felt there was scarcely a chance to save that waning country which anxiously awaited the fate reserved for it by the Kremlin.

Rumanian political leaders, even those of liberal opposition to Antonescu, were not aware of the danger they faced. Juliu Maniu, Transylvanian-born leader of the Peasant Party, and George Bratianu, National Liberal Party leader, believed as late as 1943 that they would be able to regain not only Transylvania but even Bessarabia at the Peace Conference. They looked forward to a reconciliation with the British and the Americans that would assure them protection against the Russian advance. Four groups of Rumanians, no longer having confidence in the insight and statesmanship of their prewar liberal leaders, tried to organize elements which would be ready to take over at the hour of Rumania's collapse. The Patriotic Front, the National Liberation Front, the Anti-Fascist Committee of the Struggle for Peace, and the Communist Party competed for the chance to save their country.

It was not easy for Rumanians to see with any clarity in the midst of terrible and extreme political and social decomposition. The fear of Russia, on the one hand, blocked Communist influence; on the other, the same fear caused Rumanians to affirm Communism as the one means of escape from total dismemberment, believing it the better part of valor to give themselves up to the mercies of a victorious Soviet Union which indeed would have a vital say in the future political and social organization of the Balkans.

Bulgaria's position as Hitler's satellite was rendered even more desperate by the death of King Boris in 1943. Boris had tried to convince his people, despite close military and economic collaboration and despite the benefits received by this collaboration, that Bulgaria was not a part of the Axis. He managed for three years to reduce Bulgaria's participation in the war to the harsh, merciless policing of the conquered Greeks and Serbs. The country benefited by territorial gains in Macedonia and Greece—King Boris assured his subjects of a "most advantageous" position—and by paper profits through increased exports to Germany. Boris, in short, kept a warring nation out of the war: the Bulgarians have done no fighting and their country's economy is intact.

Indeed, all would have been serene but for memories of the past that troublesomely intruded on their present satisfactions. In the past they chose the losing side, and they worried lest World War II prove no exception. Boris and his propagandists tried to reassure them, pointing out that the increasing extermination of the Serbs—massacred by both the Axis and the Croatian Ustashi— would make the Bulgarians the most numerically important Slavs in the Balkans. The implication was that the outcome of the war would not be nearly as relevant as this fact.

Boris' cunning was employed in a twofold task: he was attempting to reassure the Bulgarians of a bright future, and he was doing his very best to convince Hitler that Bulgaria had already contributed all that she was able to contribute to an Axis victory.

Undoubtedly Boris was the shrewdest statesman in the Balkans, perhaps in all Europe. The list of those whom he outwitted during his quarter-century reign is a long one.

For years he used his personal charm and eloquence to convince both French and British diplomats and newspapermen that his only aim was to guard Bulgaria's neutrality. When he spoke to the French or to the British, he was always anxious to emphasize that on his mother's side he was a descendant of Louis-Philippe, the last Bourbon king of France. When he talked to the Germans, however, he quite naturally became a Saxe-Coburg. As to the Bulgarians, he continually insisted that he would never repeat the tragic blunder of his father, Ferdinand, who brought Bulgaria into the First World War on Germany's side.

He had long been preparing the Bulgarian-Yugoslav rapprochement with Alexander of Yugoslavia. This rapprochement resulted in a pact of "eternal" Bulgarian-Yugoslav friendship. It lasted just five years.

Boris could boast of having outwitted even the Vatican. When he married Victor Emmanuel's daughter, he promised the Vatican that only the heir-apparent would be Orthodox, while the other children would be Catholic. However, as his first child was a daughter, and he could not risk waiting for a son, who arrived four years later, he made her Orthodox, despite the protests of the Vatican.

Boris, always extremely publicity-minded, launched the quip about himself that in a country in which the army was pro-German, the peasants pro-Russian and the queen pro-Italian, he was the only pro-Bulgarian. And indeed, he succeeded in making many Bulgarians believe that he alone could guarantee for Bulgaria the most advantageous position at the lowest possible price. However, his greatest diplomatic achievement was the maintenance of relations with the Soviet Union. To obtain Hitler's authorization not to break Bulgarian-Soviet relations, he used the legend that the Bulgarians would never fight Russia, although they certainly fought her in the last war. As compensation he declared war on the United States, not anticipating that this distant enemy would send Liberators to bomb his capital.

Boris valued his relations with the Soviet Union so highly that he maintained one of his most trusted men there: Ivan Stamenov, who was sent to Russia in 1940, and who was his special adviser on foreign policy. Boris had professed for many years that he and his country had nothing to fear from the Soviet Union. Communism, he declared, could not succeed in an agricultural country like Bulgaria. But reports from Bulgaria indicate the steady progress of the *Bulgarska Rabotnicheska Partia* (Bulgarian Communist Party), which naturally is illegal, but which already numbers 50 per cent of the Bulgarian workmen. The progress of the Communists is especially rapid in Macedonia, northern Bulgaria, and Plovdiv, and they could claim credit for some of the most important acts of sabotage committed in Bulgaria. Executing the instructions of the Central Committee, the Communists have, since March 1942, joined the Bulgarian official youth association *Branik,* organized by Boris on the pattern of Hitler's *Jugend* and the Fascist *Balillas.*

However, Boris was not a man to be frightened by Communist progress in his own country. He undoubtedly believed that his secret police along with his army were strong enough to prevent any outbreaks of large-scale revolt. His main domestic aim was to keep the peasants satisfied by furnishing them all essential commodities at a low cost. Low prices were managed with the help of a special sinking fund, constituted by taxes on goods exported to Germany at high prices in Bulgarian paper levas.

One of the paradoxes of Boris' cunning foreign policy was that he tolerated the ideological foothold of the Soviet Union in Bulgaria to maintain diplomatic relations with her. Boris was only too well aware of the danger which his country, and particularly himself, would face at the hour of Hitler's defeat. He was consequently very shrewdly preparing his diplomatic reassurances. His minister to London, Momchilov, after Bulgaria's declaration of war against Great Britain, resigned and stayed on in London where he conceivably might be in an advantageous position to render precious service to Bulgaria if England has a decisive voice in the organization of Southeastern Europe. Should the political future of the Balkans be determined by Moscow, however, Boris would still have a chance, no matter how slight—for he would be able to present to Moscow a record of the best possible relations with the Soviet Union.

Bulgarian propaganda, with Boris as its supreme chief for the past twenty-five years, was highly successful until 1943. The Bulgarians succeeded in creating in certain American circles a reputation as "Balkan underdogs" who in peacetime are abused by their neighbors and in wartime by their rulers. The Serbs, for example, have always been so sure of the integrity of their cause and so suspicious of the intentions of other countries that they sometimes estranged their most valuable foreign friends by unjustified harshness. The Bulgarians, on the other hand, realized the controversial aspects of their cause, and strove continually to gain as many friends as possible by very skillful propaganda, either direct or indirect.

The supreme ambition of Boris was to see his dynasty, even before his country, harvest the fruits of Bulgarian propaganda, as well as to make credible the legend that he was not responsible for Bulgaria's stand in this war, that he was a victim of his pro-Nazi high officers. After giving Hitler all aid short of actual fighting, Boris stalled for time. In July 1943 his agents in Switzerland spread the fantastic rumor of a conflict between Boris and his Prime Minister, Bogdan Philov, whom Boris had allegedly accused of being responsible for dragging Bulgaria into the war on the losing side. A conflict between the shrewd king and this archeologist who had neither political ideas nor principles could only be likened to a conflict between a cat and a mouse.

The premature and mysterious death of Boris in September 1943 put an end to the prodigious career of Europe's most enterprising statesman, who for years had amazed all of Europe, his own people, and perhaps even himself by his incredible performances on the diplomatic tight rope. The Bulgars lost in Boris their main centralizing factor. They were much more divided on internal policies than their Serbian neighbors. Their dream of greater Bulgaria which they realized under the Axis may still exist for them as a point of concentration. They know, however, that this "great Bulgaria" will disappear with the Axis, and those among them who

can read the diplomatic skies wonder what will become of even
the more modest, prewar Bulgaria.

Boris' son, a helpless six-year-old child, Boris' brother Cyril,
a political and moral nonentity and a Balkan-style playboy to
whom even the official leadership of the Red Cross could not be
entrusted, and Boris' sister Eudoxie who next to Boris possessed
the best political mind of the family but who had no backing in
the country—none of these will be able to save either the dynasty
or Bulgaria. The German dynasty of Coburg, which twice within
a generation brought Bulgaria into the war on the losing side, was
indeed doomed.

As to Bulgaria, her future was more nebulous than ever. Very
likely Moscow, which still had its envoy in Sofia, knew more about
the nation's future than Washington or London. The renewed
bombings of Sofia were hard blows to the already shattered morale
of the Bulgarians. Their main hope, if not their only one, was the
Soviet Union. For one of the Soviet's international chiefs was
the Bulgarian Communist, George Dimitrov, leading figure in the
Reichstag fire trial, who the Bulgarians hoped would become their
advocate at the peace table.

Turkey entered the present war as a non-belligerent ally of
Britain and France. In 1940, after the collapse of France, she
began to exchange her status of non-belligerent ally for that of
benevolent neutral. In 1941, three days before the German aggression on Russia, Turkey signed a friendship treaty with Germany
and became neutral. Throughout 1942 Turkey remained "correctly
neutral" while closely watching military developments in both
hemispheres.

After the Casablanca Conference in 1943, when Churchill went
to Adana to confer with President Ismet Inonu, Turkey reaffirmed
her neutrality but added the old note of benevolence. After the
Allied victory in Tunisia, Turkish neutrality became increasingly
benevolent while remaining officially quite correct. And after the
Cairo talks of December 1943 between Roosevelt, Churchill, and
Inonu, it seemed certain that the days of Turkish neutrality were
numbered. The Turks had no particular desire to abandon their

status of neutrality which, owing to the incomparable shrewdness and skill of their diplomacy, had insured them the greatest possible advantages. But with the war entering its final stage, and with its outcome ever more certain, they were brought to the conclusion that cautious and intelligent neutrality, which assures unquestionable advantages in wartime, pays no dividends at peace conference negotiations. On the contrary, the neutrals may suddenly discover at the end of the war that the delayed bill for their neutrality expenses may exceed the dividends which they cashed during the war years.

Turkey was certainly not too anxious to apply for membership in the United Nations. She knew by the experience of her two allies of the Balkan Entente (Greece and Yugoslavia) that the membership dues in the United Nations were high and had to be paid in "blood, sweat, and tears." The supreme task of Turkish diplomacy was consequently to delay as long as possible the hour of final decision, and to reduce the United Nations' membership dues to a strict minimum. From this point of view, Turkish diplomacy might indeed be satisfied with its record.

In June 1939 Turkey signed friendship treaties with Britain and France, which resulted in important British loans and the cession by France of the Sandjak of Hatay with Alexandretta harbor. In October of the same year she concluded a mutual assistance pact with those two powers, mainly as assurance against possible unpleasant consequences of the Soviet-German pact of August 1939. In January 1941, after talks between Anglo-Turkish general staffs, the Turkish press not only emphasized that Turkey would defend her borders but stressed that Bulgaria and Greece were being considered by Turkey as her "vital defense zone." But in February 1941, Turkish diplomats signed a non-aggression pact with Bulgaria. And on March 24, 1941, Turkey obtained assurances from the Soviet Union of complete neutrality, based on the Soviet-Turkish pact of 1925. Three months later she signed her friendship pact with Germany.

In 1941 Turkey, exporting tobacco, fruits, vegetable oils, and a certain amount of copper to Germany, also promised to deliver to her precious chrome which had hitherto gone to Great Britain and the United States. Germany was to get 90,000 tons of chrome, half of which was to be shipped in the first three months of 1943. But the Turks stipulated that before the shipments were to begin, Germany should supply them with $18,000,000 worth of arms and munitions. As it turned out, Germany was unable to deliver. While Turkey was embarking on this deal, she was the recipient of American Lend-Lease.

Turkey's main advantage, of course, has not been assured by her skillful diplomacy. Rather it is the result of the basically opposed moral attitudes of the two sets of belligerents. Turkey lived for more than three years fearing possible Axis aggression; but the Turks always knew that the Allies would not force a passage through Turkey, even though such a military action would hasten Hitler's defeat by as much as a whole year. Though there has been some justifiable impatience both in Britain and the Soviet Union over the persistence of Turkish neutrality, and though echoes of it have sometimes been heard in the United States, on the whole Turkish foreign policy has been understood in Washington. It was known there that Turkish public opinion, while approving government efforts to keep the country out of the war, hopefully anticipated the victory of the United Nations. It was known also that Marshal Cakmak, chief of the Turkish General Staff, never lost confidence in Great Britain, not even in the darkest days of 1940-41. It was known, furthermore, that Turkey's chief worry, her uncertainty over Moscow's postwar aims, was one of the main reasons for her hesitation in joining the United Nations.

It was very hard for Turkey to make this decision. In 1943 the Turks felt reasonably sure that the threat of German aggression had passed. On the other hand, they knew that they had no territorial aspiration to satisfy by their participation in the war. Certain Turkish circles may have toyed with the idea that a show of tough, unyielding neutrality would ultimately result in the cession of the Dodecanese Islands as payment for their final participation in the war. Even if such an idea had found sympathetic ears in Britain, it could hardly be acceptable to the United States. Turkey may have historic claims upon the Dodecanese Islands, now an Italian possession, but their population is overwhelmingly Greek and their cession to Turkey would be in contradiction to the principles of the Atlantic Charter.

In the fall of 1943, the Soviet Union grew especially impatient over Turkish hesitation, and Soviet diplomacy decided to exert pressure on her. *War and the Working Class,* most aggressive of Soviet publications, warned the Turks in unequivocal terms.

After the Moscow Conference, Anthony Eden invited Turkish Foreign Minister Numan Menemencioglu to Cairo. Eden spoke not as Britain's Foreign Minister but as a representative of the Big Three. He explained the general diplomatic and strategic situation and requested that Menemencioglu inform the Allies whether Turkey intended to live up to her treaty with Britain in helping to shorten the war. Eden was not as categoric as the Russians wanted and expected him to be. He left the choice between active participation in the war and a "Portuguese-style" assistance, that is, putting Turkish bases at the Allies' disposal, and allowing the Allied Navy the use of the Straits.

The Turks were evasive. They explained they were very anxious to live up to their agreements but, they pointed out, they required guarantees of both a military and political character. Istanbul, a city of wooden structures, would be an easy prey for Nazi bombers based in neighboring Bulgaria. They required reassurances and guarantees that after the war the Soviet Union would respect Turkish possession of the Straits.

The Teheran Conference, with its pledge to respect the independence of Iran, served as a basis for the moral guarantee which Turkey wanted from the United Nations. Roosevelt and Churchill gave Inonu all the assurances he wanted in Cairo. If the Soviet Union was inclined to respect, along with Great Britain, the freedom of the land route to India, there was no reason why she could not, and would not, respect the sea route from the Black Sea to the Mediterranean. Despite all these new assurances, Turkey refused to reconsider her neutrality. Her attitude resulted in a deterioration of her relations with Washington and London. But she tried to increase her security by improving her relations with the Soviet Union.

Turkish-Soviet relations were consequently expected to improve. They were on the road to recovering the cordiality of past days when Kemal Ataturk, who hung his own Communists, had cooperated closely with Moscow in international politics. Furthermore, Turkey was alert to Soviet policy in the Near East. She has always feared Soviet interest in Arab problems, and has little sympathy for a Pan-Arabic Federation. When a nephew of the Mufti of Jerusalem arrived in Istanbul in 1942, the Turks, not caring for the idea of pro-Arab agitation on their soil, requested that he and his friends leave for Greece. Turkey lives in a nightmare of finding herself squeezed between the Soviet Union and a Pan-Arab Federation, particularly if they should be mutually sympathetic.

The great hope of the Turks has always been the restoration of the prewar Balkan Entente, which would eventually lead to a Balkan Federation. Kemal Ataturk and King Alexander of Yugoslavia laid the cornerstone for such a federation. The Turks hoped for the realization of this cherished scheme, but their awareness of international complications and their first-hand experience in power politics made them regard with skepticism the possibilities of realizing it.

If, in the future, the liberated Balkan nations are given the freedom to determine their own policy, they will undoubtedly agree on the necessity and desirability of restoring the Balkan Entente, with its own Monroe Doctrine—the Balkans for the Balkan peoples! Whether they will have that freedom is a question that can only be answered on a world scale.

XI: Arab Aspirations and World Politics

THE problems of Eastern Europe constitute a sore spot on the United Nations' "inside front." But there are equally grave problems still farther to the East, and solving them is a matter of vital concern for all the United Nations.

The arrival of American forces in North Africa brought the United States in direct contact with the Arab-Moslem world. For the first time America faced the religious, intellectual, and social center of the 275,000,000 Moslems in Asia and in Africa, with ramifications in the Balkans.

The war brought American forces to the Near East. The 1,200-mile pipeline which the United States government plans to build for the exploitation of American-owned oilfields in Saudi-Arabia and in Kuwait and Bahrein at the Persian Gulf might call American forces back to the Near East for the defense of vital American economic interests in the postwar world. However, the Near East is not only the world's greatest oil depository by which the United States can replenish its domestic reserves, threatened by exhaustion within the coming decades. The Near East is also the crossroads for naval and air communications between the three continents of the Eastern hemisphere. If the United States intends to take her place in postwar international communications, she will have to assure for her ships and clippers the right to use naval and air bases in the Near East.

For the time being, most of those bases are directly or indirectly controlled by the British. If the Italians are not allowed to return to Libya after the war, the British and perhaps the French will control the most important air and naval bases in this part of the world. The British, moreover, control the greatest part of the fabulous Near Eastern oil reserves. Therefore the British view without enthusiasm America's increasing interest in Near Eastern affairs. Intelligent Englishmen realize that in the long run they will certainly benefit by American interest in this area. The day may not be far away when Britain will welcome American participation in the exploitation of Near Eastern oilfields and air and naval bases for their adequate defense against any external threats or any internal troubles. But the immediate reaction is that of traditional British opposition to a young, active, enterprising, and powerful competitor who could threaten what has amounted to an economic and political monopoly which Great Britain has been able to maintain between two wars in the Near East.

Germany, which in both wars eyed Bagdad—once the terminal of the projected transcontinental railway Berlin-Bagdad—will be eliminated from the Near East. And Italy has discovered that her Libyan and Ethiopian Empire, of which her Fascist regime was so boastful, has been built on sand.

France will maintain her position in North Africa. But she is far less certain of preserving her influence in Syria and Lebanon, where the British might believe it would serve their interest to support and control the aspirations of the Syrians and the Lebanese, who with increasing impatience claim independence of French rule.

Prior to the present war the United States was not directly interested in the Near East. Americans looked at these lands through the eyes of missionaries or oil men. For many younger Americans, moreover, the Near East is still veiled in the romanticism of Lawrence of Arabia. This American approach to the Near East had a humanitarian, economic, and sentimental basis, but was devoid of political implications. It contained no imperialistic threat. It created a reservoir of good will toward the United States on the one hand, and on the other hand inspired many illusions in the minds of Near Eastern populations.

The present war, which for the first time in history brought American soldiers into contact with the peoples of the Near East, has made serious leaks in the reservoir of good will and destroyed some of the illusions fostered until lately in the peoples of this area. Soldiers are generally less pleasant and more troublesome visitors than missionaries, college teachers, oil prospectors, and even journalists. But many Near Eastern peoples still believe that the United States, which for so many years played Santa Claus in the Near East by bringing hospitals and schools to them, will after the war bring something more precious than public health and education—political independence and freedom from want. This political independence was pledged by the United States to the people of both the Near and Far East when Roosevelt and Churchill met with Chiang Kai-shek in Cairo and Stalin in Teheran.

From Cairo, hub of the Moslem world, the Charter of Freedom came to five hundred million people in Eastern Asia, among whom are fifteen million Moslems in China and fifty million Moslems in the East Indies. And the pledge given at the Teheran Conference to Iran, when the United States endorsed the British and Soviet promise to respect the postwar independence of Iran, has reinforced the confidence of the Near East, which looks toward the United States as a fair and powerful referee in their conflict with the Western powers.

However, the United States has not been viewed since 1943 by Near Eastern peoples as the only possible referee. Another potential referee, the Arabs believe—less fair, perhaps, but possibly more powerful because of its proximity to them—has appeared on the troubled political horizons of the Near East. After twenty-five years of absence Russia made a triumphant re-entry into that area, in which her influence had once been very great. After having consolidated her traditional influence in Northern Persia, the Soviet Union opened an important Legation in Cairo, which is soon to be followed by Soviet diplomatic representation at Bagdad, Damascus, and Beirut.

The conference of all Moslems living in the Soviet Union, which took place early in 1944 at Tashkent, was widely commented upon in the Near Eastern press, which increased its space allotments for Soviet war communiqués and Tass dispatches. While Moscow can make use of the All-Slav Congress for Eastern Europe, nothing, indeed, prevents her from reserving a similar part to be played in the Near East by the numerous Moslem national groups in the Soviet Union.

The Soviet Union is no longer looked upon by the Arab people as a Communist state. The Arabs think of Russia much more in terms of power politics than of ideology. They believe that Great Britain's days as the great power of the Near East are numbered, and that only two really great powers will emerge after the war:

the United States and the Soviet Union. The United States is too far away from them. The Soviet Union is closer, and consequently they look to Moscow as the capital of "the great state of tomorrow."

Britain's main supporters in the Near East have been feudal landowners, often more anxious to defend their economic and social interests than to realize the national aspirations of their peoples. The Soviet Union, which once believed that it could raise against those landowners the discontented peasantry, knows now that she cannot expect much from the inert, unorganized, illiterate, and often fanatical masses, who are distrustful of any foreign element.

The new supporters of the Soviet Union in the Near East are to be found among the nationalist Arab youth, which has not been seduced by Communistic propaganda. But this Arab youth appears to be impressed by the new military prestige of the Soviet Union, and sees in the new Soviet constitution, with its solution of the nationalities problem, a real power of attraction. It must be recalled that the Arab youth has never known a really liberal approach to political and social problems. Democracy—which for Egyptian and Iranian intellectuals was personified by France—was defeated in 1940. Britain is in the eyes of the Near Eastern populations an imperialist oppressor. The United States is for them the "ideal democracy," though it may revert to its former isolationism. The Soviet Union offers them an attractive combination of socialist and nationalist factors. If the United States fails, they believe that the Soviet Union should help them to obtain after this war the realization of the promises made to them by the British during the last war, and which continue to be unfulfilled. Consequently, they look to the United States and the Soviet Union for the materialization of their aspirations.

What are those unfulfilled British promises, and what are the Arab aspirations?

There are three British "promises" in the Arab dossier. In 1915 Sir Henry McMahon, British Commissioner in Egypt, who prepared the Arab revolt against the Turks, wrote a series of letters to Hussein, Sherif and Emir of Mecca and great-grandfather of the present boy king, Faisal II of Iraq. In those letters, handed to Emir Hussein by Lawrence of Arabia, Great Britain expressed a readiness to recognize Arab independence in territories in which Britain was "free to act without detriment to France." Those territories were in an area stretching east to the Iranian borders and south and west to the Indian Ocean, the Red Sea, and the Mediterranean, with the exception of the possessions of Syria lying to the west of the districts of Damascus, Homs, Hama, and Aleppo. The text of those letters have since been variously interpreted by Britain and by the Arabs.

In the summer of 1918 seven Arab leaders domiciled in Cairo sent a memorandum to the British government asking British guarantees of postwar Arab independence. The memorandum of the seven Arabs begged for a "clear and comprehensive" definition of British policy with regard to the future of the Arab countries as a whole. The British government answered that Britain would work for the liberation of Syria, Palestine, and Iraq from Turkish rule and "would assure the freedom and independence of those countries." It even pledged that "no regime would be set up in any of them which was not acceptable to their populations." In November 1918 a joint Anglo-French declaration proclaimed the identity of French and British war aims in the Near East, and defined those aims as the "complete and final liberation" of the populations living under the Turkish yoke. The Arabs were assured that they would have "national governments chosen by themselves in the free exercise of their will."

However, when Prince Faisal, younger son of the Emir Hussein, arrived at the Peace Conference in Paris as chief spokesman of the Arab cause in behalf of his father, he encountered three main influences which were opposed to the realization of Arab aspirations. British imperialistic interests in Iraq and Palestine, French imperialistic interests in Syria, and Zionist interests in Palestine were not co-ordinated. Each opposed in varying degrees, however, the realization of the promises so generously given by the British to Hussein and Faisal during the First World War.

While Faisal was in Paris, the British set up administrations deriving their immediate authority from the military command in Syria, Palestine, and Iraq. Iraq was treated as one unit and placed under a single administration, with a British civil commissioner at its head. The remainder of this territory was divided into three parts, comprising Palestine in approximately its present frontiers under British control, the interior of Syria from Aqaba to Aleppo under Arab control, and thirdly, the Lebanese and Syrian seaboard from Tyre to the confines of Cilicia under French control.

In these areas, however, Great Britain and France had acquisitive designs which seemed to be foreshadowed in their administrative arrangements. Before going to Paris, Faisal visited London, where he was informed that the French government had taken strong exception to his administration of the Syrian area to the east of the territories under French control. He was further informed that the French objected to the proposal that he represent his father's independent Arab kingdom of the Hejaz at the Peace Conference. Finally, he found himself the target of a determined offensive in London on the subject of Palestine. Faisal's position was a very difficult one. His friends in Whitehall pressed him to endorse British and French plans which were not only extraneous to the summary instructions issued to him by his father, but which were also in conflict with the general and somewhat inflamed feeling already aroused in Syria by Anglo-French policy. Faisal allowed himself to be persuaded that his chances to defend himself against the French would be greater if he could satisfy to the fullest possible extent all British wishes.

In January 1919 in Paris, Faisal presented the Arab case in a brief statement and in a longer address before the Peace Conference. He emphasized the principle laid down in the Anglo-French agreement of "the consent of the governed" and took his stand on the McMahon pledges and the Anglo-French Declaration. From the outset his arguments met with temporizing and constant opposition, and finally in April he sailed for Syria to resume control of affairs at Damascus pending further developments. In Damascus he found the Arabs restless and anxious about their future. A group of responsible Arab leaders came forward with a proposal for the formation of a national assembly. Elections were held in haste. The opening session was attended by 69 out of a total of 85 elected delegates representing Syria and Palestine, whose deliberations resulted in a set of resolutions defining the national aims of Syria, Palestine, and Iraq, which were passed with almost unqualified unanimity. These resolutions recognized the independence of Syria—in which Palestine as part of Vilayet was included—as a sovereign state with the Emir Faisal as King, and recognized at the same time the independence of Iraq.

Neither the French nor the British were disposed to accept those resolutions. In August 1919 Faisal was invited to visit Europe once more. Further negotiations between the French and British took place. Yielding to pressure, Faisal finally agreed at the end of November 1919 to accept a provisional Franco-Arab arrangement which recognized French occupation of the Lebanon and the rest of the coastal regions of Syria as far north as Alexandretta and agreed also that the Arab state to the east of those regions would henceforth turn to France for "any assistance it might require."

By signing this agreement, which meant nothing less than the dismemberment of Syria, Faisal weakened his position in the eyes of the Arab world; and at the same time he weakened his position with the French and British by his persistent claims to control the eastern portions of Syria. When he returned to Syria he was coldly received by the Syrians and finally accepted the resolution of the general Syrian Congress, passed on March 8, 1920, proclaiming the independence of Syria, Palestine, and Lebanon as a sovereign state and a constitutional monarchy with Faisal as King. At the same time a meeting of Iraqi leaders had passed a similar resolution concerning Iraq and chose the Emir Abdullah, Faisal's brother, as its first monarch.

The Arabs believed that they had thus blocked the imperialistic designs of Britain and France. But in April 1920 the final blow to Arab aspirations came with the establishment of a French mandate over Syria and Lebanon, and British mandates over Palestine and Iraq.

Unrest mounted throughout the Arab world. Faisal was urged to attack and drive the French out of Syria. The French prevented the revolt by ousting Faisal. On July 14, 1920, the French presented Faisal with an ultimatum demanding military control over the Rayaq-Aleppo railway, reduction of the Arab Army, unqualified acceptance of the French mandate, and adoption of the French currency system. Faisal accepted, but the French General Gouraud nevertheless occupied Damascus and requested that Faisal leave the territory immediately. He complied on July 28, 1920. With the flight of Faisal the aspiration of the Arabs for independence and the establishment of an Arab state or federation of states came to an end. Faisal was finally persuaded to accept the crown of Iraq under British mandate. His brother, the Emir Abdullah, became ruler of Transjordania, a tract of land to the east of the Jordan River and the Dead Sea.

The Arabs believed that their cause was flagrantly betrayed by the British. They lived in an atmosphere of deep-rooted suspicion of French and British interests in the Near East. They could not, on the other hand, arrive at an agreement with the Zionists on the Jewish problem in Palestine. Indeed, only one genuine attempt was made to do so when in 1919 King Faisal and the Zionist leader, Dr. Weizmann, tried to find a common ground of understanding. It is therefore the more astonishing that, living with those accumulated grievances which have been most skillfully and constantly exploited by Axis propaganda, the Arab leaders in the Near East, with the exception of the Mufti of Jerusalem and his supporters in Palestine, and Rashid Ali Gailani and his friends in Iraq, remained generally deaf to the seductive appeals of the Axis.

The Arab leaders tried to credit themselves with the fact that even in the darkest hours of this war they believed in the final victory of the United Nations. On the other hand, though they were deceived by the Allies in World War I, they believed that this time the principles of the Atlantic Charter would be applied not only in countries bordering on the Atlantic Ocean but also along the shores of the Mediterranean Sea.

All Arabs are agreed upon the necessity of independence for Arab lands. Some would welcome a unified Arab empire or kingdom. Others would prefer to win individual independence for separate Arab states as a step toward a federation. Many have come to the conclusion that they cannot fulfill what they believe to be their historic mission unless they are strong—and they realize that they can be strong only in unity. Many Arabs are convinced that their domination by Western powers is no longer a necessity and should therefore no longer be tolerated. The Arab nations, they believe, could and should assume responsibility over their destinies. Their unity would make this task much easier.

The rising standard of education in Arab countries has made the Arabs increasingly conscious of their common heritage in language and culture. Frustrated economically and politically after the last war, the Arabs have developed a passionate desire to prevent such frustration after this war.

The urge for Arab unity, which began to develop in the latter part of the nineteenth century, expressed itself at the Arab Conference in Paris in 1913 and the conference in Damascus in 1919 —both landmarks in the history of the movement. But the mandatory regimes during the period between 1921 and 1939 stimulated narrow local nationalisms—Iraq for the Iraqis, Syria for the Syrians. They retarded but did not altogether halt the trend toward unity.

London and Paris did not view this Arab trend with much sympathy. Arab unity might well represent a threat to British and French oil interests and to imperial communications. Recently the British appear to have had a change of heart. In the spring of 1941 Anthony Eden declared that Britain would favor Arab unity if the initiative were taken by the Arabs themselves. Immediately discussions were opened in each of the Arab lands. Statesmen and their emissaries traveled from one country to the other, sounding out leading Arabs as to their views on federation. Several conferences were held in Egypt, where delegates from all Arab lands came to exchange their views.

The recent Lebanese crisis has called the attention of the West to the growing desire on the part of the Arabs to realize their dreams of independence. These troubles, at the same time, have helped to stimulate among the Arabs ideas of solidarity. Broadly speaking, thoughts on Arab unity have oscillated between two extreme views: the "Pan-Islamic" and the "Cultural Alliance."

The Pan-Islamic view calls for the unity of 50,000,000 Arabs from the shores of the Atlantic to Iran. This would be only the first step, however, toward the eventual cohesiveness of all the 275,000,000 Moslems in Asia and Africa. The Axis has favored this view, which also has been championed by a number of reactionary and uncompromising religious leaders opposed to all Western and Christian thought. They would favor a return to the Caliphate and elimination of all Western influence from the Moslem world.

The Cultural Alliance represents the opposite extreme. Its partisans favor an organization of the present Arab countries into small but independent states joined by loose cultural bonds. They argue that this organization can best preserve the individuality of many contending minority groups in Arab lands and prevent dangerous clashes.

Between these two extremes lie most of the schemes which have been advanced recently by different Arab leaders. Some Arab nationalists favor a federation that would be built up only gradually. They would begin by bringing together Syria, Lebanon, Palestine, and Transjordania. This federation would later be linked by economic and, if possible, political ties to larger Arab states such as Iraq, Saudi-Arabia, and eventually Egypt. Special measures would be drafted to take care of the Jewish minority in Palestine and the Christian minorities in Lebanon. A second group favors a larger federation which from its inception would include Iraq and, if possible, all free Arab states to the south on the Arabian peninsula. A third group has more ambitious plans for a cultural and economic federation which would embrace all Arab states from the Atlantic to the Iranian border, the Persian Gulf and the Indian Ocean. This federation would include all Arab states in North Africa from Morocco eastward, as well as Egypt and various states in Syria, Mesopotamia, and Arabia proper.

It is interesting to note that while the British and French mandatory regimes have worked against Arab unity by stimulating local nationalisms, the British-American Middle East Supply Council, which devoted a great part of its activity to the co-ordination and rationalization of the economic effort in the Near East, contributed to the establishment of an economic solidarity in the Moslem world by focusing the attention of Arab leaders upon the economic interdependence of their various states.

The extent and form of future Arab federation is but one of the two fundamental problems which confront Arab nationalism. The other problem is that of leadership within the movement itself.

This is a delicate problem which obviously will be conditioned—among other considerations—by the boundaries of the future federation.

Several families in the Near East aspire to that leadership. The Hashimite family of the Sherif of Mecca includes King Faisal II of Iraq, his uncle-cousin the Regent Abdul Ilah, as well as the Emir Abdullah of Transjordania. This is one of the oldest families in the Arab world, which can trace its origins to the Prophet and is closely associated with the Arab nationalist movement. There is secondly the mighty figure of King Ibn Saud of Saudi-Arabia, often described as the great leader of Puritanism in the Moslem world. Finally there is the royal family of Egypt with King Farouk, who would not decline the honor of heading an Arab federation.

The clash of personalities among the Arab leaders is a powerful factor working against the successful federation of Arab states. These leaders do not know one another well enough, and many of them mistrust each other. Ibn Saud is suspicious of the Egyptian Premier, Nahas Pasha, and of the Iraqi Premier, Nuri Pasha; he never fails to see the British imperial shadow back of them. Furthermore, the two Premiers are suspicious of each other. This conflict and mistrust goes beyond the leaders and touches the common people as well. The Arab by nature is individualistic. He has not yet succeeded in disciplining himself to the extent of submerging his individual interests to a larger cause.

There are at least five other factors working against the realization of Arab federation. The disparity in the degree of modernization has been called "the problem of the tent and the town." It involves the difficulty of finding the same economic ground and a common cultural roof for the nomad of Transjordania or Saudi-Arabia and the settled man of Cairo, Beirut, or Jerusalem. Then there are narrow nationalisms and separatist movements fostered by mandatory regimes; the presence of the French in Syria and the Lebanon; and Zionist aspirations in Palestine, in spite of Zionist assurances that a Zionist Palestine would not block an Arab federation. Finally, the economic self-interests of large portions of the Arab world may dictate a policy of association with powers outside the orbit of that world. This is particularly true of the

North African Arab states such as Morocco, Tunisia, and Algeria, and somewhat true of Egypt and the Sudan.

Whether or not the Arab peoples are able to achieve their federation, some adequate solution of their complex problems—which will be examined in the following chapters—must be found if after the war the United Nations are to build a decent and lasting peace.

XII: *The Custodian of Unpaid Promises*

Iraq

IRAQ regards herself as the foremost champion of the Arab cause by virtue of her religious, cultural, political, and historical prestige. Bagdad, the capital, is an ancient intellectual and cultural center of the Arab-Moslem world. The ruling family, of the Hashimite dynasty, descends from the Prophet himself, and also from Emir Hussein. Hussein's descendants possess the promissory notes given by the British when Colonel Lawrence was preparing the revolt in Arabia. Some of these notes have been paid in part. Others have been completely forgotten by the British.

When Faisal lost his great Syrian kingdom, the British offered him as compensation the smaller kingdom of Iraq, under their mandate. This mandate over Iraq was endorsed with a guarantee of eventual independence. Faisal was formally proclaimed King in August 1921. His reign lasted for twelve years, until his death in September 1933.

Faisal was able to see Iraq through all the stages of her constitutional formation and political emancipation. This gradual process of emancipation was marked by the conclusion of treaties of alliance with Great Britain in October 1922, January 1926, December 1927, and June 1930. The decisive 1930 treaty, concluded at Bagdad, promised British sponsorship for admission of Iraq as a sovereign independent state to membership in the League of Nations—the treaty coming into force when Iraq was accepted by the League. In October 1932 Iraq was formally admitted by the unanimous vote of the fifty-two nations present.

Relations between Britain and Iraq's rulers had previously been entirely harmonious. But seeds of trouble had been sown. A conflict over national autonomy was developing between the Assyrian Christians settled near the northern frontiers of Iraq and the Moslem rulers in Bagdad. The uprising of the Assyrians, who as

Christians expected to be supported by the British, resulted in
their being savagely massacred by a small military clique in power
in Iraq. Suppression of the uprising was used by this clique to
establish military control over the kingdom. This miltiary control
created a chronic political instability through attempts to discredit
the Iraqi politicians. Anti-British feeling increased in the country,
as Bagdad became the heart and soul of the Arab nationalist movement. The death in 1939 of Faisal's son and successor, the young
King Ghazi, in an automobile accident did little to improve the
situation. He was succeeded by his infant son, the present boy
ruler, Faisal II, under the regency of his uncle, Abdul Ilah. The
pro-British Nuri-as-Said Pasha, who as Minister of the Interior had
bucked the dangerous intrigues of the Iraqi Chief of Staff in April
1939, became Minister of Foreign Affairs.

When the war began, Iraq, unlike Egypt, did not break diplomatic relations with Germany. The presence of Nuri in the government was considered by the British as sufficient assurance of Iraq's
benevolent neutrality. The German Legation at Bagdad, however,
was determined to capitalize the Arab resentment against the
British. They found a precious ally in the Grand Mufti of Palestine.
An intransigent Arab nationalist, the Grand Mufti fled Palestine,
and after his expulsion from Syria, took refuge in Iraq in 1940.
The combined propaganda effort of the German Legation and the
Grand Mufti, both equally eager to arouse discontent over British
influence throughout the Arab world, scored a success when the
pro-British Nuri Pasha found himself obliged to resign early in
1941 because of a conflict over the application of the Anglo-Iraq
treaty.

His successor, Rashid Ali Gailani, continued to do lip service
to the British, while secretly reversing Nuri's pro-British policy.
In May 1941, aided by a small group of senior army officers, Rashid
Ali prepared to throw Iraq wholeheartedly into the Axis camp.
The general revolt of the whole Arab-Moslem world was to begin
in Bagdad.

This revolt was undoubtedly encouraged by German military
successes and German propaganda. Basically, however, it was an
anti-British revolt. The British moved their forces into Iraq, restored Nuri Pasha, and gave to former pro-British elements a

precarious control over the restless, turbulent, and discontented people. Rashid Ali fled to Iran and, followed by the Grand Mufti, found refuge in Germany. From their new haven, through Nazi shortwave broadcasts, the two men tried to achieve those subversive objectives which they had failed to realize in Bagdad. To their surprise and chagrin, the broadcasts had an unexpected result: the Bagdad government accepted them as grounds for a declaration of war. It was the first time that radio broadcasts constituted a *casus belli.*

The pro-British cabinet of Nuri Pasha, pressed by the British, explained that the persistence of broadcasts hostile to Iraq and its interests was evidence that Germany was attempting to create "differences and disunity" among sections of the population, and was endangering public peace and order. The Iraq government could therefore not tolerate the use on the air of "expressions prejudicial to the honor of the Royal Family," designed to undermine their prestige as well as public morale. Neither could the Iraq government tolerate the encouragement given by Nazi Germany to Iraq's exiled politicians "to overthrow by force of arms the constitutional system of their own country." As a result, Iraq declared war on Germany, applying for admission to the United Nations. Since her admission in January 1943, Iraq has considered herself the most appropriate champion of the Arab cause before the Western powers. But the interests and aims of Iraq cannot be understood without a proper understanding of the country and its people.

Iraq is a land of striking antitheses which constantly affect the mentality of all groups and classes living within its boundaries. There is the eternal contrast between cultural traditions of a fabulous antiquity, dating back to before the glorious days of the Caliphate, and the limited political experience of a people inured for thousands of years to a succession of Oriental despots. The fabulous antiquity has created a sense of extended intellectual and religious continuity. The lack of political experience—the Iraqi Arabs were emancipated only in 1919 from Turkish domination—prevents the people of Iraq from enjoying full sovereignty in an independent state of their own creation. Their pride in a great past is tempered with doubts in the present and anxiety over the future. Their cultural assurance is colored by a paradoxical sense of political insecurity.

The obvious desire of the Iraqi leaders to direct the Arab nationalist movement and their equally obvious determination to exert increasing intellectual and political control over the Arab-Moslem people reveal confidence and pride. But lack of stability and insecurity are clearly visible behind the rapid, successive cabinet changes, the various shifting pressure groups within them, the susceptibility of the different regimes to foreign influence, the bitter and fanatical hostility to Zionist claims. Political insecurity on the home front, however, cannot be explained by the absence of political experience alone. It is due, as well, to racial, cultural, and religious differences between Moslem Arabs and the minorities under their control, especially the Assyrians and the Kurdish tribesmen in the north. The serious conflicts between these minorities and their Arab rulers, however, are not as upsetting as the endless rivalries between the Moslems themselves.

The governing classes in Iraq are predominantly adherents of the Sunni (Orthodox Moslem), with Bagdad as the seat of its power. But the population in general favors the dissident Moslem doctrines of the Shiah, with its centers of Karbala, Nadjef, and Samarra, second in sacredness only to Mecca, and to which thousands of holy pilgrims go annually. Hostility between Sunni and Shiah is perpetually latent in Iraq, and could, with little provocation, cause grave political upheavals. It must be said in passing that these latent hostilities do not interfere with the fundamental unity of the Moslems when they are confronted by non-Moslem or foreign opposition; further, beneath the surface there is a fundamental religious unity centering around the cities of Mecca, Cairo, Damascus, and Jerusalem, places sacred to both sects. Sunni and Shiah, governors and governed, are further divided by economic and social cleavages that stem from the complicated Iraqi economy. Vast reaches of desert barely support a nomadic population of herdsmen who are disdainful of the sedentary agriculturalists— farmers who have tilled the soil in the rich, fertile valleys of the Tigris and Euphrates for more than a thousand years. In contrast to both nomads and farmers are the pleasure-loving urban classes of Bagdad, Basra, and Mosul. Desert wanderers are ruled by their shrewd and able sheiks; agricultural settlers, who form a semi-feudal and servile group, are dominated by a small number of powerful landowners. The urban masses are controlled by small political cliques in the larger cities. These social divisions, which cut clearly across economic distinctions, create a kaleidoscopic assortment of conflicting religious, economic, and social interests which have left an indelible impression on the temperament of the Iraqi people.

Cultural pride, religious zeal, mutual distrust, and class distinctions are the characteristic result. But the Iraqi virtues outweigh these faults. Though a great many Iraqi Arabs are illiterate, their leaders are progressive and genuinely anxious to weld disrupted elements into a homogeneous state. Most of these leaders are alert and highly intelligent, with enormous reserves of vitality —though, like many Arabs, they are sometimes reluctant to undergo sustained exertion of any sort. The Iraqi have a keen sense of humor, are brave, and with proper leadership make stern fighters.

The main task of Iraqi statesmanship is that of eliminating temperamental, economic, and political obstacles standing in the way of the nation's development. The national growth of Iraq, in turn, is bound together with the development of a healthy Arab nationalism. Two fundamental problems emerge: the extent and form which Arab nationalism is to assume in the political sphere, and who the men will be to guide the movement.

The royal family of the Sherif of Mecca claims leadership of the nuclear federation. As to the extent and form of this federation, Nuri Pasha advocates the union of Lebanon, Syria, Palestine, and Transjordania into a Greater Syria with close ties to Iraq. All other Arab nations would be free to join in a loose federation with this nucleus.

In 1943 Nuri Pasha conferred in Cairo with Nahas Pasha, the Egyptian Premier, and he also sent a cabinet minister to visit Syria, Palestine, and Transjordania. He has been extremely active in Cairo preparing the exchanges of views on Arab federation. He believes that Iraq's rank in the United Nations now makes it possible to present the promissory notes Iraq holds for payment at the "Atlantic Charter Bank"—the same notes they were unable to cash at Wilson's "Fourteen Points Clearing House."

Other Arab leaders naturally follow with interest the attempts of Nuri Pasha to obtain this long-overdue payment, and they will be delighted if he succeeds. It is far from certain, though, that they will be disposed to let him get control of leadership in the Arab federation for Iraq and the Hashimite family. Ibn Saud, king of independent Saudi-Arabia, has only limited confidence in Nuri Pasha. He also has little love for the Hashimite dynasty which he ousted from their original kingdom at Hejaz. Ibn Saud knows that Great Britain cannot completely abandon Iraq, first leg of the Empire's continental road to India, and depository of British-owned oilfields which, after the last war, the British guarded so jealously from their American and French partners. Ibn Saud believes there will be found, behind any federation scheme advocated by Nuri Pasha, the imperial shadow of England. And Ibn Saud, whose voice has many powerful echoes throughout the Arab world, is convinced that an Arab federation will be realized only when Arab nations are completely free.

XIII: Poet and Puppet

Abdullah of Transjordania

THE Hashimite family, custodians of the unpaid promises, claim that Iraq since 1932 has been an independent state. They cannot claim the same status for the tiny 4,700-square-mile state of Transjordania, carved out by the British in 1922 for Emir Abdullah, when the latter was obliged to cede his kingdom of Iraq to his brother Faisal, expelled by the French from Syria. Abdullah, in his own way, has been as closely identified with Arab nationalism as his father, Hussein, and his brother, Faisal. He spent his youth in Istanbul, where his family stayed for eighteen years as "guests" of the Sublime Porte. They were, in fact, hostages, designed to secure the loyalty of the Hashimite family to the Sultan. Following the Young Turks' Revolution in 1908, Abdullah and Faisal returned to Istanbul as representatives of Mecca and Jedda to the new Turkish Parliament. Elected Vice-President of the House, Abdullah championed the rights of the dissatisfied Arabs. When World War I broke out, he made contact with the British in Cairo and became, along with his father and brother, one of the most active and influential leaders of the Arab revolt, which also paved the way for the downfall of the Ottoman Empire.

T. E. Lawrence predicted that Abdullah would be politically more useful to British ends than the other members of the Hashimite family. Indeed, Abdullah got on quite well with the British, although he might have had grounds for resentment. For the British had failed to live up to any of the promises made to him, to his brother, and to his father. They had permitted the French to oust his brother from Syria in 1920, and in 1924 they had allowed Ibn Saud, Wahabi ruler of Nedj, to drive his father out of Hejaz which, since time immemorial, had been the domain of the Hashimite family.

As a matter of fact, Abdullah was more affected by the ousting of his brother than by the expulsion of his aged father. For with Faisal unseated, Abdullah was obliged to relinquish the throne of Iraq to his brother, even though he had been elected to it in 1920. The semi-independent Transjordania was very meager compensation for a man who had already seen himself as King of Iraq and who had been prepared to drive the French out of Syria. But being a very practical man, Abdullah accepted Transjordania. He let the British build for him on a hill near Amman—his capital, scarcely more than an oversized Arab village—a handsome palace which he covered with rows of lights so that it resembles a Coney Island amusement park. The $60,000 annuity which he receives from the British assured him a comfortable existence. He installed huge distorting mirrors inside his front halls so that he can "see his guests as they really are." When the venerable sheiks visit him, he mounts them on bicycles and speeds them down the palace halls.

A lavish entertainer, Abdullah has been criticized both at home and abroad for extravagance and misadministration. He is perpetually in debt, unable to pay his tradesmen, but determined to let the British solve all his financial problems. His extravagance led to a rebellion among the native tribes in 1923 which caused Great Britain, a year later, to take more direct control of the country. Since then his kingdom has been governed by the British as if it were a crown colony.

Abdullah gives the impression of being perfectly satisfied with the arrangement, and devotes most of his time to riding and to shooting; he owns one of the finest stables of Arab horses in the Near East, and he is a crack shot with rifle and revolver. He also writes flowery poems—he considers himself one of the greatest living Arab poets; and his published volume *Man Ana* (Who Am I?) traces the literary history of the Arabs from the time of the Prophet to the Emirat of his late father in Mecca. He plays chess for relaxation and is famous for his wit and keen sense of humor.

Behind this amiable exterior is concealed the mind of a perhaps naïve but certainly most ambitious politician. The oldest living member of the Hashimite family, Abdullah believes that both his rank and the fact of his being the only surviving participant in the British-Hashimite negotiations of World War I qualify him, rather than his nephews in Bagdad, to demand from Britain that they pay their long-overdue note. Furthermore, Abdullah is convinced that the Allies will win the war, a belief not shared by his Cambridge-educated son, Tallal.

Abdullah has never forgiven his brother for having taken away from him the kingdom of Iraq. He has no love for Faisal's descendants, but when they were forced to flee Iraq in 1941 because of the pro-Nazi coup of Rashid Ali Gailani, he gave asylum to the Regent, Abdul Ilah, and to other pro-British officials of Iraq. He issued proclamations denouncing Rashid Ali's conduct, and ordered the Transjordanian Arab Legion to aid in putting down the German-inspired insurrection.

His behavior was unequivocally pro-British despite the fact that he has an old personal account to settle with Winston Churchill. In 1921, when Abdullah was ready to move against the French, Churchill, then presiding as Colonial Secretary at a conference in Cairo, invited him to Jerusalem where he was given an ultimatum. He was to call off his attack against the French and renounce his claims to the Iraqi throne; the British in turn were to install him as ruler of the new state of Transjordania. Abdullah, never forgetting that Churchill had promised him the Iraqi throne, felt betrayed. But he undoubtedly felt that it was wisest to accept. As a consequence, Abdullah holds strong anti-British sentiments, but he has buried them deep, concentrating his hatred of the "Western traitors" openly on the French.

He apparently is extremely anxious to create for himself a perfect record which he expects one day to present at the peace table. He believes he will be in a position to remind Churchill that he had been promised Syria, if his conduct in Transjordania was compatible with British interests, and if his record shows evidence of unswerving loyalty to the British Empire during World War II. He has illusions that Britain will fulfill her World War I promises, and her claims for himself nothing less than the crown of an independent federated Arab state embracing Syria, Lebanon, Palestine, and Transjordania.

Abdullah is not very much concerned with the other Arab states. He would not object, however, to a unified block of Arab states around his "greater Syria." He believes that Great Britain, when the postwar talks occur, ought to disregard French claims to North Africa and Syria, and that a bloc of Arab states should be created under native "royal family" rule. This Arab bloc would be allied to the British Empire, which, in turn, would stand behind the Arab Federation. The British Navy would control the sea lanes from Gibraltar to the Red Sea, and then Abdullah would become the British Empire's powerful puppet ruler over the entire Arab world.

In his ambitious dreams, Abdullah has apparently forgotten the indignation created among the Arabs by the agreement he signed in 1928, which thoroughly subordinated Transjordania's political and economic life to British "advice." Abdullah was accused of betraying the oppressed Arabs in order to advance his own personal interests.

Ibn Saud, who has disliked Abdullah more than any other member of the rival Hashimite family, will exert all his power to block the ambitions of a man whom he has both distrusted and despised as a British puppet. Abdullah, on the other hand, is imbued with the importance of the services he has been rendering the British Empire. Used by the British as a buffer against the expansionist dreams of Ibn Saud, he believes that, with British support, he might become the most powerful factor in the Arab world. In all likelihood, he has been blinded by his poetic imagination and his swollen political ambitions. In spite of his excellence at the game of chess, he has forgotten, or failed to realize, that during recent years he has been nothing but a pawn in the British Near East diplomatic chess game. If the British have used him as a buffer against Ibn Saud, they indeed might use Ibn Saud at any moment against Abdullah, and freeze out his claims for control over the Federated Arab States.

Abdullah, however, has immediate and concrete objectives. He is convinced of his opportunity to become the ruler of the "United Kingdom of Syria." He tried to add to his British backing the friendship of the Turks, hoping to become a neighbor of theirs after the war. He has established contact with several Syrian politicians, and he has advanced and fostered the theory that the French mandate over Syria fell when France fell. In March 1943 he even issued a proclamation addressed to the Syrian nation, in which he brought out these fundamental points:

At the close of the last war, Arabs had relied upon the Allies in general, and Great Britain in particular, to make possible the establishment of an Arab state; under these circumstances the Arabs agreed to give every possible aid to the Allies during that conflict. At the end of the war the Allies set up the machinery for the creation of an independent Iraq, Nejd, and Yemen. But Syria was left disjointed and without adequate political unity, the result of conflicting imperialist interests. However, the Atlantic Charter has now paved the way for a revival of those claims first laid down by the Syrian Nationalist Congress in 1920. These aims must be realized under Hashimite leadership.

The Emir further took the liberty of inviting Syrian delegates to a conference to be held at Amman when and as said delegates should desire. Abdullah's proclamation makes clear that he conceives this new Syria as a kingdom which would include not only Syria and Lebanon, but Palestine and Transjordania as well.

Abdullah, who claims that he "technically" rules Palestine, also has definite views on the Jewish-Arab question. He did not allow the Jews to acquire land in Transjordania, and he has opposed the British policy of allowing increased Jewish immigration in Palestine. He is determined that the Jews shall have no place in Palestine, but he is willing to allow the Jews who are already there to remain, provided that further immigration be stopped immediately. On the other hand, he would permit the Jews self-government in localities where they are in the majority, and would give them representation in the single Parliament which he proposes for the four federated states of "United Syria."

However, even Abdullah's anti-Jewish attitude and his concern with creating the impression that he is a deeply religious man— he reads the Koran daily, ceremoniously attends the Yami-ul-Husseini mosque on Fridays, and criticizes King Farouk of Egypt for allowing his wife and sisters to go unveiled—do not win him the sympathies and confidence of the Syrian and Iraqi Arabs. His appeal to Syria had little or no effect and his relatives in Bagdad remained cool, while Ibn Saud shrugged his powerful shoulders. As to the Syrians, they elected Ibn Saud's close friend Shukri Quwatli as President of the Republic. He could have little sympathy for Abdullah. Quwatli is, indeed, in favor of a Great Syrian

Republic, in which there would be no room for Abdullah and his ambitions.

The French, suspicious since the last war of British attempts to drive them out of Syria, have been somewhat uneasy about Abdullah's appeal. They are worried over the possibility that British thinking may have directed the hand of the British puppet. The British, though, who know Abdullah's qualifications and limitations better than anyone else, have banned his appeal. They believe the poetic son of the Sherif of Mecca is under complete control. They have never been very much interested, nor are they now, in his political dreams or immediate political objectives.

The British policy in Transjordania is dictated by the strategic location of the country. British control of Transjordania means control of the Iraq pipeline to the sea, of the Bagdad-Haifa road, and of the Hejaz-Damascus railway. These three decisive factors determine the British decision to remain in Transjordania, regardless of Abdullah.

XIV: Seeds of Dissension

Syria and Lebanon

ON November 8, 1943, just seventy-one days after it had been elected, the Lebanese Parliament demanded by an almost unanimous vote the immediate independence of the Lebanese Republic. Jean-Louis Helleu, French Commissioner for Syria and Lebanon, answered this demand by arresting the Lebanese President, Bishara el Khoury, and Premier Riad Solh, together with all those members of the Cabinet and the Parliament on whom the French gendarmerie could lay their hands.

Trouble flared up in the streets of Beirut, capital of the little coastal republic, trouble that served to call to the attention of the Western world several important factors. The two sister republics of Syria and Lebanon, of great strategic value as Near Eastern bases for the United Nations, are under French mandate but are not French colonies. The mandate was to have expired in 1939, but the outbreak of war postponed the realization of Lebanon independence. The revolt of the Lebanese, who had been under French influence since before the eighteenth century, when French informal protection was granted to the Catholic Maronite clergy, was an alarming sign of danger to the French colonial empire. French "strong-arm" methods strengthened the Arab desire for unification.

The Lebanon affair also fostered a revival of British-French rivalry which developed in Syria and Lebanon during the nineteenth century and seriously compromised British-French solidarity immediately after the last war. The British and Free French forces liberated Syria and Lebanon in June 1941 from the Vichy regime, and it was in this region that General de Gaulle entered into his first serious conflict with the British.

Syria's stony deserts and rocky mountains have proved to be a fatal setting for the struggle between the British and the French.

Rivals in the eastern Mediterranean for three centuries, the British clashed with the French in Syria in 1799, following Napoleon's campaign in Egypt. They were foes again in 1830, during the troubles in Syria and Lebanon. They were in different camps in 1860, too, when the Moslem Druse tribes came down from their mountain villages to attack the Catholic Maronites: the French supported the Maronites, whose priests were educated by French Jesuits, the Druses had British backing.

For one hundred and fifty years Britain dreamed of linking Egypt with India, a project France opposed because she considered Syria her spiritual province. Syria was and still is the preferred domain of French spiritual imperialism. This imperialism was supported, as everywhere in the Near East, by French Catholic missions and by the French-Jewish cultural *Alliance Israélite* which carried French civilization to the Jews in the Near East.

When World War I broke out, the British and French had no boundary quarrels in Europe, but they knew there would be keen competition in the Near East. In March 1915 they reached an agreement with regard to Constantinople, Persia, and Arabia. But when Great Britain initiated her Arab policy and, in the fall of 1915, opened negotiations with Sherif Hussein in Mecca concerning the future of Arabia, the French grew worried. Their concern increased when they learned that Sir Henry McMahon had written to Hussein in October 1915 that "only the districts situated to the west of Damascus and Homs and Hama and Aleppo" were to be excluded from the future Arab state. The French rushed Georges Picot, an expert on the Near East, to the scene, and in 1916 an agreement was reached with Sir Mark Sykes. The contents were kept secret even from Hussein, but it is known that the British promised all of Syria, Mosul included, to the French. Mosul was later ceded to Lloyd George by Clemenceau, whose foes accused him of ignoring the oil riches of Mosul. This appears to be inaccurate; Clemenceau was ready to make concessions to Lloyd George in the Near East because he needed his approval of French policy on the Rhine.

Whatever the agreement, in 1919 Damascus and Aleppo were occupied by British-Arab forces headed by General Allenby and Colonel Lawrence. The Syrians set up an Arab government at

Damascus with Faisal crowned King of Syria. Lawrence had been greatly disappointed by the Allied decision to give Syria to the French. He was also disappointed by the British decision to create the Jewish National Home in Palestine, for he considered it a breach of Britain's solemn promise to the Arabs for their war against the Turks. On the other hand, he believed—and his views were shared by many British officials—that it was a great pity to let the French hold Syria, for it created a weak link in British control of the Near East.

When the San Remo Conference of April 1920, which carried out the British-French agreement of September 1919, allotted France a mandate over the whole of Syria, the first act of the first French High Commissioner to Syria, General Henri Gouraud, was to send an ultimatum to King Faisal at Damascus. Faisal refused to capitulate. The British sympathized with him but they were unable to help him against their French allies. Lawrence and some other agents of the intelligence service considered it their duty to help Faisal. It was then that the French accused the British of attempting to provoke trouble in Syria.

Faisal was defeated in July 1920, in the battle of Khan Meisalun, and General Gouraud entered Damascus. Syria was partitioned by the French into two states: Syria, with 2,700,000 inhabitants and Damascus as the capital; the small coastal republic of Lebanon, with 800,000 population and Beirut as the capital. This division reaffirmed the administrative status which the Turks granted to Lebanon under French pressure in 1864. In that year the French wanted to protect the Catholic Maronites of Lebanon against the Moslem Druses. In 1919 the French intended to use the Maronites as the main support of their administration. Therefore, they not only maintained the separate status of Lebanon but enlarged it to the detriment of Syria. This division, along with the special favor shown to the Maronites, irritated the Moslem Arabs and later became a source of concern for the Christian Arabs themselves.

The Maronites were in the majority in Lebanon. Their capital looked like a typical French Mediterranean town; their élite spoke fluent French, and the French commissioner, who controlled both Lebanon and Syria, chose Beirut for his residence. This policy was

responsible—and the French themselves acknowledged it later on
—for all their trouble in Syria. But the French placed the responsibility on the British, accusing them of supporting the Syrian rebels.
They undoubtedly had reasons for complaint, but a good many of
them were exaggerated. It was quite natural, for instance, that the
British-controlled Arab countries, such as Palestine, Iraq, and
Transjordania would give refuge to Arab rebels from Syria; the
British could not prevent the Arabs from manifesting their racial
solidarity. On the other hand, the French authorities in Syria
took revenge by sheltering rebels from British-controlled Arab
countries, particularly from Palestine. And if French complications
in Syria caused by the favoritism shown the Maronites were of
some consolation to the British, the British difficulties in Palestine,
caused by Arab opposition to the Jews, were equally consoling to
the French.

Both France and Britain tried to minimize their troubles by
pointing out the other's difficulties. Such an attitude could not fail
to create hostility between them. The problem of the oil pipelines
—the French insisted on having their own from Mosul to Tripoli;
the British wished all the oil sent directly to Palestine—helped to
accentuate the animosity, which finally reached a climax after
the Druse revolt of 1925.

The leader of the Druses, Sultan Al Atrashi, was a friend of
Lawrence and pro-British. At the same time, the depreciation of
the French franc between 1923 and 1925 was cause enough for
the growing discontent among Arab merchants of the Damascus.
Furthermore, the French accused the British of playing up the
superiority of the pound sterling as against the depreciated French
franc.

In 1925 the Free Mason and liberal General Sarrail, sent to Syria
to redress the errors committed by his Catholic predecessors,
Gouraud and Weygand, made the mistake of bombing rebellious
Damascus. The British Consul-General promptly reported the in-
cident, and London urgently insisted on the recall of Sarrail. The
French then accused the British of permitting the Transjordanian
Arabs to assist the rebels of Djebel Druse and Damascus. They
accused the British of sheltering Syrian revolutionaries in Egypt

and Palestine, as well as playing up to the Syrian-Egyptian Prince Michael Loutfalla, possessor of a vast fortune and pretender to the Syrian throne. They even insisted that the British were supporting Fakhri Baroudi, Fascist deputy for Damascus. This accusation was obviously false. The fifty-year-old little man who organized the Syrian Steel Shirts looked for support only in Axis capitals. The French, however, could not help but see the British behind each one of their failures in Syria.

The Nazis obviously counted on this antagonism when they determined that Syria was to become the scene of Franco-British strife. They suggested to Vichy that the passionately anti-British Jean Chiappe be sent to Syria as High Commissioner. When Chiappe's plane was downed in the Mediterranean during a British-Italian air battle, Vichy sent to Syria, with the approval of Germany, the anti-British General Henri Dentz. For a year Dentz tolerated the activity of numerous Nazi agents, headed by Karl von Grobba, former German Minister to Iraq, and the eighty-one-year-old archeologist Max von Oppenheim, who was the Kaiser's private agent during the construction of the Bagdad railway and who received the title of Baron from the Kaiser and, later, "honorary Aryan" from Hitler.

But when General Dentz, upon instructions from Vichy, opened the Syrian railways for transit of Nazi supplies to the Iraq rebels, he met with opposition among the best elements of the French garrison in Syria. Colonel Collet, the best soldier the French had in Syria, served Vichy as long as he considered Pétain loyal to his armistice pledge. After several weeks of argument with Dentz, he joined the British, bringing with him three battalions of his devoted Circassians; and in July 1941 Syria and Lebanon were occupied by British and Fighting French forces under the command of General Georges Catroux.

Britain and France had, in 1918, promised both countries a national government deriving authority "from the initiative and free choice of the native populations." More specifically, they were promised their independence by two treaties with France, signed by the French Socialist government of Léon Blum in 1936 but not ratified by the French Senate. France was to assure them within three years complete independence patterned after the Anglo-Iraqi setup. The ensuing war delayed the execution of this treaty. When the Fighting French occupied Syria and Lebanon, General Catroux proclaimed their independence in November 1941. But this independence, according to the British-French agreement, was "subject to the limitations necessitated by conditions of war." The British approved both the proclamation of independence and its limitations. They furthermore agreed to recognize the continuing "pre-eminent and privileged position of France" in Syria and Lebanon.

The Fighting French adopted the attitude, later confirmed by the French Committee of National Liberation at Algiers, that as trustees of the French Republic they could not fulfill their previous obligations until the restoration of the French Republic. Both de Gaulle and Catroux officially declared that the legal situation established by the mandate would be unchanged by any proclamation of independence.

The British, who were responsible for the military security of the two republics since the Fighting French took over only the civilian administration, did not agree with the French interpretation of Syrian and Lebanese independence. Their criticism of the French attitude was motivated by their desire to appease the Arabs and prevent a possible revolt in an area of extreme strategic importance. They suspected the French of playing a delaying action and of fostering secret plans to maintain, in some camouflaged form, their control of Syria and Lebanon.

The French, on the other hand, too clearly remembered their struggle against the British for the two Near Eastern republics. They had been witness to many British maneuvers and intrigues there; they immediately suspected the British of being more anxious to eliminate the French from Syria and Lebanon than to grant independence to the two countries.

Mutual suspicions and traditional frictions were aggravated by a clash of personalities. If de Gaulle was intransigent and hard to deal with, General Sir Edward L. Spears, the British Minister to Syria and Lebanon, was even more so. ("Spears on his fingers and spears on his toes, He makes trouble wherever he goes," the British sang about their military chief in the Near East.) De Gaulle did not miss this opportunity to prove that he was and could be independent of British control.

There was a third Allied power interested in the Syrian and Lebanese situation. The United States was not politically or economically involved, but she was maintaining hospitals, schools, and a university there, and American missionaries in Syria and Lebanon were more numerous than American salesmen. And, also, because of the many Syrians and Lebanese who had emigrated to America, the moral prestige of the United States was very high throughout the Near East.

The American King-Crane Commission, sent by President Wilson in 1919 to investigate the situation in Syria and Palestine, found that the two countries wished to unite, and that the Syrians were opposed to French rule. However, this report was disregarded. Syria and Palestine remained divided and Syria, along with Lebanon, remained under the French mandate which, in 1924, was recognized by the United States.

When the British and Fighting French occupied Syria and Lebanon in June 1941, the United States was not yet in the war. Consequently, it was not consulted in this connection, nor on the British-Fighting French agreement on the limited and delayed independence of the two republics. Washington could view with approval the ousting of German and Italian agents, along with the Vichy regime, from this strategic region. However, it did not accept, and has not yet accepted, the British pledge regarding the "pre-eminent and privileged position of France."

When the United States entered the war, both the Fighting French and the British appealed for recognition of the local governments set up by Catroux. The local governments supported the appeal, but, after examining the situation thoroughly, the United States reached the conclusion that it was undesirable to comply. Opposition was based on the fact that Syrian and Lebanese independence was delimited, and that the local governments were not representative, nor were they in actual control of these areas. Control was in the hands of the Fighting French who were trying to retain it, at least until the restoration of the French Republic.

However, Washington did want to manifest sympathy with the aspirations of Syria and Lebanon for sovereign independence and to encourage them in its attainment. In the autumn of 1942, in recognition of their limited independence, George Wadsworth was accredited to them as Diplomatic Agent—a customary rank in the case of semi-independent states. Complete official recognition was withheld pending fulfillment of three prerequisites: first, that the Syrians and Lebanese must be in full control of the political machinery of their respective states; second, that they must govern by popular consent; and third, that they must be competent to fulfill all international obligations incumbent on a sovereign state.

So long as these prerequisites are not realized, the attitude of the United States, according to official sources, will be to "favor the claims of the Syrian and Lebanese peoples to complete independence as conceived in the terms of the Franco-American Convention of 1924. We do not regard the existing governments as in any sense a satisfactory fulfillment of these terms." In reply to objections that this attitude contradicted reiterated statements on the postwar integrity of the French Empire, official spokesmen pointed out that Syria and Lebanon are not part of that Empire but mandates in which French control is definitely stated to be of limited duration. Inasmuch as the conditions on which such control was based must eventually alter, or even cease to exist, the United States government presumes that independence for the two countries will become a matter for further negotiation.

The British have been less disappointed than the Fighting French by America's stand. It was, as a matter of fact, of some aid to them in putting pressure on the French. The British have always believed that the French mishandled the political and economic life of Syria and Lebanon, and they used the American attitude as an additional weapon with which to persuade the Fighting French to implement their promises so far as they could under war conditions. The French, with the past in mind, had no confidence in the sincerity of the British, suspecting them of pursuing their old Near Eastern game. The British efforts, therefore, remained unsuccessful. Friction between them grew more acute and Great Britain's opposition to the American deal with

Darlan improved Franco-British relations only temporarily. Very soon the old disagreements were resumed with even greater bitterness.

French interests have been served by the idea fostered among the Lebanese Christians that the British are supporting schemes for an Arab federation favorable to the Moslems, at the expense of Christian interests. Likewise, the French inadvertently reaped the benefits of Axis propaganda which tried to raise a mistrust of the United States among both Christians and Moslems by insinuating that Americans favored extreme Zionist claims.

The French, however, were perfectly aware that their position in Syria and Lebanon was by no means firmly established in the eyes of their Allies. The United States government has never admitted the validity of the Fighting French claim that they inherited from the Third Republic the responsibility of the mandate over Syria and Lebanon, although in practice it has accepted their *de facto* control. The British, who have endorsed French promises of independence, urged the gradual realization of those promises. And so the French found themselves obliged to prepare for elections in the two republics.

But in March 1943 General Catroux ousted the Syrian and Lebanese governments which he had appointed at the time of the conquest of Syria. The death of Taj-ad-Din-al-Kassain, President of the Syrian Republic, became the pretext for these changes. Ata Bey el Ayoubi was designated to become the Syrian Chief of State. In Lebanon, Alfred Naccache was succeeded by Dr. Ayoub Tabet. Those changes were explained by the desire to prepare the grounds for the free election of new parliaments in both countries. The elections were unavoidable: French and British were both committed to them, and the United States had given her blessings.

The Syrian elections took place in July, and resulted in a clear majority for the anti-French National Bloc party. Parliament convened in August and elected Shukri Quwatli as President of the Syrian Republic. Quwatli, head of the Nationalist Bloc is a Syrian nationalist of long standing, and is thought to be opposed to all schemes for the "Kingdom of United Syria" advocated by Abdullah of Transjordania. He is a trusted friend of Ibn Saud.

Faris Bey el Khoury, a Christian nationalist, was elected President of the Chamber. The result of the elections was the attainment of power by elements undeniably hostile to French aspirations. On the whole, the French interfered less in these elections than British and American observers anticipated.

The situation was different in Lebanon, where a serious electoral crisis broke out even prior to the Syrian elections. Lebanese separatism has been a conflicting factor in every scheme of political organization in the whole area. The position of religious minorities in the Near East has always been difficult—and union with Syria would once again make the Lebanese Christians a minority. Their main desire was for religious security, for they are still haunted by the specter of the 1860 massacres. The French mandate provided them with both security and the guarantees they wanted. The Lebanese naturally were expected to look more favorably upon the French mandate than their Syrian neighbors. Thus, the Lebanese elections, and the troubles which resulted three months later, came as a surprise to most observers in the Near East.

On June 17 the Lebanese government in Beirut promulgated two decrees prescribing the number, by religious affiliation, of deputies to be selected to the Lebanese Parliament. The previous basis on which deputies had been elected in 1936 called for a total of 42 deputies of which 22 were to be Christians (13 Maronite and 9 from other sects) and 20 Moslems (9 Sunni, 8 Shiah, and 3 Druse). Under the new decrees, 12 additional seats were to be established—divided between 10 Christians and 2 Moslems. The decrees stirred up a violent reaction among the Moslems. It was obvious that these edicts could be projected only with the approval and support of the French; and it was equally obvious that their aim was to increase the power of a single sect whose objective is a Christian-controlled Lebanon, independent of any Arab-Moslem state, and under the protection of Catholic France.

Attempts on the part of the French Commissioner, Jean-Louis Helleu, to smooth matters over, served to make the Moslem leaders more indignant and promoted further bitterness and confusion. For the first time since the last war, all Moslem groups found themselves united in defense of their common interests. The religious angle was further complicated by the disposition of Greek

Orthodox elements to side with the Moslems against the Maronites.

The arrival of General Catroux in Beirut at this critical juncture helped to re-establish the seriously threatened French control. Catroux was also called on to settle a British and French dispute over electoral candidates from the city of Tripoli. He solved the crisis by making clever use of the unexpected intervention of the Egyptian Prime Minister, Nahas Pasha, who had recommended a ratio of 29 Christians to 25 Moslems as a basis for the new Lebanese Parliament. Ayoub Tabet resigned as Chief of State and parliamentary elections were finally held on August 29.

The British accused the French of attempting to bring pressure to bear in favor of pro-French candidates. General Spears' protest was sufficiently strong to alter the course of the elections in certain areas. Moreover, nationalist elements combined to a surprising degree to defeat French-supported candidates. The Parliament, chosen under these adverse circumstances, assembled on September 21 and elected as President a former Premier, Bishara el Khoury, a Maronite Christian who nevertheless has nationalist tendencies and is not likely to accept the French mandate. It was significant that Naccache, Riad Solh, and Ayoub Tabet, all three ousted from office by the French, were elected as deputies from Beirut. The entire electoral experience indicated a serious, and surprising, decline of French influence.

On October 8 the independent spirit which animated the elections led to a 48 to 4 vote for constitutional amendments which, in effect, meant the immediate liquidation of the French mandate. This revolutionary resolution was answered by the use of arms— a method which had proved successful during the twenty-three years of the turbulent mandate. The French proclaimed martial law, arrested the President and the Prime Minister, along with many prominent Lebanese anti-French politicians, and dissolved the Parliament.

The Arab world was aroused and the sister republic of Syria was the first to express indignation. The Iraq Parliament demanded the immediate ousting of the French from Lebanon and Syria. Abdullah of Transjordania became agitated; Ibn Saud expressed his discontent. In Cairo King Farouk and Premier Nahas did not mince words in expressing their indignation, and rioting students stoned French buildings and offices. From distant India, the Moslem League insisted that the British not only assure full independence to Lebanon and Syria but to the three French North African states.

The British expressed extreme concern over this threat to order in the Near East, so potentially rich a ground for German propaganda. They strongly protested the French action—about which they had not been consulted—and demanded that the French release and reinstate the imprisoned Lebanese statesmen, threatening to take over power if the French would not comply. In Washington the State Department frowned and declared that it felt very unhappy about the incident; certain officials even termed the action a fascist measure.

The French in Algiers shrugged their shoulders and observed that so long as the British were policing India, Palestine, and Egypt, and were holding Gandhi in prison, all their indignation about the arbitrary French action in Lebanon could only be considered classical British hypocrisy. De Gaulle and the French Liberation Committee, however, realized that since they were weaker than the British they were obliged to comply with the British demand. Catroux was rushed to Syria and a compromise was worked out. The imprisoned men were released, and reinstated. Furthermore, they announced their "decision to open with the government of the Syrian republic negotiations necessary for the harmonizing of the French mandate with the regime of independence promised by France to the Levant states in 1941." And they declared that "as soon as constitutional life has been reestablished in Lebanon, similar negotiations will be open with the Beirut government."

The road to appeasement was thus opened, while an indispensable amount of French prestige appeared to be saved. The Lebanese events proved, however, that French prestige was seriously shaken; one of the most significant facts in the Lebanese troubles was the indignation of Lebanon's Maronite Archbishop over the French arrests, and his emphasis on the complete unity of Christians and Moslems in Lebanon.

The Maronites, who for centuries have been French protégés in the Levant states, have wondered whether France, greatly weakened by the war, would be in a position to resume her traditional role of protector of the Christians in the Near East. Also, the Christian Arabs in Lebanon, as well as the Moslem Arabs, undoubtedly resented an implementation of the French mandate which gave to the French some of the most lucrative sources of income in the Lebanese state. The Christian Arabs must also have been impressed by the reiterated emphasis of the Atlantic Charter in the Near Eastern broadcasts of the Office of War Information. They were encouraged to believe that the powerful United States, friend of all oppressed peoples, was pledging application of the Atlantic Charter to their own lands in the postwar world. Their claim to independence, based on French promises and endorsed by the British, found further justification in the principles of the Atlantic Charter.

For all Arab peoples, who watched with extreme interest its developments, the Lebanese situation became a test case for the application of the Atlantic Charter. The Lebanese themselves, who had allowed their leaders to set them on the road to independence, were not quite sure where they wanted to go. They wanted independence, and the Maronites, aware of its potential realization, were anxious to emphasize their solidarity with the Moslem Arabs. Still, the Christian Lebanese continued to be apprehensive of an Arab Federation, fearing that their religious freedom would not be sufficiently safeguarded or respected. They felt that their growing unity with the Moslems might make for the best defense of their interests in the postwar world, but felt, too, the desirability of reinforcing their security through the protection of a great power. Since it was a question whether France would again be in a position to resume this role, they looked toward the United States.

But by the end of 1943, the Soviet Union, potentially the greatest continental power in postwar Europe, or, more exactly, in Eurasia, had recognized the Greek Orthodox Church and re-established the Greek Orthodox Patriarch. The gesture enabled the Soviet Union, if she should so desire, to resume her traditional role of protector of the Greek Orthodox Church in the Balkans and the Near East as well. The Greek Orthodox minorities in Syria, Lebanon, and Palestine, pro-Russian until the Soviets came to power, once more

turned toward Moscow and awaited the time when a new Russian
Patriarch would come to their lands.

The Greek Orthodox Arabs were not the only ones to turn to
Moscow. Many young intellectuals in Beirut and Damascus,
exasperated by French delays and British maneuvering, and dissatisfied with the benevolent but noncommittal attitude of the
United States, also turned to the rising red star of the Soviet. These
young nationalists did not embrace Communism as a solution—
the Russia they admire is not the ideological, but the victorious,
great power, the Russia of decisive action in battle and in diplomacy. This Russia was directly interested in the fate of Persia,
Afghanistan, and Turkey. The young Arab nationalists had doubts
as to whether Russia would be as interested as was the United
States in the most strict application of Atlantic Charter principles.
But they believed that she could not, and would not, ignore after
the war the Near East's complex problems. They also believed that
their country, over which the British and the French have competed for generations, and to which the United States was present-
ing the liberating banner of the Atlantic Charter, would become a
focal point in the New Deal they were expecting in the Near East.

XV: The Over-Promised Land

Palestine

FOR thousands of years Palestine, cradle of religions, has been the symbol of the richest spiritual promise in the history of man. But since World War I the Holy Land has become a country of unfulfilled political promises made by the British to Arabs and Jews. World War II has come and the promises have yet to be fulfilled. The British, whom both Arabs and Jews accuse of deceit, do not deny their promises; they affirm, however, that both have misunderstood the precise character of their pledges. The Zionists justify their claims both by the Bible, which gives them legal title to Palestine since time immemorial, and by the so-called Balfour Declaration, which confirmed the Jews' historical ties with the Holy Land.

On November 2, 1917, Arthur Balfour, then Britain's Secretary of State for Foreign Affairs, wrote to Lord Rothschild asking him to inform the Zionist Federation that "His Majesty's Government view with favor the establishment in Palestine of a National Home for the Jewish people, and will use their best endeavors to facilitate the achievement of this object." The reservation in the declaration stated that "nothing shall be done which may prejudice the civil and religious rights of existing non-Jewish communities in Palestine."

When World War I ended, the Zionists rushed to the Near Eastern counter of the "British Empire's Bank," wishing to cash the Balfour promises. They ran square into the Arabs, who were there for exactly the same purpose. They were in possession of letters written to Emir Hussein in October 1915 by Sir Henry McMahon, British High Commissioner in Cairo, which pledged the political independence of the Arabs within certain territorial limits. But Jerusalem and Palestine were not mentioned by name in the correspondence.

228

The Arabs maintained it had been understood that Palestine was to be included in the area promised to them by McMahon. The British replied that they did not find it morally possible to include, within an independent Arab state, the Holy Land with its shrines sacred to the Moslems but still more sacred to Christians and Jews. The British pointed out that although Palestine was neither specifically included nor excluded from McMahon's pledge a scrupulous reading of the "ambiguous" language showed that Palestine was excluded by implication.

For a while it looked as though the British would be able to co-ordinate the conflicting claims and establish harmony between the Arabs and Jews in an independent Arab-Jewish state. Dr. Chaim Weizmann, leader of the Zionists, talked with Faisal, son of Hussein, who believed as late as 1919 that he would be created King of a great Syrian state, to be federated with Palestine. Faisal was inclined to favor the political immigration of Jews to Palestine and he expressed his views in a letter to Justice Felix Frankfurter, whom he had met at the Versailles Conference. He did not anticipate that the Great Syria of his dreams could be dismembered.

Despite the King-Crane Commission's findings that the populations of northern and southern Syria, including Lebanon and Palestine, desired unity within a single political state, Syria was dismembered. France received the mandate for Syria and Lebanon, Great Britain the mandate for Palestine, the Jordan Valley, and Transjordania. The Balfour Declaration was incorporated in the Palestine mandate as obligatory. In 1920 the Arabs revolted against the Balfour Declaration. Five Jews and four Arabs were killed. In 1921 trouble broke out on a larger scale, resulting in the deaths of forty-seven Jews and forty-eight Arabs. Two young nationalisms were clashing on the soil of the world's most ancient culture.

The Jews, mostly from Eastern Europe, began as early as 1860 their return to what they regarded their spiritual home. They were attracted to Palestine by a kind of non-political, sentimental, and nationalist nostalgia. In 1897, however, the first Zionist Congress at Basle, called by Dr. Theodore Herzl, laid the foundation for a political Zionism which became the modern expression of Jewish nationalism.

Arab nationalism was of an equally recent date, its nascence occurring at the end of the nineteenth century. Its first important landmark was the Arab Congress in 1913 in Paris, and its first struggle for independence—the revolt against the Turks—took place in June 1916. The Arabs were aware that they could attain independence only with British approval and aid. They were forced to accept British control as a necessary evil. But they were agitated by the appearance in their lands of a new important group with national aspirations as strong as their own, and supported by more powerful economic forces.

It is probable that the appearance of the Jews in Palestine contributed to the crystallization of Arab nationalism, which at the beginning of this century was still in a confused state. Rightly or wrongly, the Arabs considered the Jews a dangerous obstacle on the thorny road leading to their own independence. The trouble of 1921 was the first alarming expression of Arab ill humor. Yet it is unlikely that the Arabs were very much alarmed by the 60,000 Jews, as compared to the 600,000 Arabs in Palestine, plus 300,000 in neighboring Transjordania.

The British had been optimistic as to the compatibility of the commitments made to both sides; in 1921 they became worried. Winston Churchill, then Secretary of the Colonial Office, went from Egypt to Jerusalem to discuss the situation with the British High Commissioner, Sir Herbert Samuel, who, being a Jew, was especially desirous of assuring the fairest possible co-ordination between Jewish aspirations, Arab claims, and British imperial interests. Anxious to prevent a repetition of the riots, Sir Herbert Samuel searched for a policy of concession to the Arabs—and suggested the restriction of Jewish immigration. Churchill was attracted by the romantic passions of the Zionists, but was primarily concerned with the defense of the interests of the British Empire. He was for a policy of limited concession.

The third Arab-Palestinian Congress met in March 1921, and worked out what the Arabs considered their minimum anti-Zionist platform. The Palestinian Arabs asked for the creation of a national parliamentary government, to be elected exclusively by prewar Palestinians. They were thus insuring for themselves political supremacy and for the Jews an official minority status. They also called for the union of Palestine ("southern Syria") and northern

Syria. Obviously, such a program could not constitute a basis for discussions with either the British or the Jews. The Zionists interpreted the Balfour Declaration as a specific promise that Palestine would be the Jewish state. It is not certain whether Lord Balfour, and other members of the Cabinet who drafted the declaration in 1917, differed with this interpretation. However, when Zionists and Arabs clashed, British officials lectured both sides on the difference between a "home" and a "state," stressing that they had promised the Jews not the state of Palestine but simply a home in Palestine. The White Paper issued by Churchill in 1922 explained that the British government did not contemplate the subordination of the Arab peoples, or their language and culture, and they did not intend the creation of a "wholly Jewish Palestine."

The limitation of Jewish immigration, based on the principle of the economic absorptive capacity of the country, was the other major concession given to the Arabs. Churchill sugared the pill by emphasizing the fact that the Jews came to Palestine not on sufferance but as a right. Weizmann accepted this solution with reluctance, but accept he did on the theory that half a loaf is better than no loaf at all. But the extreme Zionists, under Vladimir Jabotinsky, rejected it and split away from the main Zionist body.

This British compromise, which was to be the first of a long series, satisfied neither Arabs nor Jews—and it is uncertain whether it satisfied the author himself. Churchill probably considered the compromise an indispensable surgical operation, having come to the conclusion that British commitments to the Jews and Arabs were basically incompatible and that it was necessary to make certain sacrifices in order to salvage the basic interests of all three parties, as well as the face of the British Empire. But he must also have felt that the pledge barring "a wholly Jewish Palestine" and limiting Jewish immigration did not constitute a repudiation of the Balfour pledge. Anything that went beyond would clearly do so.

This state of mind must explain his opposition to the last British White Paper on Palestine issued in the spring of 1939. He considered then that a definitive limitation or practical suspension of Jewish immigration would be a violation of the pledge, and explained that the Balfour Declaration was not an "ill-considered, sentimental act. . . . Hardly any step was taken with greater deliberation and responsibility." The British, however, published additional White Papers between Churchill's 1922 paper and the 1939 paper of Malcolm MacDonald, Minister of Colonies in Chamberlain's Cabinet. The White Paper of 1922 did not satisfy either the Jews or the Arabs, but it assured a few years of peaceful development. In 1929 the peace was disrupted by the Arab uprising known as the incident of the Wailing Wall. Jews and Arabs quarreled over the right to certain ceremonial arrangements before the Sacred Wall and 133 Jews and 116 Arabs were killed. Conclusions of the British commission that investigated the situation were published by the Shaw Commission and led to the so-called Lord Passfield's White Paper in 1930. This paper aimed at reassuring the Arabs by suggesting new restrictions on Jewish immigration—suspended during the investigation—and on the sale of land to the Jews.

A storm of protest broke out in Zionist circles. Dr. Weizmann, chief protagonist of co-operation with the British government, resigned as President of the Zionist organization. Leaders of the conservative opposition supported his position by denouncing the White Paper. Prime Minister Ramsay MacDonald wrote Dr. Weizmann in February 1931, attempting to counteract the impression produced by Passfield's paper. His letter reassured the Zionists, but alarmed the Arabs, who labeled it the "Black Letter." By the combined use of the White Paper and the Black Letter the British won a few more years of respite.

It could be of only short duration, for Hitler brutally reopened the Palestinian question. On the one hand, his persecution of the Jews in Germany and in the Central and Eastern European countries which he overran increased the number of Jews in search of a haven. For them it was quite natural to find it where the British had promised it. On the other hand, Nazi propaganda did its best to stir up the anti-Zionist feelings of the Arabs by spreading tales of alleged Zionist intentions to drive them not only out of Palestine but out of Transjordania. The Nazis played up, as well, alleged support of the Western powers for wild Zionist dreams.

Jewish immigration to Palestine, which in 1931 fell from 5,249 to 4,075, rose with Hitler's appearance on the political scene and jumped in 1933—the year Hitler took power—to 30,327. It increased and reached its peak in 1935 with 61,854. The fact that Jewish capital poured into Palestine from Germany and Poland and created a boom during a world economic crisis did not diminish the anti-Semitic terrorism nor soften the Arabs' bitterness.

In October 1933 the Arab Executive, which hitherto had demonstrated only against the Jews, staged a protest against British policy. It demanded once more the prohibition of Jewish immigration and the purchase of land by Jews. A general strike was averted, only to break out with greater fury in 1936.

The echoes of the Italian-Ethiopian conflict, the student riots in Egypt, the Arab strike in Syria, served to intensify the excited climate in which the Palestinian Arabs were living. Haj Amin, Mufti of Jerusalem, President of the Supreme Moslem Council and one of the Husseini family of landowners, became the leader of the Nationalist Palestinian Arabs. Four other Arab parties presented to the mandate government demands in the classical vein: interim suspension of Jewish immigration, revision of the whole immigration system, prohibition of transfer of Arab lands to Jews, and a democratic government which, by proportional representation, would freeze their majority status.

The British proposed a new compromise constitution to assure the Arabs of a majority representation. Both parties refused it. It was not enough for the Arabs; it was too much for the Jews.

The National Political Strike, which the Arabs declared in April 1936, lasted six months and resulted in the loss of many Jewish and Arab lives. It was ended through the intervention of neighboring Arab leaders, and because of economic considerations and the increase of British armed forces. The Arabs failed to reach their objectives; the Jews were not sure they had safeguarded theirs.

Both groups remained dissatisfied and uneasy about their future while the British made an effort to find a solution. A Royal Commission headed by Lord Peel stayed in Palestine for eight months. It tried to be sympathetic and just and it came to the conclusion that only a partition of Palestine would offer to both Arabs and Jews "a prospect . . . of obtaining the inestimable boon of peace." The Arab state was to include eastern Palestine, the southern district of Beersheba, and Transjordania; the Jews were to be allowed to build their National Home in northern Palestine and along the entire fertile coastal plain. Like all the other proposals, it satisfied neither the Arabs nor the Jews. The former insisted on an integral Palestine in which the Jews would be reduced to a minority. The latter did not refuse the principle of partition, but rejected the thesis that their nationalist aspirations and those of the Palestinian Arabs were irreconcilable.

Violence continued with increasing fervor. A British official and his police escort were murdered by the Arabs in September 1937 and the British found themselves obliged to apply strong-arm methods. The Arab Higher Committee, along with all other national committees, was dissolved. Haj Amin fled to Lebanon to continue in exile his anti-British campaign, having tied his fate to the Axis chariot.

At the end of that year the Jews armed themselves against the increasing Arab violence. By April 1938 armed bands were terrorizing the country and the whole of Palestine was on the verge of civil war. Meanwhile a new British commission, headed by Sir John Woodhead, arrived in Palestine for the purpose of drawing up the boundaries of the partition recommended by the Peel Commission. It found a condition of sporadic civil war and came to the conclusion that it would be impossible to divide Palestine so as to have homogeneous Arab and Jewish states. It maintained, moreover, that the Arab state could not be economically self-sufficient, and therefore recommended in October 1938 an "economic federalism." It recommended, furthermore, that Jewish immigration be regulated not only by purely economic but also by "political, social, and psychological considerations." A new White Paper was issued by the British government, rejecting the plan of partition.

Once more the two groups faced each other, as well as a harassed British government. The situation was critical; war clouds gathered over Europe. Hitler's armies, already in Austria, were prepared to march into Czechoslovakia. The number of Jewish refugees seeking a haven mounted. But the Jews, persecuted and assaulted in Berlin and Vienna, were assaulted in their own haven of the Promised Land.

Alarmed by the growing violence in Palestine, and having just bought a peace at Munich by allowing Hitler to dismember

Czechoslovakia, the Chamberlain government, in February 1939, · called the Jewish and Arab leaders to a conference in London. With Haj Amin in exile, the Palestinian Arabs sent Raghib Nash-ashibi, who was disposed to collaborate with the British. Ibn Saud sent his second son, Faisal. The Iraq Cabinet delegated its Prime Minister, Nuri Pasha, and Egypt was also represented.

The Palestinian Arab leaders refused to sit at the same table with the Jewish delegates and so the conference was transformed into two separate ones. What became known as the White Paper of 1939 was the result. An independent Palestine was to be estab-lished within ten years. The British government specified "that the whole of Palestine west of Jordan was excluded from Sir Henry McMahon's pledge," on which the Arab leaders based their claims for an independent Palestine. So far as the Jewish National Home was concerned, the British government accepted Winston Churchill's interpretation which specified that the Balfour Declar-ation did not contemplate that "Palestine as a whole should be converted into a Jewish National Home, but that such a Home should be founded in Palestine."

The British government tried to prove that the mandatory ad-ministration had carried out its obligation, having allowed over 300,000 Jews to enter Palestine between 1922 and 1939. It was finally decided that an additional 75,000 Jewish immigrants would be authorized to enter the National Home between April 1939 and April 1944. If conditions in Palestine would permit, the 75,000 could be increased by another 25,000 "as a contribution toward the Jewish refugee problem." But after April 1944 no Jewish immigra-tion was to be permitted "unless the Arabs of Palestine are pre-pared to acquiesce in it." This was the first real attempt to put an end to Zionist hopes. The partition solution proposed in 1936 was definitely revoked.

The White Paper of 1939, which the Mandate Commission and the League of Nations refused to approve, provoked a storm of indignation in Zionist circles that was shared by Winston Churchill, who called it a breach of faith. The Zionists called it the "Munich of Palestine." They accused the British of appeasing the Arabs just as they appeased Hitler, and of violating all their pledges in order to buy a peace which might be nothing but a

Munich armistice in the Near East. Neither were the Arabs entirely satisfied with the White Paper. Yet it was for them a new and great step on the road leading to the establishment of their independent state of Palestine.

At the end of 1943—British forces having been able to maintain order during the first four years of the war—Palestine again became tense. The Jews were growing more nervous with the approach of the fatal date in 1944 when the gates of the Promised Land were to swing shut to refugees. The Arabs were growing more excited about the same date, for they believed their independence loomed ever closer on the political horizon. This tension increased during the early months of 1944.

Both groups looked for support from the outside. The Zionists anxiously sought aid not only from the Jews scattered over the world and especially those in England and America—many of whom, while passionately sympathizing with the ordeal of their European brothers, did not favor the creation of a National Jewish state—but also hoped to enlist non-Jewish public opinion in all Allied countries.

The Palestinian Arabs sought assistance from the more powerful Arab states, whose leaders had already begun, under unofficial British sponsorship, discussions of a Pan-Arab Federation. Indeed, they did obtain the support of the Iraqi, Syrian, Egyptian, and other Arab leaders. Abdullah of Transjordania, who considered himself "technical ruler" of Palestine, continuously opposed Jewish immigration to Palestine. Ibn Saud, who for many years avoided a public statement, went on record in 1943, stating that the Jewish occupation of Palestine was an "error first because it constitutes an injustice against the Arabs and Moslems in general, and secondly because it causes dissensions and disturbances between the Moslems and their friends, the Allies." The Palestinian Arabs wanted to assure themselves a place in the Arab family. In November 1943 a delegation of Palestinian Arabs, headed by Musa el Alami, former Attorney-General of the Palestinian government and son-in-law of the Syrian Cabinet Minister Jabri, went to Cairo to participate in the discussion of a Pan-Arab Federation, following delegations from Iraq, Saudi-Arabia, and Syria. The Palestinian Arabs were spurred on by the example of the Lebanese Arabs, who were demanding immediate independence for themselves.

But while both groups were hoping and looking for aid from without, they were preparing to defend their interests by their own means. In the summer of 1943 certain Jewish groups in Palestine decided that the only way to prevent a possible slaughter of Jews was to arm the Jewish youth and to be prepared for impending trouble. Hidden arms were subsequently discovered by British authorities and the trials that followed only incensed both Jewish and Arab passions. More than half a million Jews in Palestine and a million Arabs, of whom 850,000 were Moslems, were restlessly awaiting the year 1944.

While Haj Amin el Husseini was still technically the Mufti of Jerusalem, he could not very well exert his functions from Berlin. Having helped establish, together with Rashid Ali Gailani, a pro-Nazi government in Bagdad in 1941, he had fled to Iran, whence he reached friendly Axis country. A staunch admirer of Japan, he broadcast to the Near East in an attempt to get his compatriots to fight against the Allies. Axis failure determined his own failure. Moreover, his concentration on Palestinian problems without so much as offering any constructive policy hastened his downfall as a leader. His religious education ill prepared him for political leadership. He stood for an absolutely intransigent opposition and his thinking was too strongly fanatical and too weakly political. And he was ignorant of the West, of the Western world's political and social concepts.

His absence and his diminished prestige was used by other Palestinian Arab leaders. Two parties competed for the right to represent their people. Raghib Nashashibi led the Arabs who were disposed to collaborate with the British. The more recalcitrant Arabs founded a new Independence Party, headed by Rashid Haj Ibrahim, who, though allied with the Mufti, was a commoner. The Mufti championed the rich landowners. Rashid Haj Ibrahim tried to organize the Arab middle classes, which he reached through the Arab Chamber of Commerce.

The Arabs disagreed among themselves on the way to assure their majority rights and, eventually, their independence. They

THE OVER-PROMISED LAND

were determined, however, to use every means, including violence, in order to assure those two basic ends. They justified their claims by their thirteen hundred years of Palestinian residence and by the British pledges given to them—pledges, according to the British, which did not include Palestine. Other Arab leaders supported these claims and opposed the Jewish National Home in Palestine as an obstacle in the way of Arab unity.

The Zionists, pointing with pride to the cultural, agricultural, and industrial achievements of half a million Jews who had invested half a billion dollars in Palestine, insisted that the country west of the Jordan and exclusive of the Negev (southern Palestine) could absorb an additional three million Jews. They saw the establishment of Palestine as a commonwealth where the Jews could live as a self-governing and independent people. They refuted the Arab apprehension that the Jewish National Home would block or forestall Arab unity, though they were skeptical about the probability of such an organization. They were convinced that Jews and Arabs could live side by side, each within his own state. They admitted that the Jewish state in Palestine, or even consisting of all of Palestine, could not solve the Jewish problem in general, but they were convinced that the solution of the international Jewish question was organically bound up with the solution of the problem of the homeland. They pointed to the Peel Commission's report which acknowledged the economic successes of Jewish colonization that had also benefited the Arabs. Indeed, the Peel Commission's report had stated: "The large import of Jewish capital into Palestine has had a general fructifying effect on the economic life of the whole country. The expansion of Arab industry and agriculture has been largely financed by the capital thus obtained. Jewish example has done much to improve Arab cultivation, especially of citrus. Owing to Jewish development and enterprise, the improvement of Arab labor has increased in urban areas, particularly in the ports. The recreation and anti-malaria work undertaken in Jewish colonies has benefited all Arabs in the neighborhood."

The Jews further pointed out that while in the last twenty years Jews had increased by some 400,000, the Arabs had increased by half a million—from 600,000 to 1,100,000. In no neighboring country could the Arabs boast of such proportional increase. The Arabs did not deny that they had benefited by the cultural and social achievements of the Zionists in Palestine. But some of them claimed, perhaps through wounded national pride, that they would have realized the same achievements, provided they had had the disposal of half a billion dollars. The point was that nearly all of them refused to pay for these achievements by the loss of their majority status. Since Jewish immigration threatened this status, they were determined to oppose it. The economic power of the Jews threatened them in the possession of their lands and they wanted an interdict on the sales of their lands to the Jews in order to protect themselves against the temptation of high prices which the Jewish buyers offered them. Recognizing the political and economic superiority of the Jews, the Arabs of Palestine believed that only a majority status, guaranteed by constitution, could adequately safeguard them.

The Zionists, on the other hand, were determined not to accept a minority status in Palestine—their ancestral country into which they had put, along with 500,000 Jews and $500,000,000, all their faith in the resurrection of the Jewish nation. It was for them the country in which three million of their European brothers, persecuted and ruined, could find both a haven and a nation of their own. They recalled that of the total of 550,000 Palestine Jews, 32,000 enlisted in the British Army. This was more than 6 per cent, and was equivalent to an enlistment of eight million in the United States. They recalled, too, that while many Arabs were lending an interested and often hopeful ear to Axis propaganda, and some of them, such as the Mufti of Jerusalem, actively served the Axis cause, the Jews, first victims of the Axis aggression, had become the "forgotten ally."

Both sides were intransigent; both were convinced of the integrity of their cause. The British, sincerely unhappy over this dilemma, looked in vain for an enduring solution. They knew that 550,000 Jews in Palestine would not accept a minority status; that the 1,100,000 Arabs, strengthened by the support of neighboring Arabs, could not be deprived of their majority status. Their main aim during the war had to be to maintain order in the Near East, an area of vital strategic importance. All other considerations were subordinated to this objective. And they hoped to maintain this order until the Peace Conference, at which time they would have to face the problem as one of the major issues in the winning of the peace. With traditional faith in the miraculous efficiency of compromise—a faith which has not been shaken by all their failures in Palestine—the British hoped that both the Arabs and the Jews would let their political reason become stronger than their nationalistic passions. They hoped that some Arab federation scheme would reassure the Palestinian Arabs by offering a greater guarantee than a majority status. They hoped, on the other hand, that some general solution of the Jewish problem would reduce the importance of Zionism in the eyes of the Jews. And they hoped to find allies in non-Zionist Jewish circles.

In October 1943 the American Jewish Committee withdrew from participation in the American Jewish Conference in New York, stating that it was dominated by Zionists who were demanding the establishment of a Jewish Commonwealth in Palestine, and who were subordinating all other Jewish issues to "the problem of the political structure of Palestine." The American Jewish Committee specified that in regard to Palestine it approved "an international trusteeship responsible to the United Nations" which would safeguard the Jewish settlement and the Jewish immigration, but it expressed, at the same time, the firm conviction that the world problems of the Jews "cannot be achieved through Palestine alone and certainly not through overemphasis of the political constitution of Palestine." This statement was sharply criticized by the Zionists, who believe that solution of the world problems of the Jews is impossible without "the recreation of the Jewish homeland in Palestine."

While the Arabs and Jews faced each other in Palestine with growing suspicion and antagonism, their hands already clutching the hidden arms which each group had managed to obtain, and while the Zionist and non-Zionist Jews argued about the possibilities of Palestine as a solution of international Jewish problems, a new and extremely important political factor loomed on Palestine's troubled horizons.

The Soviet Union was beginning to manifest her interest in this area. When in September 1943 the Soviet diplomat Ivan Maisky left

London where he and Anthony Eden made preparations for the Moscow Conference, he stopped at Cairo and Jerusalem for talks with Greek Orthodox leaders. And in December, the Patriarch Sergius, head of the Soviet-recognized Greek Orthodox Church, announced that he planned a visit to the Holy City at the very moment when Stalin was to meet Churchill and Roosevelt in Iran.

Russia's claim to being protector of the Holy City had led to the Crimean War, and Britain could not be sure whether Russia's reappearance on the scene now was as a friend or potential foe. The attitude of the Soviet Union on the thorny dilemma was not clear. In 1943 she officially recognized the Greek Orthodox Church at home, and she viewed with little sympathy the activity of the Zionists within Russia, who, as a party, had been banned. It was not clear however, whether the Soviet Union was inclined to continue her internal anti-Zionism in order to win over the Arabs, many of whom are greatly impressed by the recent rise of Soviet prestige. Certain Soviet diplomats privately disclosed their disappointment with the Arabs, accusing them of being basically receptive to Fascist propaganda.

More clear, of course, is the fact that the Soviet Union, desiring a postwar organization which will safeguard her European and Asiatic borders, will have to recognize this heterogeneous Arab-Moslem-Jewish world with its multiple and conflicting schemes, and will have to aid in bringing an equitable solution to the tragic problem.

XVI: Word, Sword, and Oil

Ibn Saud of Saudi-Arabia

In 1901 a twenty-one-year-old Arab, living as a landless exile in Kuwait at the Persian Gulf, boldly set out into the desert with two hundred men. His purpose, a highly serious if adventurous one, was to recover the principality of Nejd, once ruled by his grandfather, Emir Faisal, and lost by his father and uncle. His mission was successful and with the recovery of Nejd, a fabulous career as religious leader, conqueror, and statesman was launched.

Forty-three years have passed since then, and Ibn Saud—or Abdul Aziz Ibn Abdulrahman Ibn Faisal Ibn Saud—is the triumphant ruler of the largest of all independent Arab states. Saudi-Arabia, of which Nejd is the nucleus, consists of all the Arab states in the Arabian peninsula with the exception of petty principalities on the southern and eastern coasts.

While Ibn Saud still lives, history has given him a place as the greatest of Arab conquerors and as one of the greatest of Arab rulers. Because he built his empire by word and sword, because the Wahabi religious doctrine (the Puritan movement within Islam) inspired the fanaticism of his fighters and laid down the social bases of his empire, Ibn Saud has been compared to Mohammed.

Far more striking is the parallelism between Ibn Saud and Napoleon. Through all Europe Napoleon carried on the tips of his bayonets the principles of the French Revolution; through all Arabia Ibn Saud carried on the edges of his swords the principles and the "pure word" of the Prophet. Napoleon conquered Rome, Eternal City of the Catholic universe; Ibn Saud conquered Mecca, Sacred City of the Moslem universe. Napoleon built up modern European nationalisms by destroying the residue of medieval conceptions of principalities; Ibn Saud built up Arab nationalism by extending the Wahabi theory eliminating all tribal distinctions.

242

But the parallel can go only so far: Napoleon was finally defeated by British coalitions; Ibn Saud escaped complete subordination to Great Britain by granting oil concessions to American corporations.

Saudi-Arabia has rich oilfields at El Hasa. For Arab countries, oil is their greatest economic asset. But politically it is a liability, attracting oil men who bring with them a mandate or "sphere of influence" to protect their interests. The British have established such a sphere in southern Persia to protect their oilfields on the Persian Gulf. They placed Iraq under their mandate to develop the oilfields north of Bagdad and to build the Iraq pipeline to the Mediterranean. They viewed with little pleasure the French occupation of Syria; but they obliged the French to cede to Iraq the province of Mosul with its rich oilfields.

Ibn Saud has never refused British gold when it could help him to become more powerful. But always he carefully avoided committing himself, and he considered it dangerous to accept British gold in exchange for oil concessions. Ibn Saud met the British in his youth, when he was a landless but ambitious exile at the court of the Sheik of Kuwait, and very early became aware of the value of British support. The Sheik was a protégé and friend of the British. The young Ibn Saud also became Britain's friend.

The British watched with interest Ibn Saud's successful efforts to create a new national Arab community by organizing groups of "militant salvationist agricultural colonies." He transformed the nomads into settled agriculturists. Protecting the sheiks on the shores of the Persian Gulf, the British were pleased by the pacification of adjoining territories. In December 1915 Ibn Saud concluded a friendship treaty with Britain. This friendship, however, did not exclude growing suspicions, provoked by increasing British support of Hussein, Sherif of Mecca and Ibn Saud's greatest rival in the Arab world. But even after he fully realized that the association between T. E. Lawrence and Hussein's family left little hope for British support, he did not rise up against the British. He waited for a better time, and, in expectation of that better time, devoted himself to the consolidation and extension of his power.

In 1919, at the battle of Turaba, he defeated Hussein's son, Abdullah, but he did not yet consider it the time to settle accounts with Hussein. And in 1922 he acquired access to the Syrian desert.

Both Iraq and Transjordania, ruled by his rivals and enemies, sons of Hussein, became accessible to his fanatic and well-disciplined forces.

A conference was called at Kuwait in 1923, for the British Foreign Office was concerned over the increasing threat to its protégés, the Hashimite family. But the conference arrived at nothing: Hussein and his sons refused to recognize in Ibn Saud's growing power any threat of danger. Old Hussein, confined to his Hejaz kingdom, while his sons Faisal and Abdullah ruled over Iraq and Transjordania, could not forget the great Pan-Arab dreams that Lawrence had inspired.

Kemal Ataturk, pursuing his social reforms in 1924 separated the Turkish state from its theocratic base and abolished the Caliphate, the nominal religious leadership of all Moslems. Hussein immediately claimed the title of Caliph. And Ibn Saud, as if this was too much for him, invaded the Hejaz. The defeated Hussein abdicated in favor of his son Ali; the British, who in 1916 had promised him and his sons the leadership of the Arab world, brought him to Cyprus, where he ended his life full of great ambitions and still greater disillusionment.

In 1926, in the Great Mosque of Mecca, Ibn Saud, the Wahabi ruler of Nejd, was proclaimed king of the Hejaz. In 1927 he signed a treaty with Great Britain which recognized the complete and absolute independence of the King of the Hejaz, and of Nejd, and all its dependencies. In 1932 the kingdom of Hejaz and the kingdom of Nejd and its dependencies became Saudi-Arabia. Having established his authority throughout the theocratic Wahabi Empire, and having gained complete control of the Holy Cities of Mecca and Medina, Ibn Saud found himself in a position where he could contemplate the great world about him without fears for his lands or for the security of his own authority. Great Britain, first to recognize the exceptional qualities of Ibn Saud, cultivated his friendship and supported the stability of his ruling house. Britain claims an interest in Saudi-Arabia greater than that of any other power. She has indeed a dominant position in all countries, excepting the Yemen, that surround Saudi-Arabia. On the other hand, among the tens of thousands of overseas pilgrims who yearly visit the sacred cities of Mecca and Medina, and whose expenses constitute one of the main sources of income for Saudi-Arabia, about half are either British subjects or protégés.

As to Ibn Saud, his forty-three years of experience as conqueror and statesman has taught him to value British friendship and to be suspicious of Britain's intentions. That combination of feelings has determined his policy toward Britain, with whom he has always been anxious to maintain the friendliest relations. There have been a number of disputes over his eastern and southeastern borders and conflicts with the British-protected Abdullah of Transjordania, but they have always been under control. Finally, there has been, and still is, the possibility of a conflict over Palestine. Ibn Saud has avoided any interference in the Palestine situation, but he has observed closely the Palestinian developments and, in 1943, he departed from his traditional cautiousness to express publicly his anti-Zionist views.

Unable to forget that for many years the British supported his Hashimite rivals, he is undeniably aware that a clash with Great Britain might be disastrous not only for him but for his family and the future interests of the empire he has built. He is therefore anxious to avoid a clash but he is nonetheless grimly determined to defend his interests and those of his family by not allowing Britain to extend her influence in Saudi-Arabia, and by fighting British support of any other Arab leader in any possible schemes of Arab federation.

Ibn Saud's relations with Britain have, therefore, been tinged with suspicion. He has been reluctant to enter into treaties, conventions, or protracted negotiations with states other than his nearest neighbors, and he did not heed those of his advisers who wished to see Saudi-Arabia a member of the League of Nations. On the other hand, he believed he had found in the United States a potential defender of his country's integrity against the British attempts which he is always fearing—whether rightly or wrongly.

In 1933 he made a move to assure Saudi-Arabia's economic independence, granting the Hasa oil concession to the Standard Oil Company of California. A few years later he was pleased that control of a British company, which since 1934 held a concession to prospect for gold and other minerals, passed into American hands. Early 1943 brought him real gratification: the United

States appointed a Minister to Saudi-Arabia, with residence at Jidda.

In the fall of 1943 his son Faisal, Viceroy of Hejaz and acting Foreign Minister of Affairs, accompanied by a younger brother, visited the United States. A good will tour, it was nevertheless calculated to plumb the depth of America's devotion to the Atlantic Charter, as well as to discover the extent of the friendship and support to be derived from the leasing of Saudi-Arabia's oil wells to the United States, and how effective that support would be. A few months later, political circles in Washington, the oil industry's lobby, and the press throughout the country were passionately discussing whether the American government should invest $150,000,-000 for a pipeline which would help to exploit the American-owned oil concession in Ibn Saud's country.

Ibn Saud's relations with the Soviet Union have been distant and correct. He had no fear of Communist ideology because he was convinced that the religious and social doctrines of Wahabi completely satisfied his people. He relaxed restrictions which he had earlier placed on direct imports from Russia, and he watched Moscow's mounting interest in Near Eastern affairs.

France interested Ibn Saud in so far as she held mandates over Syria and Lebanon, and was the protector of Morocco and Tunisia as well as Algiers. The fate of Syria and Lebanon was of greater concern to Ibn Saud than the future of Morocco, Tunisia, and Algeria. Before the fall of France, he avoided interference in Syrian and Lebanese affairs. But the election in 1943 of his friend Shukri Quwatli as President of the Syrian Republic marked the beginning of a new era in Saudi-Arabian relations with Syria.

It was to be expected, therefore, that Ibn Saud would give his not inconsiderable support to all of Quwatli's attempts to achieve an independent Syria, and to assure her a just place in the Arab Federation. As for Quwatli, it is known that he wants federation of Syria, Saudi-Arabia, and Iraq. But, it is believed, he is waiting for Ibn Saud to declare his position publicly.

Ibn Saud's relations with Iraq were not very cordial during the first years of the reign of King Faisal I. Faisal could not forgive this rival, who in 1924 had driven his father from the family domain at Hejaz. Owing to British influence, however, their relations improved, and in 1930 they met on a British sloop in the Persian Gulf. The meeting resulted in a treaty signed under British auspices.

With the death of King Faisal in 1933, there ended the most bitter phase of the long rivalry for leadership in the Arab world. Faisal's son, Ghazi, could not be regarded by Ibn Saud as serious competition. Fear of Italy, which had been engendered by the Ethiopian War, and fear that Iraq might be drawn into an alliance with Iran and Turkey, both hostile to Saudi-Arabia, encouraged better relations between Saudi-Arabia and Iran. In 1936 the two countries signed a Treaty of Arab Brotherhood and Alliance. Translated into the diplomatic language of Western powers, it was a consultation treaty; both parties pledged to consult each other should either be the object of aggression by a third state.

In 1943 Ibn Saud still believed that Nuri Pasha, pro-British Premier of Iraq, lacked the freedom and authority necessary for discussion of an Arab federation. He felt disposed, however, to consult with him and with the other Arab leaders, to find out whether the Arab world was really approaching the maturity requisite for such a federation.

The ambitions of the Emir Abdullah of Transjordania have scarcely been of a nature to arouse benevolent sentiments in the breast of Ibn Saud. Since the death of Faisal, he has represented the incarnation of the Hashimite family's hostility toward the creator of the Wahabi Empire.

The British, who intervened to improve Ibn Saud's relations with Iraq, exerted a similar pressure on his relations with Transjordania. A treaty of friendship was signed in 1933, in which the British guaranteed the fulfillment of all obligations undertaken by Abdullah. Over a period of a dozen years, Abdullah was gradually emancipating himself from complete British domination—a process that should have given Ibn Saud satisfaction. He was, however, far from pleased. Abdullah, British protégé, was less dangerous than Abdullah, independent candidate for the throne of a United Syria, backed by the prestige of the Hashimite family. Ibn Saud did not take Abdullah very seriously, but he could not ignore his ambitious plans and their probable support by the British, who might very well prefer a greater United Syria headed by their own man to Ibn Saud's potentially antagonistic Wahabi Empire. Ibn Saud, therefore, relied on his friend Quwatli to see that Abdullah's dreams never became more than just that.

Ibn Saud's relations with Egypt have been strained for years. Saudi-Arabia did not even receive recognition from Egypt until 1936. This absence of diplomatic relations was the result of a long-standing hostility between the late King Fuad of Egypt and Ibn Saud. Despite the lack of official relations, however, many Egyptians made their annual pilgrimage to Mecca and Medina. But Egypt considered herself the protector of the Sacred Cities, and this attitude, emphasized by King Fuad, was one of the reasons for the opposition between the two countries.

When, in 1936, Egypt finally recognized the "complete sovereignty and independence" of Saudi-Arabia, together with the incorporation of conquered Hejaz and its sacred cities in the Wahabi Empire, Ibn Saud was compelled to guarantee to the Egyptian government the privilege of "keeping the two Mosques of Mecca and Medina in repair." He strongly resented this guarantee, but he had been obliged to give it as the price for recognition of his empire.

He consistently opposed the slightest indication on the part of Egypt's ruling house toward assuming any titles or prerogatives which might automatically increase their prestige in the Arab world. He refused to recognize in them any superiority over other Arab leaders; he has, therefore, regarded with the greatest mistrust young King Farouk's aspirations to lead the Pan-Arab movement. However, he could not possibly ignore the discussions in Egypt in 1943, even though he suspected the British of playing a game with which he could not sympathize. He sent his close friend and adviser, Yasin Pasha, to confer with Egypt's Premier, Nahas Pasha; and in Jidda he received a special envoy from Nahas Pasha. He did not declare his hand and did not express a definite desire to assume leadership in any sort of Arab federation. He was apparently waiting for a more auspicious opportunity.

On the other hand, he has on several occasions swung all the great might of his influence against those less cautious and more openly ambitious than he—those who dared make a bid for leadership. He was determined to block the road to leadership, both to his old rivals of the Hashimite family and to the ruling house of Egypt. Moreover, he made clear that he could visualize a federation only among absolutely independent states.

From his point of view, neither Iraq nor Egypt was an entirely independent state, and their complete independence was the indispensable condition for the successful realization of any federation schemes. He knew that many Iraqi and Egyptian leaders viewed a federation as the best possible political means of achieving their independence. Unity, they felt, would increase their strength and would allow them to reach their twofold objectives of federation and freedom from foreign influences. They were, therefore, disposed to accept even a British-inspired, or British-sponsored, federation. But Ibn Saud believed that Saudi-Arabia's adherence to such a federation would weaken his country's independence more than it would help the semi-independent Arabs to obtain complete freedom.

An ardent Arab patriot, he was naturally prepared to help the other Arabs in their fight for independence; but having always been cognizant of political and strategic possibilities, he was not disposed to commit the great Arab empire he had been building for forty-three years to a dubious federation. Moreover, he was aware of the crucial test his empire would be confronted with after his death. His thirteen sons could provide a magnificent opportunity for an adequate successor to emerge and thus assure the survival of the empire. But thirteen sons could also divide the empire. The kingdom of Nejd had been lost precisely because of family quarrels between his own father and uncle.

By the sword, and on the Word of the Prophet, Ibn Saud built his empire. By extremely modern methods of oil concession, he attempted to consolidate his empire and make it economically independent. But this greatest Arab conqueror and modern statesman knows only doubts as to the future of his empire. For it flourishes in a world of power politics where the Arab populations, struggling for their freedom, may provoke explosions that will rock the entire Near East, including Ibn Saud's Saudi-Arabia.

XVII: Paradoxes on the Nile

Egypt

THE victory of El Alamein saved Egypt. The successful occupation of North Africa by the Allies liquidated the Axis threat to the Nile Valley and permitted Egypt to continue in full security as the great military base for Allied operations in the Middle East and the Eastern Mediterranean.

Egypt commands the vital communications of the British Empire through Suez to India and to South and East Africa. Her cities have long been headquarters of both the British Eighth Army and of the Eastern Mediterranean fleet with its great central base at Alexandria. Egypt is the focal point to which supplies for the Middle East are sent from America and Britain around the Cape of Good Hope and through the Red Sea, making it the headquarters of the Middle East Supply Council. Moreover, her capital is becoming an important political center. The Greek Government-in-Exile has been transferred to Cairo; the Yugoslav government followed; the British Minister of State to the Middle East has his seat there. And it was in Cairo that Roosevelt and Churchill met with Chiang Kai-shek. Beyond all this, Egypt is a vital center of Arab intellectual and religious life. Her culture and her wealth—it is the richest of the Arab countries—augment her importance as the geographical keystone among the Arab nations. Her prestige is great not only among Arabs but in all of Islam. Consequently, British policy in Egypt is determined by many factors besides Egypt's strategic importance and Britain's interest in the Suez Canal.

At the outbreak of the war Egypt was on the way to realizing complete independence along the lines laid down by the Anglo-Egyptian treaty of 1936; this pact was gained chiefly by Wafd, a nationalistic party headed by Mustafa Nahas Pasha, its leader since

the death in 1927 of the fervent Egyptian nationalist, Zaghlul
Pasha.

For many centuries a dependency of the Ottoman Empire,
Egypt gained virtual freedom during the nineteenth century. In
1882 the British moved in, nominally to support the Egyptian
Khedive against a military uprising. But it was also a measure
calculated to protect interests of the foreign holders of Egyptian
bonds, most of whom happened to be British and French. British
occupation was then described as temporary, but soon it assumed
an air of permanence and led to considerable friction between the
Egyptians and the British. In 1914 the weak ties which still bound
Egypt to the Ottoman Empire were cut, and she was proclaimed a
British protectorate. This was a severe blow to Egyptian hopes of
independence. However, Wilson's Fourteen Points renewed and
stimulated them. If independence was promised to other Arab
states which were hardly ready for it, Egypt, the Egyptians believed, should be the first to achieve it.

During the first fifteen years of the twentieth century, Cairo was
an important center of Arab nationalist aspirations. When
Zaghlul Pasha was jailed by the British in 1919, a serious uprising
ensued. Once these disturbances subsided, the British government
tried to solve the Egyptian problem by a unilateral declaration
terminating the former protectorate and declaring Egypt an independent sovereign state. The 1922 declaration, however, reserved
for Great Britain important rights and privileges. She was assured
control of defense, protection of foreign interests and minorities,
and security of communications to her Eastern Empire through
Suez. She preserved, moreover, her condominium over the Egyptian Sudan. Finally, England managed to maintain unofficial control of Egypt's foreign policies.

The Italian conquest of Abyssinia, which endangered Egypt's
security, was used by the British in 1936 to bring a coalition delegation under the leadership of Nahas Pasha to London, where a
new treaty was negotiated which looked toward the liquidation
of the British military occupation and the relaxation of British
protection of foreign interests in Egypt. Britain, however, reserved
the right to maintain troops necessary for the defense of the Suez

Canal Zone and for the control of the Sudan for a limited period of time, until Egypt was felt to be strong enough to assume these responsibilities herself. A permanent Anglo-Egyptian Alliance, included in the 1936 treaty, assured Britain of Egypt's co-operation in case of war. And when the war came, Egypt broke off relations with all Axis powers, allowed Britain to use her territory for military and naval bases, and became the non-belligerent ally of Britain and later of the United Nations. Thus Egypt fulfilled her diplomatic obligations; and Britain, only too well aware of the extreme complication of Egyptian politics, declared herself satisfied. Egyptian nationalists, however, were not.

There are roughly six discordant elements in Egypt's political life, whose basic antagonisms and temporary alliances make a proper understanding of internal affairs extremely difficult. There is, first, the Palace, but there is also the Moslem religious hierarchy; the landowning and commercial aristocracy, often falsely referred to as the "Pashas"; an educated and well-to-do middle class; a small but increasingly influential lower middle class; and the peasantry or fellaheen, who constitute over 90 per cent of the population.

Among these groups the fellaheen, although they constitute the largest element, are certainly the least vocal. They are controlled by the landowners whose interests are, for the most part, closely allied to large vested British interests, and of whom the peasantry are deeply suspicious. Hardened by two thousand years of oppression, the fellaheen are superstitious and in general fanatically devout. They are a world apart in their manner of life and thought, and owing to their great numbers they constitute a force of appalling social inertia. Bitter experience and a deep religious faith have taught them resignation in the face of adversity. Mud, ceaseless toil, disease, and overpopulation are their heritage. Today their political importance is negligible. Tomorrow it could become enormous.

Just as the fellaheen are subordinate to the landowners, so the lower middle class are indebted to many elements among the upper classes for patronage and favor. Those among them who have developed a sense of political consciousness include petty government officials, small landowners, shopkeepers, petty merchants, and students. Certain members of this group are apt to be politically influential out of all proportion to their number. In consequence, they are frequently used by factions among the upper classes to give vociferous expression to a variety of selfish political objectives. This is especially true of the student groups who are constantly used by the King and the Prime Minister and even by the religious leaders as a weapon in their feuds.

Above this group are the educated, well-to-do middle classes from which most of the top government officials and leaders of the political parties are chosen. Great diversity of political opinion is a principal characteristic of this small but influential element, which includes hidebound reactionaries along with the best liberal leadership to be found in Egyptian politics today.

Leadership is also to be found among the aristocracy, which is composed of the descendants of the old Turkish ruling classes and also of certain purely Egyptian families. Most of this group are landowners on a large scale. Some of them are Christian Copts. In general, they form a social rather than a political group, which on account of its wealth exerts a profound influence upon every phase of Egyptian life.

Equally influential is the great Moslem religious hierarchy entrenched within the walls of the Azhar—the Moslem University in Cairo. This institution is one of the oldest medieval universities surviving into modern times and attracts students from every part of the Islamic world. It is one of the greatest of all reactionary forces in Egyptian politics. At present its interests are clearly allied to those of the Palace.

The group known as the Palace includes the King and his personal advisers as well as politicians animated solely by personal ambition. In reality, it might also be said to include a majority of the Moslem hierarchy. All these groups are, for the most part, sophisticated and primarily loyal to their own interests. They exert a powerful influence upon the young King, who is not without a certain amount of ability in his own right, but whose actions are closely directed and watched by such men as Sheik Maraghi, until recently rector of the Azhar, Ahmad Hassanein Pasha, and formerly by Ali Maher Pasha, who is at present secluded in enforced retirement under British pressure.

Allied successes in North Africa have won the superficial favor and reluctant support of the Palace, but have never inspired any genuine loyalty toward liberal or democratic ideals. On the other hand, it is impossible to ignore the Palace, owing to the important position held by the Royal family in popular esteem and especially by the present King, Farouk I, throughout the Arab Moslem world.

Principal opponents of the Palace at present are the Cabinet under the leadership of Mustafa Nahas Pasha. Prime Minister and leader of the Wafd, he has consistently allied himself, since the outbreak of war, with the British in opposition to the Palace but in line with the Treaty of 1936. In so doing, Nahas has placed himself in a paradoxical situation. The Wafd was first created to fight against the British for Egyptian independence. Later, however, Wafd and the King became rivals for the favor of the Egyptian people. Both Nahas and Farouk claimed to represent the interests of the middle and lower classes. Meanwhile the British were quick to seize the opportunity offered to them in the struggle which ensued. They threw their weight behind the Wafdist leaders in opposition to the King. The alliance thus formed between Nahas and his former British adversaries has survived all storms up to the present time. By means of this alliance, Nahas became Prime Minister and remains in office to this day. He has, however, paid a heavy price for his success. His private following and public popularity have both been steadily on the wane.

Most important has been the loss of those followers recruited from religious, professional, and lesser commercial elements among the population. These elements now lend intellectual substance to a variety of political factions other than the Wafd. Some of them are embittered intellectuals, without property or social position, who often overestimate their own capacities. They are informed by an excellent press, and are quick to detect propaganda. As a whole, they resent the presence of the British in Egypt, although they would probably prefer them to any others. They easily dominate the political activities of the illiterate fellaheen, whose political potentialities may become very important in the world of tomorrow. They regard this world of tomorrow in terms always of Egyptian independence, generally of Arab independence, and in some cases of Arab federation. The Egyptians themselves are barely conscious of their racial ties with other Arab peoples. They are ignorantly anxious to head an Arab Federation, but they do not know how to achieve dominance.

Chief symbol of their confused aspirations is in many cases King Farouk, who sees himself as the future leader of a great Pan-Arab federation and regards the British as a primary obstacle to the realization of his dreams. The King has only the remnants of a political party in the Egyptian Parliament, although he has always found politicians prepared to do his bidding. Among these men are Makram Pasha and Ali Maher Pasha, who was formerly Chief of the Royal Cabinet and, until his arrest by the British in 1943, the King's chief spokesman. Makram was opposed to the Palace for years. Finally, however, he deserted Nahas and went over to the King. Farouk is also in high favor with the army, and many higher officers would out of personal loyalty support his Pan-Arab or Pan-Islamic sentiments. Some of them might even be induced to join with the King is an effort to overthrow the Wafd.

In his desire to block the ascendancy of the Wafd and destroy the power of Nahas, King Farouk connived with Makram Pasha in the spring of 1943 to drop a political bomb which might have put an end to Nahas' career. A "Black Book," circulated among political and official circles, accused Nahas Pasha and other Wafdist leaders of corruption. This "Black Book" had such repercussions throughout the country that Nahas was forced to defend himself before both the upper and lower houses of the Egyptian Parliament. There has recently been a second "Black Book." Only a few copies were distributed and little is known about its content. Presumably charges were similar to those leveled against Nahas in the first book.

The political prestige of Nahas was shaken for a while. Very soon, however, it was restored when discussions of Arab Federation began in Cairo, with Nahas taking the leading part in them. The British, who for a time have been reserved in their support of Nahas, again extended to him their backing. It has not been established whether Nahas Pasha in his rivalry with the King tried to improve his political prestige by bidding for leadership in an Arab Federation for Egypt—a leadership which Farouk was reserving for himself—or whether he has been pushed on the road leading to an Arab Federation by the British who, once having realized that this Federation might become a reality, would prefer to have it built up by leaders with whom they have been able to establish co-operation. This appears at any rate to have been the suspicion which rose in Ibn Saud's mind when he saw Nahas Pasha and Nuri Pasha work together on the realization of plans for an Arab Federation.

The aspirations of the majority of Egyptians are concentrated on winning their independence. The interest of the fellaheen is centered in a passionate desire for increased economic security and improved social conditions. Cotton prices, on which this security depends, interest them more than the political ideas of Ibn Saud. The Egyptians are too fully aware of their economic and cultural superiority over other Arab-speaking states to pay much attention to Pan-Arab ideals. In general, they prefer to limit their influence in the Arab world to cultural, religious, and possibly economic spheres.

In so far as their political aspirations are not concerned with internal social and economic problems, they concentrate upon the realization of complete and absolute national independence. Four goals loom on the horizon of that independence: to take over from the British the defense of Suez; to control the Sudan, where the waters of the Nile are regulated and where the Egyptian middle class would find employment; the evacuation of all foreign troops and, immediately upon termination of the war, Egyptian participation as an independent state at the peace table.

Those purely nationalist ambitions are of far greater importance to the Egyptians than the Pan-Arab aspirations of their King. Yet, even in Egypt, Pan-Arabism is not a movement to be lightly ignored. The Arab Union was formed in Cairo in the spring of 1942 under the leadership of Fuad Abaza Pasha. Members of the Union, who view their organization as the nucleus of a powerful Pan-Arab group, have drawn a clear distinction between Arab "Unity" and Arab "Union." Arab Unity is defined as the political union of Arab countries under a single head. Arab Union is supposed to be the economic and cultural union without the necessity of definite political ties. Unity, they believe, is no longer practical, since no Arab country would submit to the domination of another.

"Union" is not only practical but essential for Arab survival. The distinction has not been accepted by everyone. Some Pan-Arab Egyptian nationalists think of actual political unity among the Arabs. The activities of the Union have been followed, however, with sympathy by the King and his advisers. Fuad Abaza Pasha and his Union do not go along the Pan-Arab road as far as King Farouk would like to go, but the King is still able to consider them allies. They help him in diffusing the Pan-Arab idea among the Egyptians.

On the other hand, King Farouk was both aided and handicapped by the series of conferences among Arab leaders which took place during 1943 in Cairo. The fact that all the conferences were held in Egypt, and that even the great Ibn Saud sent his envoy, emphasized the importance of Egypt in the Arab world and consequently enhanced Farouk's chances for a Pan-Arab union under his own leadership. However, the fact that Arab conferences were prepared by his Prime Minister and rival, Nahas Pasha —and that they were British-sponsored—undermines Farouk's chances to satisfy his personal ambitions.

A paradoxical situation was thus created during 1943 in the Nile Valley. The leader of the nationalistically minded Wafd, created to fight the British, became an ally of Britain. The King, whose Prime Minister became his rival, encourages politicians who in their turn accuse his Prime Minister of corruption. The Prime Minister helps the King in that he works for an Arab Federation and arouses interest in that Federation among the Egyptian people. And the Prime Minister works against the King by taking personal leadership in the Pan-Arab discussions and allowing the British to inspire and direct such discussions.

There is no love lost between the King and the British authorities in Egypt. The only force which has been effective in keeping the King in check is the British Ambassador, Sir Miles W. Lampson, recently created Lord Killearn. When in February 1942 a crisis broke out because of the British demand to oust the Vichy Legation in Cairo, the British Ambassador forced King Farouk's hand, obliged him to break diplomatic relations with Vichy, and installed the present Wafdist Cabinet.

The King finds it hard to forgive his Prime Minister for allying himself with the British Ambassador. The King must therefore follow the Arab conferences which, with Nahas presiding, take place in Cairo, with the secret hope that some opportunity might offer him the chance to get rid of his Prime Minister and harvest for himself all that Nahas Pasha has sown in the Pan-Arab field. It is not impossible though that Nahas, allowed by the British to sow the seeds of Arab Federation under their surveillance, may try, when the harvest is ripe, to take all of it over to the Wafd's barn, oblige the British to recognize Egypt's complete independence and, thus becoming the real national leader of Egypt, definitely subject the Palace to the Wafd or, if the Palace should resist, eliminate it.

Further evidence of the bitter rivalry between Farouk and his Prime Minister has recently been revealed in the closing of Azhar University and the enforced resignation of its Rector, Sheik Maraghi. Struggles to take the lead in schemes for Arab Federation are, in this new conflict, matched by struggles to win the support of the Moslem hierarchy. This struggle has been going on behind the scenes for a long time, but it finally came into the light during the visit in January 1944 of the Lebanese Delegation, when certain groups of the Azhar students manifested their support of Farouk, and others proclaimed both Farouk and Nahas Pasha.

Rivalry between Farouk and the Wafdist leader for a dominant position both in Egypt and in the Arab world is a factor which must be kept constantly in mind in any consideration of Arab problems in the Near and Middle East. The British have used this rivalry skillfully throughout the war to consolidate their own position, and even to prepare the ground for an Arab Federation which would not conflict with their own plans for the Near East. But if the rivalry between King Farouk and Nahas were to come to a head before, or during, the Peace Conference, it would create a difficult situation not only for Britain but for all the United Nations.

XVIII: Complexities and Perplexities

French North Africa

When in November 1942 American soldiers landed in Morocco and Algiers, they discovered a new world with an alien culture and an unfamiliar religion. They also found a lack of comfort that could not be compensated by the abundance of local color which was often dimmed by the dust of centuries. North Africa looked to those soldiers like a stage set that had been prepared for the great and somber adventure of war. It also served as a waiting room for their departure to Europe. They settled themselves as comfortably as they could in that unfamiliar and unreal world.

Curiously enough, Americans at home also had a tendency to regard North Africa as a stage set against which was enacted the extremely complex and often unpleasant imbroglio of a French political drama wherein an assassinated French admiral and two French generals played leading roles. It is quite natural that the audience focused its attention on the complicated action and not on the dusty set. The set, of course, was not designed for the American military forces nor prepared especially for the drama. It has been in existence for centuries, and it will outlive for as many centuries the present conflict.

Millions of North Africans live and work in the hope that their still confused aims will some day be realized. Both Frenchmen and Americans are foreigners to them; they do not know yet how and when they can get rid of these intruders. They vaguely hope that the day will come, but only a few among them actively work to bring that day closer.

Of the total French North African population of 16,190,000 (1936 census), the native Arabs and Berbers number 14,516,000. Their political status differs greatly from one country to another. Algiers, conquered by the French in 1830 and divided into three departments, is an integral part of continental France. Its French settlers and native Jews, franchised by the so-called *Loi Crémieux* of 1870, sent deputies and senators to the Parliament in Paris.

Tunisia, governed by a Bey, has been since 1881 a French protectorate. It lives under a regime of disguised annexation, with an administration in which higher French officials have gradually substituted their own authority for that of the Tunisian ministers, while French *contrôleurs civiles* absorbed the power of the Moslem caids (judges), and the French gendarmerie replaced the native Spahis.

Morocco, conquered in 1912, has been better organized than Tunisia, due to the colonial genius of Marshal Lyautey, who described himself as a Royalist who brought an empire to the French Republic. It is also a French protectorate with a native government controlled by the Sultan, but it enjoys greater freedom than Tunisia.

The Arabs and the Berbers in all three parts of French North Africa have in common their religion, to a certain extent the same culture, and the same deep-rooted opposition to foreign rule and exploitation. Nationalism to them is largely an instrument through which improvement of their immediate material welfare may be achieved. Some have even accepted Communism, despite its fundamental opposition to the religious and social doctrines of Islam, as a political weapon of revolt against foreign imperialism. They are, however, divided by the innumerable conflicts between nomadic and sedentary tribes, plainsmen, and highlanders, and between Arabs and Jews in the cities.

North Africa is predominantly inhabited by Berbers, whom the Arab conquerors succeeded in Islamizing and, in part, Arabizing over a period of five centuries. A non-Semitic people of undetermined origins, the Berbers have lived along the southern shores of the Mediterranean from time immemorial. Their national stock has been further confused by intermarriage with Arab conquerors and Negro slaves. They range in appearance from tall, light-haired, blue-eyed men in the regions of the Atlas mountains to dark brown Negroid types in the south.

Over a period of more than a thousand years Berbers and Arabs struggled for supremacy, although wars and intermarriage combined to make it difficult to draw any clear distinction between them. Many Berbers were linguistically, culturally, and religiously assimilated by the Arab invaders. Literary Arabic, the sacred language of both Arabs and Berbers, has fulfilled the same unifying function as the Islam faith.

On the other hand, the differences between them were complicated by the conflict between nomadic and sedentary peoples, the traditional conflict between the "tent and the town" in the Arab world.

The bulk of this population, Arabs and Berbers—nomad, peasant, and townsman alike—are primarily concerned with squeezing a bare living from the land. The illiterate and hungry masses in French North Africa are not very much interested in the Pan-Arab movement. Pan-Arab aspirations are, however, fairly strong among the intellectual minority, which some day might play a leading part.

The nationalist parties, with their constant agitation for a variety of conflicting political programs, form a very small element in a population indifferent on the whole to the larger political conceptions of nationalism and Pan-Arabism. Yet this element is of an importance far in excess of its trifling numbers, for almost all the intellectual leaders in North Africa belong to it. This fact, frequently overlooked by many observers, must constantly be borne in mind in any discussion of nationalist movements in this area. Throughout all North Africa, nationalist parties are determined to Arabize the Moslem population in its entirety, not only religiously and linguistically but psychically and politically. Some of these nationalist parties have even tried to win over the Berbers by convincing them that they are of pure Arab stock.

In Algeria the Pan-Arab movement is fostered by the conservative *Association des Oulémas Algériens,* whose program calls for the independence of all Arab nations, the fusion of these nations into a North African bloc, and the entry of this bloc into a federated Arab empire. The association, divided since 1937 into two parts and advocating nationalism on a strictly Moslem and Orthodox basis, has been mainly responsible for the agitation against the *Loi Crémieux.* This decree was issued in 1870, when France needed all possible support in her war against Prussia. Its aim was to secure the ties between France and Algeria by increasing

the number of French citizens there. There were two Crémieux
decrees, both signed on the same day, in October 1870. The first
declared that all Jewish natives of the departments of Algeria were
French citizens. The second authorized the Moslem natives to
apply for French citizenship by a simple declaration that they
placed themselves under the "civil and political laws of France."

Very few Algerian Moslems, however, made use of this right
which was extended to them. Islam is not only a religion. It is
also a legal system. Acceptance of French laws would be equiva-
lent, in the eyes of the Moslems, to the rejection of Islamic laws.
The French laws—the *Code Napoléon*—did not recognize the Moslem institution of polygamy, the Moslem privilege of the initiative
of divorce reserved to husbands only, the right of Moslem fathers
to give their sons or daughters in marriage without their consent,
and the Moslem inheritance laws establishing the supremacy of
the male descendant.

After the First World War, in order to facilitate and encourage
the naturalization of Algerian Moslems, a new law was created.
The Moslems were no longer obliged to reject their Islamic laws.
The only condition imposed upon them by the new law was to
be a monogamist or a bachelor. As economic conditions in Algeria
forced the overwhelming majority of the Moslems to a reduced
budget which could afford only one wife, it was to be expected
that many Moslems would be willing to benefit by the new law.
Actually, however, they did not. The new law with its complicated texts gave the impression that they would be snared in
French "red tape." And apparently they mistrusted the status of
the citizenship which was offered to them.

With the awakening of Arab nationalism, the Algerian nationalist parties used the Crémieux decree, and especially the fact that
one of the four signatories, Senator Isaac Crémieux, was a Jew,
for anti-Jewish agitation. Also the fact that in the North African
cities trade and especially money-lending was concentrated in
Jewish hands greatly stimulated this agitation. Algerian nationalists declared that they considered the Algerian Jews as part of
their community. They accused the French of having favored the
Algerian Jews for the purpose of making them a bolstering force
in French nationalism. Nazi propaganda therefore found a more

or less favorable ground in North Africa even before the war. Naturally its influence increased with the support of Vichy ideology after the collapse of France. The Crémieux decree was abrogated by Vichy in 1940 with a retroactive clause. Algerian Jews, who for three generations had been French citizens and who fought in three French wars (the Franco-Prussian War and World Wars I and II), overnight found themselves deprived of French citizenship.

After the Allied landing in North Africa, the local French administration, strongly anti-Semitic even before the war, opposed for more than a year the restoration of the *Loi Crémieux* and the re-establishment of French citizenship to those Algerian Jews who had lost it. They maintained that restoration of the law would provoke a revolt among the Arabs, propagandized for over thirty months by Vichy and Nazi broadcasts, and this, they argued, would compromise the security of the Allied forces in North Africa. However, under increasing pressure from both American and British public opinion, the *Loi Crémieux* was finally restored in the summer of 1943, and no troubles resulted. The indignation of the Algerian Arabs has apparently not been as great as some elements of the French military and civil administration believed —or wished to believe. It is also probable that the presence of the Allied troops contributed to prevent any outbreak of trouble. In December 1943 the French Committee of National Liberation recommended the bestowal of French citizenship on the Moslem élite without demanding the rejection of the Islamic laws. It was the counterpart of the restoration of the Crémieux decree.

Prior to these events, radical nationalist groups in Algeria had been dissolved, only to reorganize and be dissolved again. The most lasting group was constituted by dissident elements of the *Association des Oulémas Algériens,* which in 1937 formed the *Réforme Musulmane.* This group has been rather quiet in recent years, and has tended to place its emphasis on religion rather than on politics.

In Tunisia the center of nationalist agitation was the *Destour* party, divided into two groups, *Vieux Destour* and *Neo Destour.* The *Neo Destour* has been a source of serious concern and trouble to the French. It appeared to have instigated the riots which took place in Bizerte during 1937 and in which the Lebanese agitator, the Emir Shekib Aslam, played a very active part.

The *Destour* carried on treasonable dealings with Fascist Italy, which untiringly tried to used eighty thousand Italians settled in Tunisia for anti-French agitation and as a pretext for the justification of Italian claims on Tunisia. On the other hand, radical elements of the *Neo Destour* put to use the Communist concept of the class struggle; transplanted into Moslem countries, the struggle against an exploiting class automatically became a struggle against the European.

Until the Allied occupation, the native government in Tunis was controlled by Sidi Mohammed el Mounsaf, known as the "Peasant Bey." Member of a dynasty going back to 1691, when a military revolution ousted the Turkish regime, the Tunisian Bey was popular among his people. He himself was not pro-Axis, but members of his family had been influenced by Italy and Fascist propaganda. He accepted Axis domination, was unable to hand Tunisia over to the Allied forces, and went into exile. The pro-Vichy administration in Tunisia must be held greatly responsible for the Peasant Bey's attitude.

He was succeeded by Sidi El-Amine, youngest son of Sidi Mohammed el Habib Pasha, who ruled Tunis from 1922 to 1929. The new Bey is known more for his hobby of painting than for his political ideas. It is as yet impossible to say what influence he may have on the future of Tunisian nationalism.

In French Morocco, conquered in 1912, the native government is controlled by the Sultan, the namesake of the former Bey of Tunisia, Sidi Mohammed. A member of the Alaouite dynasty which dominated Morocco from the end of the seventeenth century, he is a Sherif or descendant of the Prophet and as such has great religious as well as political power. Waning French prestige temporarily increased his power. General de Gaulle and General Georges Catroux, Co-ordinator of Moslem Affairs, have done their best, however, to reduce the Sultan's authority to its former proportions.

The power of the Sultan is exerted under the surveillance of the French Resident-General in Morocco, who is Minister of For-

eign Affairs to the Sultan and head of the French administration.
Important religious functions are delegated to the Sultan's brothers and half-brothers, or khalifas, in Fez, Marrakesh, and Tiznit.
Civil and judicial administration is in the hands of a grand vizier
and a subordinate council of viziers who, in turn, control officers
in the various cities, towns, and tribes. Under these men a hierarchy of lesser native officials work in close collaboration with a
French Counsellor in charge of Sherifian affairs, French members
of the Municipal and Native Councils, and the extremely powerful
Bureau des Affaires Indigènes (Office of Native Affairs). Co-ordination, however, does not always imply co-operation.

The spirit of independence is undoubtedly stronger in Morocco
than in Tunisia or Algiers, for the Moroccan tribesmen still live
with memories, as recent as 1912, of their struggles for independence. Successive revolts of many tribes prevented complete
pacification for two decades. Yet many Arabs in Morocco appreciated the colonial genius of Lyautey, who knew how to win their
confidence and, on certain occasions, even the affection of the
conquered but proud people. Unfortunately for France, the fine
spirit of Lyautey and of his military aides did not always pre-
vail in the French civilian administration. Too often it was impressed by economic interests, represented in North Africa by
powerful French corporations, rather than by the legitimate interests of the native population.

Several Pashas, great feudal landowners more interested in the
increase of their wealth than in the welfare of their country—for
example, El Glaoui, the Pasha of Marrakesh—have been willing
to play the game of both French and British capital. Nationalist
propaganda in Morocco consequently found a favorable soil for
agitation, emphasizing the exploitation of the country which it
often exaggerated to serve its own purposes.

Arab nationalism is propagated in French Morocco by the
Comité d'Action Marocaine, centered around the great College
at Fez. Supported by left-wing politicians in France for a time,
its leaders, Abd-al-Jalil and Allal-al-Fasi, were arrested and exiled
in 1937. It has been revived as the Nationalist Party under the
same leadership and is in close contact with the *Unidad Maroqui,*

a highly developed nationalist party in neighboring Spanish Morocco, nominally under the Sultan of Morocco, but since 1912 ruled by Spain.

The *Unidad* strenuously combats all influences hostile to strictly orthodox Islam. It campaigns to encourage loyalty to the reigning Alouite Sultan and his family, fights Berber influence throughout Morocco, propagates Arabic, opposed foreign rulers of any sort even though they be Moslems, and fosters a program of social and educational reforms. Another important nationalist organization, *Bureau de Défense Nationaliste,* is directed by Ibrahim al-Wazzani who has used only legal means in his defense of the Arab cause but has never ceased to expose and condemn French colonial intentions toward Islam in general, and the North African Arabs in particular.

Though the French military administration in North Africa boasted of having had the entire Arab nationalist organization under its control at the time that General Giraud was supreme French authority in North Africa, it appears that French control has been efficiently tightened and consolidated since the French administration has been taken over by General de Gaulle. The Arabs have an innate respect for military power. The Sultan of Morocco was considered by the French as altogether loyal. When, however, the Sultan realized that General Giraud was essentially an American protégé, he indicated to both American and British authorities that he regarded the French protectorate over Morocco as having lapsed owing to the condition in which the French found themselves at that time. France herself needed the protection of a great power, the Sultan reasoned, and could hardly be expected to protect Morocco. On the other hand, he was ready to concede that French Morocco was not ripe for complete independence. He was therefore willing to accept foreign protection by a combination of powers to include the United States, Great Britain, France, and possibly Spain.

The intransigeance of de Gaulle toward both the United States and Britain since he took over the administration undoubtedly impressed the Sultan of Morocco, as well as the other Arab leaders in Tunisia and Algiers. It is even possible that his uncompromising attitude was to a great extent determined by the need to manifest to the North African Arab population that France, although weakened, still had sufficient strength to fight for her prewar position among world powers. From this point of view the French "strong arm" policy in Lebanon might be seen as inspired by the same desire to impress not only the Arabs of the two sister republics on the shore of the Eastern Mediterranean, but the Arabs of North Africa as well.

There is, however, an essential difference in the status of the North African countries. Syria and Lebanon are republics under the French mandate, and they have been repeatedly promised their independence. Tunisia and Morocco are nominally independent states under the French protectorate, with no date whatever set for the expiration of the protectorates, and Algeria is incorporated into metropolitan France. Certain Arab aspirations, especially in intellectual circles, are common to all those countries. Curiously enough, the University of Paris became a rallying place for young Arab intellectuals living under the French protectorate and mandate. The custom of sending their sons to Paris brought leading Moslem families of French North Africa into close contact with Pan-Arab leaders from the Middle East. The spirit of Arab revival was brought to North Africa by books and newspapers, by returning pilgrims and students, some of whom had attended Egyptian and Syrian universities.

The Moslem world at an early date claimed as its own the Arab world of North Africa. Fez, with its great college, Marrakesh, the great economic center in French Morocco, and Kairouan, the holy city in Tunisia, are only slightly less important than Bagdad, Damascus, and Cairo, the great Arab centers of the Near and Middle East. The Islamic Congress was always attended by North African delegates. Egypt's acquisition of independence in 1936, the activity of Pan-Arab agitation from Egypt, Syria, and Palestine during the Tunisian disorders of 1937, the disturbance in Palestine in 1938, the steady rise of Wahabi power under Ibn Saud in Arabia—all served to arouse at least momentary enthusiasm among North African Moslem intellectuals.

In 1943 the Arab Union of Fuad Abaza Pasha in Cairo established a North African Committee. This fact is significant for it shows the extent to which Moslems in North Africa look to Egypt rather than to any other Moslem country for leadership. It is also important because it would appear to give substance to rumors that certain nationalist elements in North Africa anticipated the formation of an African Moslem bloc under Egyptian leadership to extend from Dakar to Suez and from Tetuán to Timbuktu. Nevertheless, the total effect of Pan-Arabism in North Africa may very well be insignificant for some time to come, and for several reasons.

Morocco continues to lack adequate contacts with the rest of the Moslem world; so does Algeria and so, to a lesser extent, Tunisia. Also Pan-Arabism can appeal to only a fraction of the Moslem people in this area. The Arab-speaking populations of North Africa were not nationalistic minded in the sense that nationalism is understood by the Western mind. Nationalism, in which they see primarily a means to improve their immediate material welfare, is not founded on a conception of loyalty to a Moroccan, Tunisian, or Algerian state. More frequently it is confused with loyalty to specific political or religious leaders, and is generally understood as such by these leaders. Though at the present time only the educated classes in the towns have been affected by the Pan-Arab appeal, it must not be forgotten that under the stress of adverse economic or political conditions, this small group could conceivably stir up the more apathetic and ignorant Moslem majority. An additional Pan-Arab weakness is its lack of leadership and a sense of unity, although in recent years Spanish Moroccan chieftains attempted to cultivate ties with Egypt and thus gain something of that country's prestige.

Again, though the Arabs in North Africa have serious grievances with regard to their economic status, they cannot deny the civilizing action of the French, particularly in Morocco. French prestige has benefited by comparison with the control exercised by the Italians since 1912 over neighboring Tripolitania and Libya. The horrible atrocities they perpetrated on the Moslems in Libya are too recent to be erased from memory. Mussolini's pretentions of becoming the protector of Islam only emphasized the shallowness of Italian imperialist designs. And finally, there is the fact that Moslem energies continued to be deflected from Pan-Arab ends by petty local squabbles with the Berbers, and the continuation of friction between the French governors and these "slaves of slaves."

The fate of Moslem aspirations is more an enigma in North Africa than anywhere else in the Moslem world. Additional formulation and clarification of these aims will depend largely upon political developments in North Africa itself, upon the zeal of those Moslem leaders who desire to bring North Africa into the framework of Pan-Arabism, and perhaps most important of all, upon economic developments. For it is a harsh fact that the Pan-Arab movement in North Africa has made itself defined only at times of acute trouble and, more particularly, at times of severe economic depression. The economic self-interest of the North African bloc of Arab states may dictate a policy of association with powers outside their orbit. Pan-Arabism can hardly become a serious factor so long as the united interest of French factions, backed by British and American policy, demonstrates to the restless native population that the Western powers will brook no interference for the duration of the war in their absolute control of the political situation from one end of North Africa to the other.

The fate of North Africa in the postwar world is another matter. What it becomes and how it will unfold is a question mark. Its partial and qualified answer is found in yet another question mark—for North Africa is inextricably bound to the future of the French Empire. What the Fourth Republic will become, and what its position on colonies and mandates will be, will determine to a great extent the destiny of all North Africa.

XIX: The Testing Ground

Iran

THERE are a number of places in the world that are testing grounds for the sincerity of United Nations' policy and postwar plans. Iran is an outstanding example.

Iran, more commonly known as Persia, has been for the last hundred and fifty years the foremost arena for the power politics of both Russia and Great Britain. When, after a century-old rivalry in Asia, Britain and Russia were able to reach an agreement over Persia in 1907, this agreement made possible the British-Russian alliance against the Germans in 1914. When the Soviet Revolution broke the British-Russian alliance, the two powers immediately clashed in Persia. And in the present war, when Britain and the Soviet Union found themselves once more in the same camp, the first place in which they established co-operation was Persia, where their forces moved in in August 1941.

The Persians, who know their history, believe that their only hope of survival is in British-Russian rivalry. Their greatest fear is agreement between those two great powers. "When the British Lion and the Russian Bear move together," wrote a nineteenth-century Persian poet, "the fate of Iran will be sealed."

By the Russian-British agreement of 1907, Persia was divided into three zones. The northern provinces were reserved for Russia's political and military influence. The southern regions, in which Britain obtained rich oil concessions, were placed under her control. Between these two spheres there remained a kind of "no-power's land." In this mountainous terrain, inhabited by the old and aristocratic Bakhtiari tribes—the Scots of Iran—the Persians felt more or less their own masters.

When this agreement ended in 1918 with the Soviet Revolution, Persia feared even more the threat of a Bolshevized Russia. In the northern provinces the Red Army fought the British who were

attempting to hold onto Baku's oilfields and the Persians benefited
by the reopened conflict. When hostilities ended, the Russians
aided the soldier-usurper Riza Khan to ride the wave of anti-
British sentiment, to liquidate the degenerate dynasty of Kadjara,
and to seize for himself one of the world's most ancient thrones.
Once on the throne, Riza Khan proved to be a very adroit politician; he became the "strong man" of Persia, shrewdly playing
the Russian Bear and the British Lion against each other. He
modernized his country and, making the most of the nationalist
pride of his people, restored the ancient and glorious name of
Iran. He fought cleverly for its economic emancipation; but while
he always kept his nation's interests in the foreground, he never
forgot his own. As an individual he was bound to become rich
faster than his country.

The Persians, poor and ruthlessly exploited by a small group
of landowners and politicians, disliked him, but having been exploited by rulers for over two thousand years, they had grown
accustomed to it. Throughout her long history, Persia has risen
to greatness only under the leadership of a succession of strong
men, generally usurpers, whose power rarely survived more than
three generations. There has never been any sense of national
unity; only the influence of domineering personalities has been
able to shake the Persians out of an innate national lethargy. So
far as Riza Khan is concerned, the Persians no doubt considered
that it was preferable to be exploited by one of their own people
than by the British or Russians.

Riza Khan found an economic ally in Germany. Commercial
travelers and technicians from the Reich flooded the country,
bringing with them old truck engines, and making dynamos and
setting up electric installations. Not as well off as the British, they
lived on an economic level only a little higher than that of the
Iranians. Nor were they as powerful as the British, with the result that instead of treating the proud Iranians as natives, they
took pains to flatter them.

When Hitler came to power, these Germans became loyal Nazi
Party members and, while they grew in strength, they pretended
they had no aim but to prosper by helping the Iranians rid themselves of British and Russian economic control. Nazi propaganda

successfully exploited Iranian national pride with tales of close
kinship between Aryan Germans and Indo-Aryan Persians. Fearing the Russians and hating the British, the Iranians began to
look upon the Germans as their saviors. They hoped for the day
of Germany victory which, it seemed to follow, would bring them
complete independence and a major role in settling the future of
the Middle East.

When in August 1941 the British and the Russians moved into
Iran, it was logical for the Iranians to fight them, but their resistance lasted only three days. Riza Khan, obliged to abdicate,
was sent by the British to the remote island of Mauritius.

His son, Mohammed Riza, who succeeded him, is young and
inexperienced, but autocratic by instinct. The rich landowners
disapprove of him as the son of a man who led them to the brink
of ruin; the multitude of the poor population have little love for
him because they wrongly regard him as a British puppet. Son
of a usurper, he will survive only so long as he can overcome the
suspicions of both elements. He is opposed not only to the corrupt
politicians in the *Majlis* (Parliament), but also to the corrupt and
selfish landed classes. It is undoubtedly next to impossible to judge
his true character and ability until after the war, for until then, if
then, he will not be free to act. At the present, he can only mark
time and wait the departure of the forces of occupation. Then, it is
possible, he may step in and take over, along with his band of
young military followers.

His Prime Minister, Soheili, despite his youth, belongs to the
old gang of self-interested politicos. He is reputed to be pro-
Russian, but he is probably as little pro-Russian as the Shah is
pro-British. Both of them, along with the army officers on whom
the Shah relies, are essentially pro-Persian, and therefore aligned
against the British and the Russians.

While the Iranian Army is still permitted to operate against
rebellious tribes, order in the land is insured by British, Russian,
and a smaller number of American troops. Iran has become Russia's Burma Road, along which moves the stream of American-
British supplies for Soviet forces engaged in a victorious struggle against the Nazi aggressors. It is as well the back door to the
Caspian Basin which the Russians have thus sealed against pos-

sible German attack from the Middle East. The British moved in not only with the purpose of helping Russia, but to be sure that the presence of Russian troops in Iran would not endanger their sphere of influence on the Persian Gulf. The American troops are present only to protect and expedite American supplies to Russia via Iran. Thus, today, three of the four major United Nations have troops on Iranian soil. And it was at Iran's Teheran that the historical meeting of the Big Three took place.

The Russians have isolated the five northern provinces of Azerbaijan, Gilan, Khurasan, Mazanderan, and Gurgan, and have closed their borders to all travelers, Persian, British, and American alike. They have stripped these provinces, the richest in the land, but so cleverly as to avoid the economic chaos now apparent in areas under British control. The economic situation in the Soviet-occupied north is even superior to what it was in the days of Riza Khan. On the other hand, the Russians have not destroyed the local government organization, preferring that the corrupt Iranian officials discredit themselves in the eyes of their subjects.

The class conflict has been indirectly projected into an already highly complex situation. While landowning classes are afraid of Communist expansion, peasants in the north have no reason to complain about their uninvited foreign guests. And the disappearance of the young Shah's tax collectors in the north have contributed more to prestige than the presence of the Russian traveling theatrical shows.

In the British-controlled south the situation is quite different. The British have stripped the region as mercilessly as the Russians stripped their zone, but without the astutely adequate compensation. The tax collectors continue to make their rounds in southern Iran; the old feudal officials still suppress the will of the people; the wealthy landlords hoard food with impunity in the face of a food crisis, aggravated by the appearance of Polish refugees released from Russia who are compelled to remain in Iran until they can depart for other havens. The entire economic situation is grave.

The Iranians received from their uninvited guests the promise that Russian and British troops would be evacuated six months after the war. They wonder, however, whether this pledge will be respected. They know they can no longer receive German aid and that German defeat is only a matter of time. Their last hope is the United States. The Americans who came to their country, often at the request of the Iranian government, had no territorial or political ambitions. Many of them have even undertaken altruistic enterprises. The first American advisers arrived in Persia as early as 1911, when W. Morgan Shuster, heading a group of five experts, came to reorganize the administrative and financial agencies of the Persian government. Russia and Britain, resenting the success of the Shuster mission, compelled the Persians to send Shuster and his aides back to the States. Another group, led by Dr. Arthur C. Millspaugh, came to Persia in 1924 at the invitation of Riza Shah. The Millspaugh mission stayed for five years and was quite successful in reorganizing Iranian finances.

At the same time American oil firms—(the Standard Oil Company of New Jersey and the Sinclair Oil Corporation)—became interested in the development of the north Iranian oilfields. In the spring of 1937 Iran granted a concession of 100,000 square miles to the Seabord Oil Corporation of Delaware and its subsidiary, the Amiranian Oil Company. The British and the Russians, however, did not view with sympathy the development of independent American oil interests in a country where Britain controlled the Anglo-Iranian oil concessions in the south, and Russia regulated the northern route over the Caspian Sea. In July 1938 the Amiranian corporation withdrew from the concession, leaving the Anglo-Iranian Oil Company, which, despite legal limitations imposed upon it by Riza Shah, was a state within the state of Persia, unrivaled in the country.

In 1943 Dr. Millspaugh, at the head of an American financial and economic group, was again in Iran as Administrator General of Finance. Other American experts supervised food administration and agricultural missions, or served as municipal policy advisers. A group of American military experts, led by Major General Clarence S. Ridley, acted as advisers to the Iranian Army, while another military group, under Colonel H. Norman Schwarzkopf, aided the Iranian government in its administration of the gendarmerie.

Almost all these missions were provided at the request of the Iranian government. Their members came to Iran as employees of that government, and were in no sense of the word dependent upon, or subject to, American policy. They were supposed to assure a disinterested international co-operation, a type which might easily become a pattern for postwar reconstruction. In certain respects they were even supposed to illustrate how the broad terms of the Atlantic Charter might be successfully implemented through the appointment of foreign advisers to alien governments at the specific requests of those governments.

In view of the Russian-British occupation, a clash between American missions invited by the Iranian government to assist in solving its administrative problems and the occupation authorities was almost inevitable. The main difficulties arose because the five Soviet-controlled rich northern provinces were sealed tight even against the Iranians. The striking contract between their relative prosperity and the food crisis and inflation in the British-controlled south became the trump card for Soviet propaganda.

American advisers to the Iranian Food Ministry complained that the Soviets only with reluctance released a meager 4,000 tons of wheat for Teheran at the time of the bread riots, and they reproached the Russians for having aggravated the food crisis by buying grain in the open Iranian market. As a result of a discussion between the Soviet authorities and the American Food Adviser, Assistant Adviser Rex Vivian was removed from Tabriz in northern Iran, and several American Army Intelligence officers who tried to check the amount of Russian grain purchases in the open market were expelled from Persia at the demand of the Russians.

American financial aides, in an effort to halt the mounting inflation, came into conflict with the Russians over a loan of $50,000,000, requested by the Iranian government on the advice of Dr. Millspaugh with the approval of the British. The Soviet ambassador denied the need for the loan on the grounds that the financial needs of Iran could be met by her own resources. The Soviet ambassador also handicapped Dr. Millspaugh's activities by twice postponing "indefinitely" his appointments.

The American financial advisers wondered whether Moscow hoped to see the American-planned financial program discredited or whether, in the interests of propaganda, the Soviet Union did not want Iran financially obligated to any foreign nation other than herself.

The delicate situation was complicated by the Iranian demand for membership in the United Nations, provided the application of the Atlantic Charter to Iran were guaranteed by the United States, Britain, and the Soviet Union. Both Britain and the United States welcomed that demand, and Moscow finally gave her consent.

On September 9, 1943, Iran declared war on Germany, and a few days later was admitted to the United Nations. The Iranian declaration, of course, did not change the material aspect of the war. Hitler gained approximately fifteen million new enemies or, to be more exact, the United Nations gained fifteen million new allies; but in so far as each United Nation can claim the benefits of the Atlantic Charter, Iranian membership constituted a new moral liability.

Nevertheless it was heartening to know that the Soviet Union had agreed to share this common United Nations' liability. It enforced the Soviet promise, extended along with the pledge of Great Britain, to respect the independence of Iran and to withdraw all foreign troops six months after the end of the war. This manifestation by the Soviet Union of her good intentions in Iran was the more important since it followed rumors of an alleged Soviet plebiscite in two of the five northern Iranian provinces for the purpose of their incorporation into the U.S.S.R. These rumors proved to be without foundation.

To the British, the postwar status of Iran is of greater significance than that of any Balkan country with the exception of Greece; it is of even more consequence to them than the future of Czechoslovakia or Poland. Iran is not only the depository of Britain's most fertile oilfields; she is also the land route to India. But absorbing Iran is one of the earliest ambitions of Russian expansionism. An ultimate meeting of minds between Britain and the Soviet Union is therefore impossible without some specific agreement on Iran. Any sign of co-operation there is important in itself, but far more so as a symptom of the definitive shape of future Allied co-operation.

From the American point of view, Iran and her postwar status is a moral rather than a political problem. The American government, with the Atlantic Charter as the cornerstone of its foreign policy, finds itself in a difficult and uncomfortable position in Iran. British and Russian policy here always has been, and continues to be, determined by their particular political, economic, and strategic interests. The United States, with considerable moral prestige among Iranians, is viewed by them as the guarantor of British and Russian vows to keep hands off their affairs after the war. This weighty responsibility has been rendered even more delicate by the double status of Americans in Iran.

Some Americans—the military missions—came to Iran to help their Soviet allies by assuring the needed supply of equipment and food. Others—the civilian missions—came to help the Iranians to reorganize and overhaul their administration. These two essentially different aims ran counter to each other. American military authorities, busy facilitating the flow of war supplies into the Soviet Union, were not anxious to intervene in Iranian political affairs. American missions assisting the Iranian government conscientiously defended Iran's interests, and thereby found themselves in conflict not only with the occupation authorities but on certain occasions with the American military officials who considered Iran an exclusively military problem.

If, after the war, the British and the Russians respect their promises, the prestige of the United States, a little shaken by the conflicting aims of Americans in Iran, will increase proportionately. Rightly or wrongly, the United States will be credited with the exertion of friendly pressure on her allies for the enforcement of the charter.

When Roosevelt, Churchill, and Stalin met at Teheran, they recognized the political importance of Iran as a testing ground by devoting to it a most significant passage of their communiqué. They emphasized "their desire for the maintenance of the independence, sovereignty and integrity of Iran." In this communiqué the United States endorsed the Soviet-British pledge as a concrete expression of the principles of the Atlantic Charter. But its double significance lies in the fact that the United States found it possible to endorse this pledge in a Middle Eastern border state adjacent to the Soviet Union.

Both the British and the Russians must have realized that by maintaining their "influence" in Persia they would risk frictions which might compromise British-Soviet collaboration in the post-war world. They must, therefore, have come to the conclusion that the moral solution of withdrawing from Iran would be at the same time the most advantageous one. This solution was to have been expected since both Moscow and London had agreed to Iran's admission to the ranks of the United Nations. The Teheran communiqué emphasized in concrete terms the application of Atlantic Charter principles, to which Iran has been entitled since that date.

The Iranians were elated: they felt they were the first nation to have won both the war and the peace. But Iranian success was supposed to mean success for all the peoples of the United Nations. The eternal contest between hard political realities and moral principles had been resolved into something of a satisfactory solution. It would perhaps be erroneous to believe that the solution found there will be automatically applied to all other nations.

The difference in each case will necessitate variants, and even entirely different application. But the pledge to Iran was basic, and the fact that a solution could be established was undeniably the greatest political and moral achievement of the United Nations. The achievement was the result of long and arduous work. Joseph E. Davies, on his second mission to Moscow, tilled the soil. Cordell Hull sowed the seed. At Teheran, Roosevelt reaped the harvest. Before this harvest was taken to the United Nations' barn, however, clouds reappeared in the political skies. The United Nations were still in search of final agreement on the program for peace.

XX: The Not Too Far East

In 1904, just before the Russo-Japanese war, a Russian general declared that "Far Eastern affairs are decided in Europe." Despite the revolutionary changes in Europe and Asia during the past forty years, Soviet strategists continue to reiterate that opinion.

British and especially American statesmen can hardly be expected to share this Russian view. Allied strategists, however, appear to accept it to the extent that they have agreed with their Soviet colleagues on the necessity of defeating Hitler first. This theory naturally could not be approved by Generalissimo Chiang Kai-shek; it became the major source of friction between China and the Big Three, sharpened, of course, by the Soviet Union's neutrality in the Far Eastern war.

Those American circles compounded of prewar isolationists, who still insist that America's only war is the one against Japan, have refused to understand the paradoxical situation in the Far East. Why, they wondered, should the United States devote so much effort to helping the Soviet Union—which was not fighting Japan— and not give increased assistance to China which was bearing on her extensive but weak shoulders the Japanese aggression? These antagonisms and misunderstandings are inevitable consequences of the different status of the Big Four in the Far East.

China is the important, integral part of the Far East. After generations as an arena and object of power politics, since the Chinese revolution in 1911 she has tried to transform herself from a semi-dependent state with foreign economic and strategic outposts into a great sovereign power able to organize the Far East. Coveted by Japan since 1894, she refused in 1915 to accept the twenty-one Japanese demands which would have made her a Japanese protectorate. Although she was powerless to defend Manchuria in 1931 or to prevent the extension of Japanese rule over Northern China during 1935-37, after seven years of devastating

279

war China was still able to tie up one-fourth of Japan's land forces.

Pressed by superior forces and with inadequate aid from her allies; ravaged from within by political, social, and military conflicts; ill-fed, ill-clothed, and ill-equipped—she continued to fight stubbornly for her survival.

She is grateful to her allies for their limited assistance, for she knows that she cannot win her fight without them. But she does not trust them unreservedly; she is uncertain of their postwar plans. China realizes that Britain and France will be reluctant to abandon their imperial status in the Far East. She gratefully remembers the help extended by the Soviet Union in 1923 to the Nationalist Canton government; but she bitterly remembers the civil war in 1927 that resulted from the marriage of the Nationalist Kuomintang primarily interested in reuniting and modernizing China for her national resurgence, and the Communist International, which intended using the Chinese nationalist revolution as a step toward a proletarian revolution, from which would emerge a revolutionary Asia against the imperialistic Western powers.

Following the rupture between the two groups in 1927, the Soviet advisers were expelled from China. But their seeds had fallen in fertile ground. The Chinese Communist Eighth Route and New Fourth Armies, commanded by Communist General Mao Tse-tung, control the Northwestern area, with Yenan as its capital and a population of approximately twenty-two million. The Communists and their followers fight to liberate their country from the Japanese invaders. But once the Japanese are driven out, they would like to settle the old score with Chiang Kai-shek, who, since the 1927 episode, has lost their confidence and is regarded as a foe to any progress beyond the nationalistic framework.

Will the postwar Soviet Union be different from the Soviet Union of 1927? Chiang Kai-shek has reason to hope so, but he has no definite assurances. He does not know whether the Russia that in 1943 made the encouraging move of evacuating the province of Sinkiang, will look to the re-establishment of her former economic and perhaps even her political privileges in Manchuria, when it is liberated from the Japanese puppet regime.

For Russia claims also to be a part of the Far East. In her expansion policy and in her search for a warm sea outlet, Russia reached the shores of the Pacific Ocean. She found Japan determined to bar the way, and Czarist Russia's defeat by Japan in 1905 was the prelude to her collapse in 1917.

After the 1917 Revolution, Japan, on the pretext of defending the social order in the Far East, tried to establish her control not only over Manchuria but over Russia's Far Eastern Maritime Province. The United States, which had sympathized with Japanese opposition to Russian expansion in 1905, opposed Japanese expansion in 1918 and insisted on the withdrawal of Japanese forces from Russian soil.

For twenty years the Soviet Union and Japan have been "hereditary" enemies in the Far East. On several occasions armed conflict between the two countries appeared inevitable. Japanese expansion in Manchuria threatened the Soviet protectorate of Outer Mongolia. The controversy over Far Eastern fishing waters, leased by Russia to Japan, has been a perpetual source of friction. The Chinese Eastern Railway in Manchuria, which Russia finally was compelled to sell to the Japanese puppet state of "Manchukuo," has been another cause of conflict. Disagreement over Japanese concessions in the northern part of Sakhalin Island and over Russo-Japanese trade, which by 1939 had become practically nonexistent, made relations between Moscow and Tokyo still more tense.

The border incidents which took place in the summer of 1938 on the Manchurian frontier had the appearance of a "curtain-raiser" to a Soviet-Japanese war. Japan at that time seriously considered the possibility of such a war, and approached Germany, to whom she had been tied since 1936 by the Anti-Comintern Pact, with a proposal of joint action against the Soviet Union. But Hitler, already engaged in the "pacific" conquest of the Sudetenland and in preparing his military moves against the Western powers, turned his back on the proposition. Anxious to avoid a two-front war, Hitler, too, came to believe that Far Eastern affairs would be decided in Europe.

In the spring of 1939 Moscow, then negotiating with Britain and France, discovered that the British were as anxious as Hitler and the Russians themselves to avoid a two-front war. Moscow wanted to include the Far East in an all-embracing agreement with the Western powers. But the Japanese warning to Britain against such an agreement with Russia impressed the Chamberlain government.

Thus, in the fateful summer of 1939 each of these nations, apparently realizing that war was imminent, abandoned efforts to prevent what seemed to be inevitable, and turned its attention to limiting the conflict to one front. Above all, each tried to protect what it believed was its most vulnerable area.

The British, French, Germans, and Russians were all in agreement on the danger of a two-front war and on the "priority" of European over Far Eastern problems. As a result of this situation, each was bound to consider every other nation an unreliable ally. The same mutual suspicion developed between Germany and Japan.

Tokyo, vexed by Berlin's refusal to move against Russia in 1938, refused in the spring of 1939 to accept Berlin's invitation to join in a move against the Western powers and their Far Eastern possessions. Her refusal contributed to the Nazi-Soviet pact which determined the immediate withdrawal by the Japanese from the conflict which had developed during the same summer on the Manchurian border. While continuing her fight against China, Japan was anxious to avoid war with Russia. The Soviet Union publicly and officially expressed the hope that China would be victorious over Japan, but resolved not to become involved in a Far Eastern war.

The European war opened to Russia possibilities to restore her western pre-1914 boundaries, but it was also loaded with serious dangers. The fall of France increased the Western danger for her, and by the same token offered new possibilities to Japan in the Far East. Tokyo's war lords felt that the defenseless French possessions in the Pacific would be easy prey, and that once occupied they would become a comfortable springboard for the realization of unlimited Japanese ambitions in the rich South Pacific area, whose white masters were now either defeated in their metropolitan countries—France and Holland—or engaged, as Britain was, in a desperate struggle for survival. Japan signed the Three Power

Pact with Germany and Italy on September 17, 1940, and on September 23 her troops marched into French Indo-China.

Duly informed by Berlin and Tokyo on the new Three Power Pact, Moscow opened negotiations with Tokyo. Both nations were anxious to reduce the risks they were sure they would have to assume in the near future. Russia was expecting a German attack, while Japan was preparing her new military aggression. In April 1941 Japan's Foreign Minister Matsuoka signed a neutrality pact with Stalin in Moscow whereby the Soviet Union pledged herself to respect the territorial integrity of "Manchukuo" in exchange for a Japanese pledge with regard to the People's Republic of Outer Mongolia.

News of this pact came as a shock to the people of China, particularly the Chinese Communists. But when, a few weeks later, Hitler attacked Russia, her eastern door was protected by Japanese neutrality—as well as by her Far Eastern Army—and she was able to gird herself for her western defense. And, when a few months later Japan struck at Pearl Harbor in her campaign for the South Pacific, her western flank was protected against a Russian attack by the Soviet Union's neutrality—and by the Japanese Army in Manchuria. Thus, in 1942 and 1943 Japan and Russia had reason to be satisfied with the mutual benefits derived from their agreement.

Early in 1944, however, with Germany nearing the end of her tether, it began to look as though Russia had profited far more than had Japan, for the Pact had allowed Russia to defeat Hitler, while offering Japan only temporary respite. And eventually the Japanese will have to evacuate not only the British, French, and Dutch possessions in the Far East, and the conquered provinces in China, but also all those territories which she acquired by war or pressure since 1894.

From the Roosevelt-Churchill-Chiang Kai-shek conference in Cairo evolved the first blueprint for both China and Japan in the postwar world. It was easier to prepare this Far Eastern blueprint than it was to work one out at Teheran for Germany and postwar Europe. Far Eastern issues are broader and less complex than European problems. While the Far Eastern peoples are more ancient than the European, the nations of the Far East are younger. There are minority problems, especially in the South Pacific area, but national antagonisms have not reached the acute intensity of those between European peoples.

Economic problems are also much simpler here than in Europe, for Far Eastern economy is still in the colonial or semi-colonial stage. Raw materials are exploited by foreign corporations which own many public utilities in economically semi-colonial China, as well as in their own colonies. The Far Eastern peoples, who have just begun to crystallize a national consciousness, look toward a parallel realization of their political and economic independence. Obviously, each is at a different stage—and on a different level— of the road to independence. Perhaps because of the reservoir of her ancient civilization and the ardor of her young nationalism, China regards herself as the coming leading power. Japan tried to establish her domination by the combined force of her army and industry, but she is on the verge of failure. She undoubtedly overestimated her striking power while underestimating the force of the Soviet Union and of Great Britain and the United States.

Conditions for Japan's reduced place in the postwar Far East were announced at the Cairo Conference. The same meeting extended to China, along with the place which she claimed in the Big Four councils, the blueprint of her postwar status. However, it was not a blueprint of the whole postwar Far East, and it cannot be described as a Pacific Charter. It was an "interim report with limited purposes" which left too many problems unsolved and omitted the mention of too many others. It gave assurances to China as to her political sovereignty. It may help China, in her search for national unity, to overcome her internal weakness. But it did not help to solve the conflict between Chiang Kai-shek's regime and Mao Tse-tung's Communist forces. This "Balkan-style" problem, amplified on the Far Eastern scale, may become a major postwar issue for the United Nations, especially if the Soviet Union—which during the war neglected the Chinese Communists in order not to compromise Chiang Kai-shek's already restricted effort—reverts to her former policy in China.

The Cairo communiqué did not indicate whether the British have any intention of abandoning their economic outpost of Hong Kong, whose strategic value proved to be inconsequential. And the Cairo communiqué, about which Stalin surely was informed although he did not sign it, left open all the problems of the Soviet Union's possible claims in Manchuria and in Korea, where, until 1905, Russia was in possession of the warm sea outlet of Port Arthur.

Pessimists fear that should Britain try to re-establish her political and economic status in Hong Kong, Malaya, Burma, and India after the war, the Soviet Union might consider herself entitled to resume her prewar push toward the warm seas, in which case the Far East would again become a stage for power politics in their most dangerous colonial form.

Optimists point out that Great Britain and the Soviet Union surmounted the equally difficult problem of Iran where Russia faced the same need of warm sea ports. They maintain that with modern methods of ice-breaking, Vladivostok is tantamount to a warm sea harbor, and they believe that the spontaneous evacuation by Russia of the enormous province of Sinkiang, until 1943 a Russo-Chinese condominium, is the counterpart of future Soviet-Chinese economic co-operation in Manchuria, and perhaps even in Korea. The optimists are convinced, moreover, that international morality in the Far East, and especially in China, will be respected because both Russia and Britain, weakened after the war, will find this attitude more advantageous. After all, a vast unified China under the benevolent eyes of the United States—which has a posi-tive economic but a negative political interest in China—may grow in strength, not in the brooding tempo of the recent past, but in leaps and bounds.

The United States, the only great power without any special political or economic privileges in China, has through her insist-ence on the open door policy become the traditional guardian of Chinese independence and economic emancipation. More severe than any other great power in condemning Japanese aggression in Manchuria, she was unable to carry this policy to its logical, militant conclusion because, along with the other anti-Japanese powers, she was not prepared mentally or materially to go to war. Now, however, the United States is in the vanguard of the Far Eastern war and is determined to see Japan crushed and totally eliminated. And while she does not desire to have Japan absorbed by China, she is determined to restore to China the territories which Japan plundered since 1895, and to insure the emergence of China as a powerful, free, and self-sustaining nation.

The pessimists wonder whether China, on recovering all her territory, will be internally strong enough to maintain and develop them. They wonder whether Stalin's consent to restore Manchuria to China has not been determined to some extent by his belief that China will be too weak to re-establish her political and economic rule in those provinces where Russian influence once prevailed.

On the other hand, among those extreme optimists who are convinced of China's ability to consolidate rapidly and develop her power, there is a small group that feels a certain apprehension in regard to her ultimate use of it. They fear that the crushed Japanese imperialism may be succeeded, after a few decades, by a powerful Chinese imperialism which, once it has successfully achieved the elimination of the Western powers' imperialistic policies in China proper, might develop a dangerous expansionist trend. In Chungking, indeed, there are certain Chinese political circles which already speak of the three great "Southern Provinces" —French Indo-China, the Dutch East Indies, and Malaya.

Indo-China was never an integral part of China—although her rulers had to pay a rather steep tribute to the court of Peking— and her population does not consider itself Chinese. But for generations China exercised a strong cultural influence on Indo-China, and Chinese nationalism undoubtedly had considerable influence between 1923 and 1930 upon the still confused but already ardent nationalist aspirations of the Indo-Chinese youth, who were bitterly disappointed in not finding at home the application of those liberal principles which had been taught them in the French universities.

It is true that the intellectual youth of Indo-China, with their frustrated national and social aspirations, were becoming extremely susceptible to Communist propaganda. This propaganda was vigilantly fought by the French police, but it penetrated not only from Moscow via Paris, but also through many Chinese Communist channels. It is therefore quite reasonable to expect that if postwar China achieves her national unity and assures her self political and economic independence after having eliminated

all outposts of Western imperialism, she might become a natural
pole of attraction for the Indo-Chinese nationalists.

While the prestige of the white man in general has suffered
greatly during this war, the prestige of the Frenchman has fared
the worst. Vichy's capitulation to Japan in 1940 and 1941 in
French Indo-China was, in the eyes of the Indo-Chinese, a fresh
blow to French moral authority, already weakened by the errors
of the French colonial administration and the mismanagement of
French economic interests in this rich colony. The French weakness facilitated the execution of Japanese aggression plans in the
Southwest Pacific. This fact is still held against the French in
United States naval circles, where the wisdom of re-establishing
the French administration in Indo-China and in other Pacific
colonies after the war is questioned.

It is true that the British capitulation at Singapore and the difficulties which they met in India in their organization of an offensive directed at Burma have not helped British prestige in the
Far East. American public opinion was shocked by British unpreparedness. But there is no question that the French position
deteriorated far more than the British. Should this result in the
loss of Indo-China by the French, the postwar status of that
country might create difficult problems. It might furnish China, if
she succeeded in emerging as the leading power in the Far East,
with exceptional opportunities for expansion.

Still another opportunity for Chinese growth lies in Malaya
where the politically unconscious and the economically unfit
Malayans constitute a minority, with the Chinese controlling the
greater part of that area's organized life. The British, who feared
the growing economic and political influence of the Chinese in
Malaya, hesitated to use Chinese troops for the defense of that
country until the Japanese forces had occupied Singapore. A great
and powerful China will undoubtedly find in the Malayan Chinese
a most active outpost for expansion. There is also a considerable
Chinese outpost in Thailand, whose value would increase enor-
mously should the Chinese be able to extend their rule or even
their influence in neighboring Indo-China.

These considerations, for the time being of a hypothetical character, explain the growing apprehension in certain Allied quarters

of the potential danger in a united and organized China, with her four hundred million population and her numerous and extremely efficient outposts in the Southwest Pacific. Apprehensions over China's possible expansion are echoed in Dutch quarters. The Dutch are proud of their colonial record in the East Indies and they are confident that they will be able to re-establish control over their liberated colonies in the postwar period. They believe that the commonwealth status, already promised the natives as a post-war measure, will satisfy all political aspirations in the Netherlands East Indies and will enable the Dutch colonial administration to resume its economic exploitation. The close postwar economic association with Australia envisioned by the Dutch will, they believe, be of mutual benefit to Australia, where Dutch capital and experience will find ready employment, and to the Netherlands East Indies, whose defense would be co-ordinated with that of Australia's northern coast.

While the Dutch do not fear the slight manifestations of desire for independence among East Indian natives, they cannot ignore what they believe China's growing power and possible expansion southward would mean to their position in the East Indies. The Chinese outposts in these colonies are not nearly so important as those in Malaya or Thailand. It is obvious, however, that a China which could succeed in expanding her control, or in establishing a kind of Far Eastern Federation including Indo-China, Malaya, and Thailand, would be bound to absorb the Netherlands East Indies.

We find in the Far East a propitious climate for mutual suspicions: China, worried over the possible intentions of her allies and especially of Russia (which might yet become her ally against Japan), fearing that her allies may curtail her political and economic sovereignty in the postwar world; and those members of the United Nations, directly or indirectly interested in the Far East, are already anxious over China's possible imperialistic ambitions. But it must be emphasized that there is a substantial difference between these mutual suspicions. The Chinese suspicions are based on unfortunate experiences of recent memory, such as Britain's unyielding approach to the question of Hong Kong. The

Allied apprehensions are merely hypothetical, and revolve around potential dangers which may never be realized, at least not for many generations. These apprehensions, formulated in British, French, and Dutch circles, and sometimes echoed in some American quarters, cannot be ignored because they might determine the shaping of Allied policy in the postwar Far East.

The United States, as the consistent advocate of Chinese independence since the Japanese aggression in Manchuria, enjoys an exceptionally strong moral position in this part of the world. The realization of Philippine independence will strengthen this position. However, it is apparent that American interests in the Pacific will be intensified after the war. Even those American circles which would like to see the United States withdraw as soon as possible from Europe's entangled and insoluble problems, will not question the necessity of maintaining a vigilant guard in the Pacific.

The defeated Japan, if Americans achieve their aims, will be placed under American surveillance. The Pacific Islands, which were handed over to Japan after the First World War, will this time become American naval and air bases. The necessity of assuring the supply of strategic raw materials—tin and rubber—from Malaya and the East Indies, and of defending the West Coast against surprise attack in the future, will extend America's defense line to a chain of new Pacific bases, and will bring America closer to the Far East than she ever has been. The term "Far East" is a European designation; Americans go west to reach the Far East—and the war has proved that it is not so far away as some of them had thought.

The American conception of the postwar Far East is being built on the necessity of annihilating Japan's military structure, of extending American defense lines, and of assuring China the possibility of becoming a strong and independent nation. This third premise will be conditioned, however, both by China's internal situation and by the attitude of America's present allies. Provided China proves herself capable of justifying American hopes, moral order in the Far East will be possible only if America's allies are disposed to respect it. Thus European powers are still the determining factors in the Far East. Consequently, agreement on the Far East cannot be achieved—and made durable—unless the

United Nations are able also to reach an agreement on the much more complex problems of Europe.

It is, of course, tempting to begin the organization of the world by trying first to solve the basic Far Eastern problems in which this country is directly concerned. But the statement made by a Czarist general forty years ago appears to be true: "Far Eastern affairs are decided in Europe." The general might well have added, "with American participation." And while Americans may disagree among themselves about the extent of this participation, there appears to be a growing determination to prevent either Far Eastern or European affairs from reaching a stage that might once more endanger American security. America—as well as other peoples of the United Nations—might not yet know how to win the peace, but they do know that there can be no real victory without a real peace.

Index

Abd-al-Jalil, 265
Abdul-Ilah, Prince, Regent of Iraq, 200, 203, 210
Abdullah, Emir of Transjordania, 196-97, 208-13, 222, 236, 243-45, 247
Abyssinia, 18, 251
Action Française, 84, 94
Afghanistan, 227
Ahmad Hassanein Pasha, 253
Alaouiti, Dynasty of, 264
Al Atrashi, Sultan, 217
Alexander I (1777-1825), Emperor of Russia, 35-36
Alexander II (1818-1881), Emperor of Russia, 41
Alexander I (1893-1920), King of Greece, 157
Alexander I (1888-1934), King of Yugoslavia, 134-36, 140, 182, 189
Alexander Nevski (1220-1263), 36-37, 40
Alexander Nevski, 36
Ali, Prince of Hejaz, 244
Allal-al-Fasi, 265
Allenby, Field Marshal Edmund H., 215
Algeria, 201, 246, 261, 263, 265-68
Algiers Committee, *see* French Committee of National Liberation
Ali Maher Pasha, 253, 255
Alliance Israélite, 215
Alter, Victor, 60-61
American Jewish Committee, 240
American Jewish Conference, 240
American Lutheran Church, 37
Amiranian Oil Company, 274
Anders, General Wladislaw, 59
Andrussovo, Truce of, 50
Anglo-Iranian Oil Company, 274
Antal, Istvan, 170
Anti-Comintern bloc, 281
Antonescu, General Ion, 180

Arab Brotherhood and Alliance, treaty of, 247
Arab Chamber of Commerce, 237
Arab Conference, Damascus, 198
Arab Conference (or Congress), Paris, 198, 230
Arab Cultural Alliance, 198
Arab Higher Committee, 234
Arab-Palestinian Congress, 260
Arab, Pan-Islamic view, 198
Arab Union, 256, 267
Arabs, 4, 86, 190-269
Argentina, 26
Association des Oulémas Algériens, 261, 263
Ataturk, General Kemal (1881-1939), 188, 189, 244
Atlantic Charter, 29, 32, 67, 275; and the Baltic States, 74; and the Far East, 3; and the Near East, 4, 197, 206, 226-27, 246, 276-78; and the Soviet Union, 61, 71, 75; and Turkey, 187
Atlee, Major Clement R., 8
Australia, 15, 17, 288
Austria, 171-74, 234
Austria-Hungary, 6, 115, 116, 117, 124, 129, 130, 131, 133, 134, 142, 167, 171-72, 174-75, 178, 179; *see also* Hapsburg Empire
Ayoubi, Ata Bey, 222

Badoglio, Marshal Pietro, 25, 96
Bahrein, archipelago of, 190
Bakhtiari, 270
Balfour Declaration, 228, 229, 231, 235
Balfour, Lord (1848-1930), 228
Balkan Entente, 167, 186, 189
Balkan wars (1912, 1913), 131, 136
Balkans, 41, 102, 128-89
Baltic States, 41, 59, 70-80
Banat, 131, 140

291

300

300

Stamenov, Ivan, 183
Standard Oil Co. of California, 245
Standard Oil Co. of New Jersey, 274
Stepinatz, Mgr., 132
Stettinius, Edward R., 18, 21
Stoyadinovich, Milan, 137, 141
Stronski, Prof. Stanislaw, 59
Strossmayer, Joseph G. (1815-1905), 131
Sudan, 201, 251
Sudeten-Germany, see Germany and Czechoslovakia
Sunni Moslems, 205, 223
Supreme Moslem Council, 233
Svinhufvud, Pehr Evind (1861-1944), 76
Sweden, 37, 77, 80, 105, 113
Switzerland, 37, 127, 176, 184
Sykes, Sir Mark, 215
Sykes-Picot agreement, 215
Syria, 91, 102, 191, 194-96, 198-200, 202, 206, 208-13, 214-27, 229-31, 233, 267
"Szeged idea," 169

Tabet, Ayoub, 222, 224
Taj-ad-Din-al-Kassain, 222
Tallal, Prince, 210
Talleyrand, Charles M. de (1754-1838), 37
Tanganyika, 137
Tanner, Väinö, 80
Tarlé, Eugene, 35
Tass, 61, 192
Tchitcherin, G. V., 52
Teheran, Conference of (December 1943), 3, 9, 29, 151, 152, 188, 192, 273, 277, 283
Teschen, 67, 124-25
Teutonic Knights, Order of the (founded in 1190), 36, 72
Thailand, 287-88
Thrace, 160, 163
Tildy, 170
Times, London, 42
Tiso, Father Josef, 119, 174
Tisserand, Cardinal Eugène, 178
Tito, Marshal Josip Broz, 128, 144-152, 163
Tolstoi, Alexey, 36

Transjordania, 197, 199, 200, 206, 208-13, 217, 222, 224, 229, 230, 244
Transylvania, 179
Tripartite Pact, 138-40, 282-83
Tripolitania, 268
Trotsky, Leon (1879-1940), 52, 176
Trumbich, Ante (1863-1938), 132
Tsirimokos, Emmanuel, 159
Tsolakoglou, General George, 156
Tsouderos, Emmanuel, 158, 166
Tuka, Bela, 119
Tunisia, 101, 201, 246, 260, 263-64, 266-68
Turkey, 40, 129, 130, 134, 142, 157, 166, 167, 185-89, 193, 194, 204, 216, 227

Ukraine, Ukrainians, 47, 49, 50, 51, 52, 53, 54, 55, 56, 58, 61, 64, 65, 66, 68, 126, 168, 177; Carpathian, 116, 125-26; Galician, see Galicia
Uniate, see Catholic Church of Eastern Rite
Unidad Maroqui, 265-66
Union of Polish Patriots (founded in Moscow in 1943), 61-62, 68
United Nations, creation of, 1-2
U.N.R.R.A. (United Nations Relief and Rehabilitation Administration), 107
United Serbian Opposition, 137-38
United States, 3-9; and the Baltic States, 70, 71, 74; and Bulgaria, 182, 184, 185; and Czechoslovakia, 118, 122, 123; and Denmark, 106; and the Far East, 279, 281, 283-285, 287-90; and Finland, 70, 75, 78; and France, 5, 7-8, 22, 25-26, 220-22, 266, 269; and Germany, 6, 9, 14-16, 37; and Great Britain, 7, 10, 13-28, 86-87, 90-91, 93-96, 107, 113-14, 190-91, 199, 207, 221, 274; and Greece, 160-62; and Hungary, 170-71; and Iceland, 107; and the Near East, 190-93, 220-23, 225-27, 236, 240, 245-46, 250, 259, 272-78; and Poland, 57-59, 61, 62, 65-67; and Rumania,